Rhyannon Styles is a journalist, performance artist and musician. Her ground-breaking *Elle* column, 'The New Girl', charts her journey from male to female, where she bares all about her experience of transitioning. In her colourful life as a performer, career highlights include a show at the Guggenheim Museum NYC, dancing with Kylie Minogue on ITV and roller skating naked at the Barbican art gallery. A star of the transgender community, Rhyannon was name-checked on *Independent*'s Rainbow List as 'One to Watch'.

Praise for THE NEW GIRL

'I watched Rhyannon Styles begin as the most inspiring and heart-wrenching cocoon I ever saw and now she is a glorious butterfly' Paloma Faith

'Love Rhyannon. Love this book. Everything you've ever wondered about transition, cocooned in an epic tale of fleeing suburbia and big city fabulousness' Grace Dent

'I loved this book – Rhyannon doesn't just shine a light on this subject, she sets off a bloody fireworks display' Cherry Healey

'I am changed for having read this – congratulations, Rhyannon, on a bold life that inspires and lifts – the world needed this truth' Laura Jane Williams

'A story that will make you smile and sob in equal measure, and challenge everything you think you know about gender, sex and fashion. Once read, never forgotten' Rebecca Root

'Rhyannon is such a great ambassador for the trans community. She writes with such class while also keeping it super real' Charlie Craggs

THE

A TRANS GIRL TELLS IT LIKE IT IS

NEW

RHYANNON STYLES

GIRL

HEADLINE

The right of Rhyannon Styles to be identified as the Author of
the Work has been asserted by her in accordance with the
Copyright, Designs and Patents Act 1988.

First published in Great Britain in 2017
by HEADLINE PUBLISHING GROUP

First published in paperback in 2018 by
HEADLINE PUBLISHING GROUP

1

Cataloguing in Publication Data is available from the British Library

ISBN 978 1 4722 4258 7

Typeset in 11.5/17.5 pt Stempel Garamond LT Std by Jouve (UK)

Printed and bound in Great Britain by Clays Ltd, St Ives Plc

Headline's policy is to use papers that are natural, renewable and recyclable
products and made from wood grown in sustainable forests. The logging and
manufacturing processes are expected to conform to the environmental
regulations of the country of origin.

HEADLINE PUBLISHING GROUP
An Hachette UK Company
Carmelite House
50 Victoria Embankment
London EC4Y 0DZ

www.headline.co.uk
www.hachette.co.uk

My memoir is dedicated to Jackie, Nadia, Venus, the cast of *My Transsexual Summer*, and all the inspiring trans people I'm so lucky to have in my life . . .

. . . and anyone who believes in the potentiality of a different reality.

CONTENTS

Prologue: Introducing the New Girl 1

1. The Lost Boy 7

2. Growing Pains 37

3. The Big Smoke 59

4. The Club Kid is Born 79

5. Life Is a Stage 100

6. The Business of Show 123

7. The B-side 158

8. Transcendence: The Beginning 180

9. Transcendence: Changes 216

10. Transcendence: A Journey 250

11. Enter Rhyannon Styles 286

12. Transcendence: Is This the End . . .? 308

Epilogue: Rhyannon Right Now 322

Acknowledgements 327

PROLOGUE:
INTRODUCING THE NEW GIRL

When I was young I had a penchant for dressing up. One of my earliest cross-dressing memories is being aged six and wearing my grandmother's heeled shoes. I would happily trot around the house pretending to be a waitress, serving food to my sister at the kitchen table. My nan's black leather shoes were four sizes too big and hung off my feet like huge boats. I called them my 'clompy' shoes. My nan hated me wearing them, but I didn't care – it felt so good.

My name is Rhyannon Styles and I identify as a transgender woman.

For those of you who don't know, trans*, transgender and transsexual means identifying as a different gender than your assigned sex at birth. In many cases, some trans* people don't identify or conform to a particular gender at all. (High five!)

Are you with me? Let's start at the beginning.

When I was born, I was assigned 'male' because of my anatomy. Then, it was presumed my gender would follow suit. Growing up, the labels of 'male/boy/man' didn't always feel accurate. Yes, I had a penis, but did my body have to dictate how I lived my life? I didn't think so.

In 2012, I'd had enough of pretending and started living. I changed roles to become the person I'd always wanted to be and I let Rhyannon enjoy the limelight at last. It was a decision that had taken years to understand and the consequences were massive!

Today I use the terms 'girl', 'she' and 'her' to define who I am. I proudly use these words to clarify my identity.

I don't know why I feel at home in a female identity. Over the years I've interrogated myself, hoping to find an answer, but I keep coming up short. It just is. I've always felt this way. I grew up dissatisfied within myself, knowing that one day I would need to make a drastic, life-changing decision on how I was going to live my life. I just didn't know how or when it would happen. It took me thirty years until I was able to fully embrace living as Rhyannon.

As I look back at my life, I believe I have always been the person I am today, although before 2012 I wasn't able to express or articulate that fully. Being transgender was an abstract curiosity to me for so long.

As a child, just like my female friends, I dressed up as

the Blue Fairy from *Pinocchio*, the super-hero She-Ra and the twins from *Fun House*. I raided my mum's wardrobe and make-up drawer, trying to fashion anything and everything into a colourful creation – I loved how this made me feel. What began as a game touched something far deeper inside of me. I couldn't see a difference between myself and the women I was creating. I knew there was more to explore. I continued to play female roles and felt at home in them. But I didn't know I was transgender – it's only now, living as the person I spent so long searching for, that I attach the word 'trans' to my stories with pride.

I was a person called Ryan and throughout my life I tried, I tried *really* hard to feel comfortable within myself, but as a male it wasn't always possible. I knew that when I wore female clothes I felt different, but I didn't know why. Beyond the wardrobe, I related to girls much more than I did men. My sensitive emotions and penchant for dressing up were characteristics shared by my female friends – I couldn't see a difference.

It was hard to translate who I was and how I felt in regard to my gender. Back then, I didn't know about gender dysphoria – a medical condition in which someone feels emotional distress (dysphoria) because there's a mismatch between their biological sex and their gender identity – although this was the reason why I felt like I did, the reason why I behaved the way I did. Whenever I expressed femininity I was told it was unnatural. I suppressed my desires and urges, so much so that sometimes I completely forgot them. My younger self felt confused and disorientated. I wasn't allowed to express myself as I wanted to, and whenever I did, I was punished. Unbeknown to me, I was growing up within boundaries that my parents, their parents and society wanted to enforce. There were rules on how females and males should behave in rural 1980s England. There was a distinct difference between the sexes and if you crossed the invisible line you were called names. I was the village 'queer' and that was bad.

As a teenager I began to identify my sexuality as 'gay'. This allowed me to be femme, fabulous and accepted in certain circles. I knew that identifying as 'gay' wasn't the full story but it was the closest option that encompassed how I felt. This identity felt comfortable for the next fifteen years.

It wasn't until much, much later that I began to see people like me that I could relate to. When Nadia won *Big Brother* in 2004, she was a transsexual being celebrated across the country and this was radical to me. I immediately identified. I knew I was transgender too, an option that had previously been an impossibility to me. Before Nadia, the media portrayed transsexuals as horror stories, only suitable for trashy tabloids, sex scandals and the punchlines of bad jokes. This negative exposure left me thinking that being transgender was shameful and wrong. Men could only be women in pantomimes, or when using drag to entertain. Transcending from male to female was beyond anything I could have imagined. I didn't know how or where to begin. In the end, the choice for me was simple: live your life as a trans woman, or die as a man.

In 2015, I began video blogging and writing about my transgender experience in a regular column called 'The New Girl' for *Elle* magazine. (I LOVE this job!) I decided to unveil my life in *Elle* because I wanted my voice to be included in the wider consciousness and on a national platform. I want to raise awareness of trans people and I want to be visible as an equally accepted member of society. The positive feedback I receive demonstrates just how much media attitudes have changed since I was growing up. Take a look on Instagram and you'll find a global community of trans people supporting each other and collectively adding to the ongoing understanding that being transgender is actually cool. We share selfies with our stories to debunk old-fashioned, dated and preconceived ideas that trans people are freaks. As individuals we are smashing existing prejudice about who transsexuals are. We are not damaged people, nor should we be forced to live a lie.

At the beginning of my transition I saw female and male as being very opposite, opposed forces. I was one, when I wanted to be the other. Navigating life as a trans woman has shown me a different perspective. I don't believe that gender is predetermined at birth and I don't believe that gender should only be reduced to female and male. I think we need to acknowledge a potentiality that more possibilities exist.

Finally, I've been conscious not to dress up these words with a pretty, stylish bow. I simply want to honestly and faithfully recall my experience in this physical body since being born on 17 March 1982 and then born again in 2012. (You know what I mean!)

The New Girl is my story. This is a memoir of self-discovery, self-acceptance and self-love.

I want to invite you into my world. Being transgender is about being true to you. For the first thirty years of my life I denied myself the opportunity to be me. It would be such a shame for anyone else to do the same.

Chapter 1

THE LOST BOY

Let me take you back to the 1980s. I've picked through the memories – some of them painful, some of them ridiculous and some so vague that I had to ask my family to fill in the blanks. What I can recall is here – the highs and the lows, the clarity and the confusion, the girl and the boy.

My childhood wasn't like everyone else's, unless you are trans too, in which case you will probably relate to nearly everything. But for everyone else, this is what it is like growing up and not knowing who you are or the person you want to be – I often switched between the roles of girl and boy in my head, unsure which one felt more secure.

These memories are tough and painful to recollect. I dodged flying potatoes and collected butterflies as I tried to navigate and understand my gender, and find a place where I felt comfortable. Quite often the only place of comfort was to be found in my own head. Within this safe space I indulged in fantasy. The only escape from the reality of my life. The voice in my head told me one thing and then society told me another. I was constantly watching over my shoulder and lived in fear.

I didn't grow up comforted by wealth and security; my West Midlands village was rural and down to earth. The people in it were honest and traditional. They held family values at heart and a great sense of community prevailed.

I had a friend called Jamie who lived around the corner. Together we'd play in my garage and build dens using old curtains and dusty deckchairs. Jamie encouraged me to steal eyeliners from my mum, who was a big fan of Avon cosmetics. I remember being obsessed by her dressing table, which was covered in lipsticks and jewellery. She was always perfectly groomed, and I remember she fashioned her brown hair into a wonderful eighties style at the time. Using her brown and blue pencils we drew spots and stripes all over our bodies to imitate our favourite characters from the cartoon *ThunderCats*. I liked to pretend I was Cheetara as we jumped around the garage, smothered in make-up, trying to save each other from imaginary baddies.

I had a *He-Man and the Masters of the Universe* duvet cover that had all the characters from the cartoon printed on it. I loved the characters She-Ra and the Sorceress of Castle Grayskull. I related to them much more than I did with the image of He-Man; to me they were so much more

On a caravan holiday in Cornwall (1980s)

representative of how I felt at the time. No matter what game I played with my friends I was always the female character. I was Rogue from *X-Men*, Daphne in *Scooby Doo* and the Power Ranger who wore pink.

My favourite Disney film was *Pinocchio*; I was in awe of the Blue Fairy. I adored how she magically appeared from inside a ball of light, and sparkled whenever she moved. The Blue Fairy ignited my imagination and I started to dress like her, or as best as I could. My mum had a long blue-green skirt in her wardrobe which I used to steal. I would pull the skirt up under my armpits and pretend it was a dress. I didn't have long hair, so I wore my red towelling pyjama bottoms on top of my head and wrapped the legs into a twist which hung down, in a childish imitation of hair. I didn't look anything like the Blue Fairy, but I felt wonderful as I floated around the house and tapped my dog on the nose with a wooden spoon, pretending to cast spells.

One day I left the house dressed in my fairy costume, jumping off the neighbours' walls and pretending to be a dazzling ball of light. I remember the Clark boys from up the road driving past me in their car. They immediately wound down the window, pointing and laughing at me; I couldn't blame them, I was putting on a great show. When my mum saw me she told me to go back inside the house. I couldn't understand why; I hadn't done anything wrong. I was happy pretending to be a fairy and making the world a better place.

On warm summer days I collected ladybirds and butter-flies. I'd explore all of my neighbours' gardens and try to catch them. Once successful, I'd seal them into a jar with a couple of holes drilled in the lid. I'd keep the jars in my room and at night I'd briefly let the butterflies out to fly around before going to sleep. The insects only stayed alive for a couple of days – I didn't know what butterflies ate so I didn't feed them anything. By the end of summer I had a nice collection of dead butterflies wrapped in toilet tissue and stuffed into matchboxes. I was mesmerised by the bright colours and patterns on their wings, I took great enjoyment from them – dead or alive.

I have a sister who is two years younger than me, called Danielle. Unlike me, she was a natural redhead who loved pickled onion flavour Monster Munch crisps. When we were kids, she'd have all the toys I wanted but was too afraid to ask for. On Saturday mornings we'd mix up the Lego and the Sindy dolls while watching *Going Live*. I enjoyed combing her dolls' hair and deciding what outfits they were going to wear. This was the late Eighties and Sindy wore amazing outfits. I remember bright yellow stiletto pumps, pink puffa jackets and leotards. My sister also owned a fashion wheel, which I loved to play with whenever I had the chance. I could quite happily sit for hours in the living room amusing myself in this way, and often my sister and I would still be in our pyjamas mid afternoon.

The village I grew up in was an idyllic playground all year round. Great Haywood in Staffordshire wasn't posh by any means, though in many ways you might believe that by walking around it. The isolated village makes for a pretty postcard of rural England, filled with old houses, National Trust halls and heritage-status buildings. On the flipside it's very heteronormative and traditional, which didn't suit me one bit.

The boys around the village didn't like me. They were jealous of my relationship with the girls. I was much closer to the popular girls than they could ever be and I became an honorary member of the girl gangs. At primary school, I remember standing behind my teacher, hidden, when I heard the school nurse ask, 'Where's Ryan?' My teacher responded, 'Probably with the girls, as always.' Although she was wrong that time, I could agree with her. You could always find me trying to do handstands against the wall with the girls.

I was an insider in the female domain; I had access to all the gossip and secrets. I knew who was writing love letters to whom, which girls had started their periods and which member of Take That was considered hot. I was allowed in girls' bedrooms when other boys weren't. I didn't know why this was; I presumed it was because I devoured their copies of the magazine *Just Seventeen*, like they did.

In the school holidays my girl gang and I would play in the woods, making rope swings from the tall trees and cooling off by swimming in the river. I wasn't actually allowed to swim in the river – my mum considered it too dirty – but I couldn't help myself; the refreshing water was too alluring. That said, even I had to admit it didn't always look very appealing. Once there was a dead cow floating on the weir. The heifer was stuck in the water for over a week and became very bloated. All the children tried to pop the inflated cow's belly, jabbing it with sticks and rocks. After seeing the dead animal slowly rot away I promised my mum I'd never swim in the river again.

There are two primary schools in Great Haywood. One is Catholic and the other is Church of England. I attended the latter. I didn't believe in God: I was told he was a man and I was instantly appalled. My mum described herself as an 'atheist', which I knew meant she didn't believe in God. Her motto was 'You'll only see me in a church for a wedding or a funeral' and I agreed. Besides, churches were freezing! Back then I thought being an atheist sounded wonderfully exotic. I preferred to go against the grain whenever possible. I decided at seven years old that Jesus and his gang were only fun when I could dress up as them for the school Christmas nativity. Even then, I couldn't be the angel that I wanted to be – a perfect example of the times.

I didn't like how gendered everything had to be at primary school, especially when it came to PE I wasn't allowed to play netball – the girls' sport – which really annoyed me because all of my friends played it. I had a penis so I was forced to play football and cricket with the people that bullied me. It was horrible. The only time the boys and girls mixed was rounders on the school field in the summer or gym inside the assembly hall when it was raining. 'Gym' consisted of various equipment left over from the 1970s. There was a climbing rope which burned your hands every time you slid down it, and a wooden frame with two long metal poles that you were supposed to do somersaults around – a task that many failed, leading to several nose bleeds. Then there was the 'horse', the purpose of which to this day I still don't understand. For a chubby six-year-old it only caused further embarrassment in front of your classmates. If you couldn't jump onto it with the help of the springboard, you were ridiculed. The only fun bit was jumping onto the bright blue crash mat which only went so far in cushioning the impact of being called a 'fairy' by my peers. Did they know I used to dress up as one?

The first time I met people from a different ethnicity was while I was at primary school. My class went to visit another school near Stoke-on-Trent. It was predominantly Asian and it came as a big culture shock. I really liked the young Sikh boys who wore fabric over their hair. I didn't know what any of it meant, but I was fascinated by the bright colours and the little bun that sat on the top of their heads. As part of the school exchange we were encouraged to swap food. I reluctantly handed over my cheese sandwiches on white bread, only to receive the same back. This experience had a massive impact on me. Their sudden presence ignited my imagination, especially as it seemed the boys were allowed to have long hair, a radical concept to me. My eyes were opened to a world beyond my village and I was curious to learn more.

Before this, I thought that people who weren't white were bad – because this is what I was told growing up. My village was so isolated, it was backwards and prejudiced. People were ignorant and racist, and these prejudices were passed down through the generations. As such they were passed on to me and I didn't know any different. But visiting this school changed everything – I could no longer believe what I had been told. To me it was obvious that the young boys and girls were exactly the same as us (cheese sandwiches and all), except they wore more earrings and bursts of bright colours. I realised there was nothing different about them at all. This is when I first began to question the voice of adults and when I started to interrogate the norm.

Another school trip also left a huge impression on me. I remember it for one reason: it was the first time I saw a punk. Technically, she wasn't a punk as this was the late eighties and she'd mixed in a slightly more 'New Romantic' vibe, but nonetheless I was enthralled. My class went for a day trip to Twycross Zoo in Leicestershire. I clocked her leaning against the llama enclosure, smoking a cigarette and looking like she didn't want to be there. Her hair was projecting off her head in green spikes, and she wore a sleeveless denim jacket covered in patches and a shiny black PVC skirt. Her make-up was like nothing I'd seen before. Her eyes were completely blacked out like a panda and her lipstick was dark red.

Again, I had been told that punks were bad. My granddad used to say, 'Waste of space,' whenever anyone of a younger generation appeared to be experimenting with clothes. But I had long since learned to distrust the conventional views of adults. In everyone else's eyes, the punks were trash but I thought she was amazing. She was the closest thing I'd seen which resembled the cartoon characters I loved and identified with. I thought about my dear He-Man bedspread and how she could easily join the ranks of attractive women. The best thing about seeing her at the zoo was observing how much she stuck out. Her attitude of not caring shone through and I was drawn to it. I didn't see anyone else like that again until I was a teenager.

My parents separated when I was four years old. I remember waking up in the night and going to the toilet. I walked past my mum and dad's bedroom and through the crack in the door I saw my mum sat on the end of the bed, crying, and my dad hugging her. Something felt wrong. It was confusing and disorientating in many ways for my sister and me. We didn't know what was happening and were too young for it to be explained.

I have few memories of living with my father as a child. My dad was the 'man' of the house and he liked to enforce rules, often making me clear my plate before being allowed to leave the table. Dad worked for an electrical firm in Stafford and liked to ride his motorbike to work. I remember him sitting on the kitchen step smoking rollies as bacon hissed and popped under the grill. We'd eat bacon sarnies drenched in brown sauce and religiously watch *Bullseye* together every Saturday afternoon. These sparse moments were precious.

Their marriage broke down because my dad had begun a relationship with a different woman. At the age of four I couldn't comprehend the fact that my dad had a girlfriend and my parents' relationship was over. As the years progressed I felt incredibly embarrassed about my home situation and carried a lot of shame around it for years to come. Not only did my gender feel unresolved, but my home life did too. After the divorce my dad settled in the next village. He remarried and some years later had two sons – my stepbrothers Adam and Matthew. I hated going backwards and forwards from house to house. I felt like I was split in two – living two very different lives. This has been a recurring theme for me.

As part of the court agreement, my sister and I attended child counselling sessions run by the local health service. Every week the counsellor liked to play a game with buttons as an initial exercise. I'd have to choose a button which represented each member of my family and one for myself. I would put my button (which was the biggest, most fabulous button I could find) in the middle of the table and everyone else's buttons around me. The more I liked them, the closer I placed them. It didn't make much sense to me at the time – just adding to an incredibly confusing period of my life – although in hindsight I can understand why I was asked to do this. I don't remember talking much at these sessions. Instead I painted pictures of how I saw myself. I always drew myself how I so desperately wanted to be: with long, beautiful hair.

After my parents separated there was a void in the house; we all felt it. My mum worked as a kitchen assistant so she often brought sweet treats home for my sister and me. After school I could gorge myself on endless bowls of cream, custard and chocolate mousse – I lapped it up. I was comfort eating because my surroundings were so uncomfortable. Little did I know then that I was using food to escape my reality and when I consumed sugar I felt good. As a result, I was a chubby child. I'll always remember my friend's mother exclaiming, 'God, you're always eating!' when I called for Adam eating a king-size Mars bar.

We lived in a semi-detached, three bedroom house in one of the three estates in the village. My sister and I supported my mother around the house whenever possible, even if we hated doing chores. There was plenty to do, ranging from hoovering and washing up to walking the dog. Our house was freezing in the winter because we had a coal fire that constantly needed attention. Every morning I would be woken up by the sound of Mum cleaning out the fireplace and getting ready to start another fire. Once a week the coal man arrived, delivering big dirty sacks of coal into our back garden's bunker. It was my job to go out into the frosty night and carry shovels of coal into the front room alongside the logs to feed the fire. It's strange to think about real fires now, but back then most people had one, and it wasn't an aesthetic choice. Neither was the clingfilm we'd cover the windows with every winter. My mum would spend hours heating up the plastic with a hairdryer, trying to get the creases out. The translucent film stretched into place around the window frames and I couldn't stop myself from poking it.

When Freddie Boswell came along, my sister and I were beside ourselves with excitement. Freddie Boswell was a small, black, scruffy poodle which my grandparents bought for us during the immediate months after my mum and dad's separation. Fred was my new best friend and he stayed with me right up until I left home aged eighteen. Fred and I had a real bond; he filled a gaping hole in my life. Whenever I skived off school pretending to be sick because I didn't want to do PE, Fred would sleep next to me on my bed all morning. When I was a teenager I used Fred as an excuse to go outside and smoke. We'd go for walks in the evenings down to the bypass just so I could secretly chain-smoke three or four cigarettes. Fred was a great companion and one of the only constants in my life. I could always be my truest self with him and he would never judge me. I revelled in the unconditional love. Fred died when I was at university, after months of suffering – I was relieved his pain was over. Looking back, I was happy to have had him in my life for as long as I did. I'll never forget how he helped me through all the turbulent years.

My mum's first boyfriend after her divorce was called Tony. When Tony came on the scene I wasn't comfortable with a male identity around the house, especially when he assumed authority and told my mum what I should be doing. I had grown to like our arrangement and I didn't want it changing. I was still too young to understand relationships and the need for people to continue with their lives.

One afternoon I was birdwatching from the kitchen window and Tony appeared. I was happy peering out at the back garden and writing down how many blackbirds, robins or wrens I'd seen. I liked looking in books at different species and trying to draw them. But Tony had other ideas. He said to my mum, 'Ryan should be doing boys' things, or playing outside.' Instead of being encouraged to watch birds and collect butterflies I was given a Subbuteo. Subbuteo is a game where you flick miniature footballers around a green felt tablecloth – for reasons unknown to me. I hated it. Up until then my only experience of it was at boys' birthday parties. Although the boys in school weren't always my friends I would be invited to their birthday parties by default – it looked worse if you didn't ask me. I was the chubby, femme-acting boy that befriended your mum and the cheese hedgehog at the buffet table. I couldn't care less about the Subbuteo tournament that was going on in the living room, it was so boring. I wanted to talk about clothes, hair and pop stars.

With the arrival of Tony and Subbuteo I was whisked into a furore of football. I played along and tried to be enthusiastic whenever I could because it made life easier for others. I would constantly have to make compromises to make others feel more comfortable. I decided that I needed the disguise of supporting a football team, so I chose Manchester United because that was Tony's team. Whenever we could afford it I would go to Man U games with Tony. One of the benefits of having Tony around was that he had a car, so we visited more places. Tony would drive us both up to Manchester and we'd watch the matches.

Before the game we'd sneak into a pub where lots of other Man U supporters would gather. This was a typical football pub, full of beer bellies, loud, foul language and St George's flags. I tentatively stepped inside, not wanting to be noticed. Tony sat there nursing his pint in silence, while I slowly sipped my flat Coke and played with the straw. I avoided going to the toilet because it was too embarrassing. I couldn't bring myself to go into the filthy cubicle and I didn't like the idea of using the urinal either. It was too masculine and I shied away from it. Instead, I sat down to wee, which felt normal to me. Once or twice a fight broke out in the pub – all credit to Tony, he quickly got me out of the way. This was the first time I witnessed male aggression and behaviour in its extreme form and I was repelled by it. Being surrounded by men singing football chants in the terraces became my worst nightmare, especially as I was always dying for the toilet. I was bored and unstimulated. I didn't know the football lingo, so I couldn't talk about team tactics, corners or penalties – it just wasn't in my vocabulary. My mum left Tony just as I was starting high school – it was the news I'd been waiting for. In contrast, her future partner and fiancé Ian only takes me to Alton Towers – we're both thrill seekers and we love sitting at the front of the rides, white knuckling together.

The only thing I liked about those football trips was getting lost around the Manchester ring road trying to find our way home in the dark. Through the misty car window, the wet concrete pavements reflected flashes of electric shop signs in writing I didn't understand. I saw people – lots of people – eating chips and sheltering under umbrellas. These were my first glimpses of city life, going about its business and sweeping past me as I headed towards the M6 and home. These fragments saturated my imagination and gave rise to a desire to explore the world beyond the confines of my village. I knew there was more to experience than countryside, nosy neighbours and football.

I loved northern seaside towns for the same reason – it gave me a glimpse of another world. Blackpool was the prime destination every year. It was all about chips, chips and more chips, with a glass of milk on the side. A week in Blackpool as a child was exhilarating. You had to battle through the crowds being swept down the promenade by the ferocious North Sea wind. I enjoyed walking around at night when the piers glimmered and shone, stretching into the vast expanse of black water. I loved the drama, the glitz and the colours. A sense of danger surrounded this small illuminated town. I didn't know if I was going to get washed away by a giant wave smashing at the sea front or picked up and carried away by a seagull the size of a swan. It made me feel alive.

My grandparents often took my sister and me on day trips to Rhyl. Granddad used to say, 'First one to see the sea gets a pound!' But we never dipped a toe into the waves because it was icy cold and a mucky brown colour. We were always desperate to go into the Sun Centre, a heated indoor waterpark with slides and a wave pool. It was rough around the edges and dirty, but this only added to its charm. I remember swimming past a chip and a plastic fork once – it wasn't quite the tropical paradise I was hoping for but it was better than anywhere else I'd been. The Sealife Centre was another attraction, complete with bellowing

sea lions awkwardly stuck in a concrete enclosure surrounded by seagulls. On a hot day, the experience was
wonderful. More often than not, it was cold and the enclosure smelt of fish.

At home during the summer holidays, I would hang out
with the girls in the woods near our house. There was a
tree in the forest which we called the 'Pigmy' tree. Its
trunk was a collage of carved hearts, acned with initials
declaring love. It was here, aged eleven, that I tried my first
cigarette, which wasn't a cigarette at all. It was a rolled-up
Double Mint chewing gum wrapper which the older girls
pretended was a cigarette. Smoking paper wasn't pleasant,
but we felt so cool pretending it was.

The boys at school and around the village picked up on
my femininity. It threatened them. One day I was called
Rachel by an older boy. Before I knew it, 'Rachel' had
become my new nickname. When I was down at the shops
with my nan or at the fruit farms picking strawberries, I'd
hear, 'Hi Rachel, you poofter!' I couldn't escape it. The
name-calling was so embarrassing. Not only was I Rachel,
I was also a 'poof'. (Poof is a poor man's term for homosexual.) I was being labelled before I'd even worked any of
it out for myself.

What started out as a joke slowly developed into a constant stream of bullying at school and around the village. At
the time I felt like the only kid in the world being targeted,

but I now know that I was not alone. According to a study commissioned by the Home Office, roughly 70 per cent of children that experience confusion about their gender identity are bullied at school. Certainly I faced my share of trouble. I was punched in the face at school by a boy because he thought I fancied him. I had to go to A&E because my eye had swollen up and I felt dizzy. When the teachers quizzed me about it, I lied – I didn't want to cause any more trouble. Another time I was chased around the Uplands housing estate by a boy who kept throwing potatoes at me. Thankfully I could run faster than him so I managed to escape unhurt, but although it might sound funny in retrospect it was incredibly frightening at the time.

Years later I asked him why he always carried potatoes in his pockets. He told me that his parents used to lock all the food cupboards in his kitchen, so he and his brother ate the raw potatoes from the garden shed. I never knew if he was telling the truth. This particular boy loved Kylie Minogue, so not long after the potato throwing incident I told him that I'd spotted Kylie down at the boatyard. (Little did I know that I would one day be performing with her!) He ran all the way down the road to the canal, in the hope that it was true. I kept out of his way for a long time after that, but it felt good getting my own back. I was particularly pleased that Kylie had formed part of my revenge plan.

I knew the boys were confused by me and they behaved

differently towards me. For example, when a fight broke out, unless they really wanted to hurt me, they wouldn't touch me. Instead, I'd watch all the other boys get beaten up while I stood on the sidelines with the girls smoking cigarettes. In essence, the boys saw me as a girl too. If they did try and throw a punch at me then one of the big girls would step in and protect me.

One way I dealt with the constant bullying was by immersing myself in arts and crafts. Through my friend Alex, I'd heard that an older woman around the corner was hosting craft evenings every Thursday night in her dining room for a handful of local children. Alex and I went along one evening, creating outfits to dress up a wooden spoon. It was a few weeks away from the annual village fête and we would enter our spoons into the 'best-dressed spoon' competition. Alex was turning her spoon into a wizard and I made mine into Worzel Gummidge, the scarecrow. After weeks of preparation I didn't win the competition, but I did come second.

I liked going to Mrs G's house. For 20p you could have biscuits and juice halfway through the evening. One week I made a picture of a killer whale jumping out of the ocean using collage. My mum turned that image into a cake for my ninth birthday. It was the best cake ever. My mum, a highly skilled craftswoman, did an amazing job cutting up the icing to look just like the original whale.

But I wasn't allowed in Mrs G's craft club for very long. After three months I was told to leave. Mrs G said, 'I think it would be better if you went and played with the lads on the green instead of coming here.' I didn't think her comment was fair but at such a young age, I was powerless to rebel against her. I had to accept her words. I was distraught to be banned from the club just because I was a boy. I liked playing with glitter, sequins and wooden spoons – I belonged there. I wasn't doing any harm, but once again my behaviour was simply a problem for somebody else.

The next week I admitted defeat, and played with the lads on the green. I was rubbish at football. I was always put in goal as an excuse for them to kick balls at me really hard. It was obvious that I wasn't one of the lads, but I couldn't be one of the girls either. I didn't know what I should do or who I could trust. I felt utterly lost.

When living became tough I used fantasy to escape my reality. I liked to be on my own because I didn't upset anyone and I felt safe. When I was alone I couldn't offend others with my behaviour and choices – I was allowed to be free.

In the early Nineties I loved Saturday-night TV. I'd sit on the sofa with my chip-shop dinner, dipping my battered sausage into a polystyrene cup filled with bright green mushy peas, while watching people wearing tight-fitting Lycra climbing walls and hanging from hoops. In the iconic game show *Gladiators* I would thrill when the host announced, 'Contenders, are you ready? Gladiators, are you ready?!' Cobra, Hunter and Warrior were firm favourites of mine with their ripped physiques and terrible Nineties hair. I've actually still got Cobra's autograph – I met him while I was queuing up for the Thunder Looper rollercoaster at Alton Towers and my jaw hit the floor. Of course, he wasn't nearly as big as he appeared on TV. I didn't want to believe he was just a human being whose real name was Mick Willson. On screen, Cobra was a high-kicking sex bomb who made my stomach feel funny. This was an early indicator that masculinity intrigued me sexually, but I was too young to really understand that I was attracted to it.

Cobra wasn't the only guy who caught my eye. There was a boy in the village who was four years older than me. I thought he was really cool and I admired him. At the end of the 1980s he was wearing baggy 'Madchester'-style clothes and wore his hair in curtains (which was a typical boy's haircut at the time). By the start of the Nineties he looked more like Kurt Cobain with longer shaggy blond hair, ripped jeans and tie-dye hoodies. His name was Tom. I asked him what the name of his haircut was, so I could have the same when I went to the barbers. He told me it was called a 'crew cut'. The next time I went to the barbers I asked for what Tom had told me, hoping to have beautiful hair like him. To my horror, the barber shaved it all off. I cherished my long hair and spent hours brushing it before school every morning. I'd been growing it for months and it was buzzed off in a matter of seconds. It wasn't a crew cut that Tom wore so well, it was an 'undercut'. I had been tricked. My hair was like a safety net to me – it was how I expressed myself and without it I felt naked and exposed. At home that night I cried when I looked in the mirror. I hated how I looked and I hated myself as a result. It took months to grow my hair back and feel happy again.

I despised male-dominated spaces, the barbers being a prime example. The barber I frequented was on the outskirts of a nearby town called Rugeley. Thick velvet curtains hung in the windows, making the wood-panelled interior intense and dark. Stepping inside demanded courage. When I opened the door and walked in I was instantly engulfed by a cloud of blue cigarette smoke. A line of working-class white men covered in faded tattoos sat on a bench waiting to go through the beaded curtain and sit in the barber's chair. Old copies of the magazine *Viz* with torn covers were strewn on the table between the overflowing ashtrays.

When I was allowed to go to the barbers on my own I remember feeling very grown-up but completely intimidated by all the men around. I never felt comfortable but I loved looking at the concoctions of products on the dusty work stations. Bubble-filled tubs of bright green 'wet look' gel, glass jars glowing with blue water and rows of bright red Brylcreem containers distracted me from the awkwardness of the situation. Instead I really wanted to be in a hairdressers. I longed to sit underneath the dryers, with my hair in rollers and sipping a cup of tea, preferably with my nan.

Whenever I went clothes shopping I was always more enamoured by the girls' section. The displays were brighter, cooler and more fun. In comparison the boys' section looked dull, bland and boring. It was so disheartening to have to sift through piles of blue jeans or black sweatshirts. Rows and rows of desert-style boots in camel colours covered the walls. Nothing spoke to me. The whole environment made me feel sick and confused.

Occasionally I would befriend boys and in these cases I started to become exactly like them. I didn't have a natural 'male' identity of my own and I couldn't magically summon one – so I had to borrow from others. I found myself asking for the same clothes they had and trying to behave like them, mirroring their every movement. When all the boys started to wear shiny 'NAFF Co. 54' jackets, I was desperate to get one, just so I could fit in. I did own one for a short time, but when it became apparent that I wanted to plait my hair instead, the jacket didn't seem to fit any more.

Pop music, like craft, was a salvation from how I was feeling. The first album I bought on cassette tape was *BAD* by

Michael Jackson. I was fascinated by Michael Jackson – his flamboyance, attitude and white socks spoke to me. He was stylish, cool and gloriously weird. He didn't seem real. He was like one of the many fantasy cartoon characters I adored and wished to be. At that age, I didn't understand the politics surrounding his identity and image; I simply took him at face value. I loved the front cover of *BAD* – I was struck by his leather jacket and his curly hair. I wore that cassette tape out and eventually the tape player chewed it up.

Every morning before school I would play 'Man in the Mirror' over and over again, singing along into my hairbrush. When I looked at my reflection and saw Ryan staring back at me, I accepted my lot. Because I hadn't heard that you could transition I told myself that I couldn't be a girl, no matter how good I felt when I dressed like one. And I didn't know how to tell people how I truly felt, so I kept it all bottled inside. With no means to identify myself as transgender and a total lack of any information, I carried on regardless.

Do you remember the neon fashion trend of the early Nineties? People wore orange, pink and yellow neon socks, teamed with towelling wristbands and headbands. Personally I wasn't interested, it was too garish for me then, even if some of my later outfits as Rhyannon were on the same crazy scale. I didn't have the courage to pull it off first time round. A girlfriend and I went to the fair in Milford one weekend, and trails of neon flashed before my eyes as I rode the waltzers while 'Rhythm Is a Dancer' by Snap! blasted out from the music system. I laughed so hard that I was crying and I couldn't see clearly. I loved being rendered powerless by the waltzers and spun into a dizzy frenzy. Those four minutes spent spinning around, making my belly feel completely crushed, was one of the happiest moments of my life.

In those days, health and safety was non-existent. We were always pushed terrifically fast by the boys managing the ride, who completely fascinated my girlfriends and me. Others in the village had an attitude of: 'Don't talk to the gypsies at the fair, they will put a spell on you.' But unlike everyone else they didn't wear neon and I very much wanted them to work their magic on me. I longed to be transformed into something else by the mysterious boys.

One thing I wished to be turned into was a beautiful mermaid. As soon as I saw Daryl Hannah in the film *Splash* I wanted to be her. I longed for her hair, her tail and the ability to swim so gracefully. I loved how she kept her identity hidden and pretended that she was just a normal gal. Ring any bells? I loved everything aquatic and dreamed of becoming a marine biologist. For starters, I joined the National Society for the Protection of Whales and Dolphins. Off my own bat I would collect money for the charity. Once I organised a sponsored walk around our local forest, Cannock Chase. Aged eleven, I walked off into the forest with a small map and a packet of Wotsits and just got on with it. I really don't know how I didn't get completely lost.

It was also at this age that I reluctantly started at 'big school'. I didn't like the idea of this; it was scary to be surrounded by new people and I didn't know what to expect. Five years felt like forever and I couldn't wait for them to be over.

The free school bus left the village at 8.15 a.m. sharp every morning. If you missed it you were stranded until the next public bus came along at 9.40 a.m. It was often a trick I pulled deliberately when my day started with double PE. It would mean I'd miss most of the first lesson and hopefully not have to set foot inside the gendered changing rooms. I hated the male changing rooms. That heady mix of pre-adolescence, testosterone, BO and Lynx deodorant made me convulse and want to hide in the corner between parka jackets. It was, as you might expect, the place where most of the bullying occurred. I was often taunted and teased, and I saw many other femme boys subjected to the same insults. Through the steam, the alpha males patrolled the tiled room like wild animals, whipping each other with towels, shaking their dicks and jabbing each other in the ribs with clenched fists.

On the bus travelling to and from school we ran riot. The older kids smoked on the back seats while us younger ones had food fights at the front. As you grew older and moved through the years, the further towards the back of the bus you could sit. The buses were trashed every afternoon. If somebody hadn't eaten their sandwiches for lunch, out they would come and get smashed on some poor child's head. I tried my best to hide, tucked away out of sight from the village honchos. Surrounded by my beloved girls.

For the first couple of years at high school I moved around different friendship groups of girls, avoiding the people I didn't like and never quite finding my place. I was drawn towards the library, where I felt safe. Instead of running away from boys on the field I immersed myself in books and let my imagination take over. I eventually volunteered in the library every lunchtime. It was a sanctuary for the social outcasts and our haven away from the name-calling and the punches. It wasn't just the boys who bullied me; in 'big school' I started receiving insults from girls. These girls were considered ''ard' by Stafford standards and it was new behaviour to me. I thought girls were my safety net, my curtain to hide behind when the boys wanted a fight. I thought that I was one of the girls and I couldn't understand why they would turn on me. All of a sudden I no longer belonged anywhere.

I felt utterly lost between the roles of boy and girl. I didn't know who or what felt more natural. I wanted to wear different clothes and do different things but this was frowned upon. Being a boy always felt like it was holding me back. The piece of flesh between my legs dictated everything. I knew that puberty was on its way as I heard other boys' voices breaking. I witnessed them slowly growing fluffy moustaches, their faces covered in zits. This all looked horribly ugly to me. I wanted to be pretty and feminine with long, lush hair.

With so many hormones flying around, people's attitudes and behaviour began to change. We began to mature and become young adults. More and more kids started to talk about sex and G-spots in the school canteen. The boys in the changing rooms bragged about 'banging' Debbie C behind the hospital. I wanted to bury my head in the sand. I didn't like what these chemicals were doing to everyone. My position was now even more precarious.

Letter to a Lost Boy:

Dear Ryan

I want to write you a letter to reassure you that everything will be OK. Let me tell you that once you come into alignment and embrace who you truly are, you will never look back.

At times, this journey will be difficult and you will want to escape it any way you can – but you must not give up. You will need to summon all the strength you can find to accept who you really are and live your life.

Your transformation will require an endless supply of determination, willpower and patience. You are going to need courage, more courage than you can ever imagine. You will face obstacles and challenges that will shake you to your core. Don't be afraid of who you are, don't let fear suffocate you forever.

My dear friend, don't let these trivial circumstances get in your way. You should take comfort in knowing that all this pain will be temporary. You have the potential to be so much more than what you are right now. Amidst the confusion and the turmoil, you will need to find clarity, composure and grace to move towards a greater and higher place of being. By doing so you will grow in more ways than you can ever imagine and life will be delicious.

Focus on what you want and keep moving towards it. You will succeed.

Whenever you're ready, I will be here for you.

I love you.
Rhyannon

Chapter 2

GROWING PAINS

On 17 March 1995, I turned thirteen and became a teen-ager. It wasn't like I suddenly grew up overnight. I still had the same life and all of the same issues. But my perspective was slowly beginning to shift and expand as I searched for more identities and possibilities surrounding what I could do with my life. Over the next five years my circumstances would change massively as I hurtled towards adulthood and the millennium.

The mid 1990s ushered in a new musical genre called 'Britpop'. Everyone had started walking around the village singing 'Wonderwall' by Oasis as opposed to the *Simpsons'* song 'Do the Bartman' from my childhood. I wasn't sure about this new phenomenon as it all felt very laddy. That changed when I saw Elastica on *Top of the Pops* performing 'Waking Up' and I was hooked. I instantly loved the tomboy aesthetic from a femme angle. The reason I didn't like

Blur, Oasis and the Charlatans was because they were too mainstream. Everyone who rejected or bullied me were fans of these bands and that really put me off. Embracing their music was a betrayal. One day I spotted a girl who lived around the corner from me wearing a pink fluffy jacket with the word 'PULP' written in big blue letters on the back. I thought she was amazing, like an alien planted into our village to alter the course of my life.

It was a big event when we erected a satellite dish onto the side of our house, just like everyone else on the street. The main reason for the satellite was so that my mum and Tony could watch the football games on Sky Sports. However, for my sister and me it brought us Nickelodeon and, more importantly, MTV. MTV was a lifeline in rural England. I was glued to the TV for hours on end. I always prolonged leaving for school in the morning because I wanted to stay at home and watch Shakespears Sister's 'Stay' video for the hundredth time. Music videos became a much-needed and sought-after education. I was thrilled to be able to finally see Michael Jackson's classic videos on a weekly basis.

MTV arrived in my life with perfect timing, as I was young enough and eager enough to absorb everything that I saw and heard. I was desperate for knowledge, however I could find it. In the days before the internet, we only had access to information about bands and music through the radio, magazines and album sleeves, so I would study them avidly, and in turn they became an important way to discover art and culture. For example, when I saw the Stone Roses' album artwork in the local library I discovered the artist Jackson Pollock. My curious imagination was being fed from all angles.

Eventually I found a group of friends who had similar attitudes to me. They were a colourful assortment of girls and boys, who liked Nirvana and Frank Sidebottom. We scrawled band names over our school bags, exercise books and ex-army shirts. We dyed our hair with food colouring and painted our nails using Tipp-Ex. I'd left the geeks behind in the library and found the rock stars. At lunchtimes we would go over to the university grounds down the road, smoke cigarettes and drink shit mix. 'Shit mix' was whatever you could steal from your parents' alcohol cupboards and bring to school. These friends weren't the type to abuse you because you were different; instead, our differences brought us together.

Every Saturday we would convene outside a record store called Mike Lloyd's in Stafford. We loved that shop because they had a great 'Indie/Alternative/Rock' section and a massive second hand area. We'd all run in clutching that week's copy of the *Melody Maker* magazine, determined to find the new single by the band of the week. One week I was after the new CD by Placebo. The lead singer of Placebo was called Brian Molko, and when I saw him on *Top of the Pops* I was gobsmacked. It was 1997 and I was fifteen years old, primed and ripe to find a new role model. Brian brought androgyny to the late Nineties with his raven-black bob, knee-length skirts and smoky eye make-up. His feminine voice penetrated my ears and infiltrated my mind. Before Brian I was in Kurt Cobain mode. My hair was chin-length and multi-coloured, I wore torn jeans and Nirvana T-shirts. I'd happily formed an identity where I felt like I was finally expressing how I felt inside. No other boy was walking around Great Haywood with long blue hair, but at this point I didn't care. If anyone said anything nasty to me I would drown them out by turning up the volume on my Walkman.

In my teenage years the bullying had eased off. The bullies had discovered their own sexuality and weed. Priorities had changed and squabbling no longer mattered. By this point everyone in the village thought I was gay and they left me to get on with it. I had few friends in the village and once I started high school, I mainly stayed in my room learning to play guitar and listening to Steve Lamacq's evening sessions on Radio One. This was my sanctuary and my playground.

I loved my bedroom. When I was fourteen I swapped with my sister, happily moving from the tiny shoebox room and into the bigger back room. I immediately painted it dark blue and silver, covering the walls with posters of my favourite bands, Hole, Sonic Youth and Babes In

Toyland. I bought a large aquarium and filled it with bright orange fancy goldfish. I burned joss sticks at night to try and disguise the smell of cigarettes as I craftily leaned out of the window getting my nicotine fix. I can't remember

In the sanctuary of my bedroom aged seventeen (1999)

exactly who introduced me to smoking – I expect it was one of the Saturday crowd.

Saturdays went like this: after my group of friends and I were done with sitting on the concrete outside Mike Lloyd Music we would head into the park. En route we would load up with bottles of cider, packs of ten Lambert & Butler cigarettes (which cost 95p back then) and temporary aubergine hair dye from Superdrug. Once situated under one of the many bridges or the bandstand in the park we proceeded to get drunk. This is what we did age fifteen, every Saturday without fail. Even when it rained and the river running through the park flooded, we'd still be there, talking about Skunk Anansie and being sick. (After downing a litre of White Lightning you'd need to puke.) After which you'd buy a bag of chips and be sick again. We thought we were cool – our behaviour was 'alternative' and we lapped it up. I'd go home on the last bus back to the village at 10.40 p.m., hoping not to vomit on the back seat or bump into anyone I knew. Once home I could sneak up to my bedroom and collapse onto my bed feeling like I was on the waltzers again, spinning out of control and dizzy. It was heaven.

I was much happier being a teenager than I was a child. Growing up was moving forward; I was able to make more choices for myself. In the mid Nineties I don't recall seeing anyone who was transgender in the mainstream. Instead I saw boys wearing girls' clothes. Kurt Cobain, Brian Molko and Boy George all wore skirts and make-up and this is what I identified with. I accepted my situation and my identity, simply because I didn't know any differently.

One small hair at a time, puberty finally crept up on me. My physical body grew in height and my voice finally broke, making it deeper. I liked my skinnier frame: after years of being called 'fatty' the growth spurt and cigarettes put an end to that. At this time of my life I didn't wish to have the body of a girl. Rather, my thoughts were occupied by what colour I was going to dye my hair and if I could afford to go and see the Foo Fighters in Wolverhampton. Dabbing Vaseline on my eyelids and cheekbones like Natalie Imbruglia suggested in *Just Seventeen* magazine and having nice soft hair which I blow-dried every morning saw me through this tumultuous period of change.

Puberty had awakened me sexually. My girlfriends all had boyfriends, and my few male friends had girlfriends. I was left out because I was a boy who had an interest in boys. There were two boys at school who had actually come out as gay and they were ridiculed and abused as a result. If I was gay – and I wasn't sure if I was yet – I didn't want to say it out loud. Being gay was a terrible crime at school, within my family and in the village – a crime I wasn't yet willing to own up to. Once I heard the PE teacher ask one of the 'out' boys, Richard, in the sports hall, 'How are your knees today, Richard?' At which point a kid jeered, 'Bent, like the rest of him!' Shamefully, the PE teacher didn't defend Richard. Instead Richard and I both turned bright red. We knew we were in cahoots on this one.

I had several crushes on my girlfriends' boyfriends. I was envious they were able to kiss each other and hold hands in public. I didn't think it was fair that I was always the gooseberry. I wanted my own man. At the same time it was incredibly confusing as I had strong desires towards girls too. These attractions were less about sex and more about friendship, companionship and mutual understanding. I liked kissing girls; their lips felt soft and tasted of sweetened lip balm. As a result of these mixed feelings I decided not to say anything about how I felt sexually because internally I still wasn't sure.

School itself was still a bore, although one exception was my art class, which I loved. I felt so at home in the art department and I wanted to live my life there with the crazy teachers. Mr Perks wore a red leather tie and drove a yellow Mini. His attitude towards me was so caring and nurturing, I wished everyone was like him at school. We could chat about anything, from the Velvet Underground to Gaudi. Beyond my family he was the first person to see how in tune I was with art and he encouraged me to take this path in life. I knew for certain that I didn't want to stay at school for A levels. I wanted to get the hell out of there. It was only art that I wanted to focus on. I resented having to revise for my GCSEs but I knew the grades would help me leave the village for good and move forward with my life. And I couldn't wait.

Leaving high school felt amazing. I was thrilled that I wouldn't have to run around a frozen rugby pitch in the middle of February or listen to Mr Kemsley teach us about crop rotation any more. My mum drove me into school on the day I picked up my GCSE results. As we walked through the school, the smell of feet lingered in the air of the corridors, mingled with a faint odour of melted cheese from the canteen. I was glad to finally be finishing this chapter of my life. It hadn't suited me at all and I was raring to move on. As a teenager and full of the usual angst I had begun to find most lessons incredibly boring and frustrating. I was pleased that my classroom days were over. Provided my grades were good, I planned to go to art college and start a BTEC National Diploma in Art and Design. I wasn't particularly worried about my results as I was certain I would get an A in art. My friend Graham turned to me after the exam and asked, 'How come you can always turn a piece of shit into a masterpiece at the final minute?' It's a skill I was particularly proud of.

Art college was the Mecca I'd been waiting for and I really let myself go. No more school buses, no more uniforms and no more teachers. You could smoke in the refectory and go to Wetherspoons for your lunch. I never missed a day of it – I couldn't wait to get there every morning, eager to soak up this new environment. Stafford art college had a great reputation. People travelled from all over the Midlands to study there and I loved it – all I could think was that this was how I wanted to spend the rest of my life. The lecturers were amazing; many of them had their own studios. It was free education from people who were passionate about what they did and it was priceless. I can't thank Jackie Mulvaney, John Mulvaney, Dawn Robertson or Cinny enough for pushing me forward. I owe a lot to these teachers who helped to shape me.

Finally, I made friends with people who knew who Lou Reed was, had bisexual tendencies and wore skirts over jeans. This was my tribe. Music and subcultures allowed me to experiment with my identity and appearance. Within my circle of friends I felt supported. They encouraged me to be as loud as possible and this felt great after years of shying away from the limelight.

As a sixteen-year-old I pickpocketed wardrobe inspiration from the people to whom I felt most connected: rock stars. But there was one exception to this rule. Madonna. I wasn't a loyal Madonna fan like everyone else. I didn't drool over her or love her every song. To me, she was just too pop. I preferred Courtney Love from Hole and Kathleen Hanna from Bikini Kill. But in 1999, Madonna released 'Beautiful Stranger' and everything changed. When I saw the music video on

MTV, watching Madonna cavorting on screen, something inside me clicked. It was the very first time that I saw a woman on television who I completely identified with and thought, 'Oh, that's me!' It was an inner connection with what I saw represented on the screen at that moment. Madonna was how I saw myself. I wanted to be her. It's impossible to say whether I felt this way because of what she was wearing or how she was dancing. At the tender age of sixteen I couldn't put my finger on the reasons behind this pivotal moment and why it has had such a lasting effect on me.

I had been learning to play the guitar, covering Nirvana songs in my bedroom for a couple of years, but I had never had the chance to play with anyone else. This changed during the second year of art college when I joined a band. We called ourselves 'Pretty Kitty'. After many weeks rehearsing furiously, our first show was scheduled at Rugeley's Red Rose Theatre, supporting a band I admired called Rachel Stamp. Rachel Stamp had been on my radar for quite some time. I had seen an image of them in the music magazine *Kerrang!* and they had amazed me. The lead singer David had bright green hair, no eyebrows and wore knee-high Dr Marten boots with skimpy vest tops and sparkling hot pants. I had never seen anything like it; it was a feast for my eyes. I loved seeing femininity expressed in that form – it was alluring and out-there and I wanted more. When I watched Rachel Stamp perform I experienced the same feelings as when I watched Madonna in that video – I related to them deeply. It wasn't just about the mix of loud glam rock and garish outfits; it was the freedom of expression that enthralled me. It sparked a desire in me to develop a style of my own.

Performing on stage presented an opportunity for me to carve out my own style and I decided to wear a dress for our Pretty Kitty shows. With our first gig looming ominously on the horizon, I wanted to find a cute babydoll slip to wear over my jeans for the show. It was an idea I'd had in mind for some time, but the only thing holding me back was finding the courage to buy one. I decided it was time to go shopping.

Charity shops seemed to offer the most anonymity. Nervously, I approached the lingerie rail inside the Sue Ryder charity shop, hoping not to draw attention from the blue-rinse brigade hunched over the tills. With a selection of four slips available I quickly swiped them off the rail and ran into the changing room – a small area tucked away in the corner of the shop, cut off with a curtain, possibly a dusty old bedspread. I tried them on as fast as I could, worried that someone would ask what I was doing. One by one I slid the crispy and smelly old slips over my head and over my clothes. I wondered how Courtney Love made them look so cool – they looked terrible on me. It was a close call between two garments but the faded lemon slip won as the fit was slightly more flattering. As I examined my reflection in the slips I felt feminine and something inside me clicked into place. I knew I was onto a winner; trying on the dresses made me feel really good.

The next obstacle was paying, which I hadn't thought about because trying the slips on had seemed like the bigger hurdle. I murmured, 'I'll take this please,' to the lady behind the counter as she looked me up and down. But I had done it. For the sum of £1.50 I had navigated buying my first dress, and as I clutched the slip close I felt very proud that I'd had the confidence to do so. When I got home I happily swished around my bedroom wearing the dress, interpreting my idols and feeling closer to my true self than I had ever done before. Discovering my identity dress by dress felt natural and comfortable.

Of course, if my mum had walked into my bedroom I wouldn't have known what to do or say – this behaviour still felt rebellious. Without a stereotypical dominating male figure around the house, I was left to my own devices. Don't get me wrong, my mum could be very strict when she wanted to be. When she found out I smoked, I was grounded for two weeks. After Tony, my mum met Steve who was a science teacher. I liked him because he gave me a cassette tape with Television's *Marquee Moon* on side A and Fleetwood Mac's *Rumours* on side B. This furthered my hunger for art, culture and Stevie Nicks.

The first night Pretty Kitty played live was a big deal for all of us. My outfit was perfect. My lemon slip was teamed with hair accessories and silver stars stuck all over my face. The overall effect totally confused the audience. I know this because my friend's dad filmed the show, and when I appear onstage you can hear two boys chatting to each other before suddenly exclaiming, 'Oh my God, it's a man!'

All of us dressed up to great effect. Sam dyed his hair peacock blue and smudged red lipstick under his eyes. Julia was wearing a feather boa and sparkly silver stilettos. Mark was wearing eyeliner and mascara with figure-hugging black clothes. I know it doesn't sound daring by today's standards, but remember that this was a small conservative town in the late Nineties. We became notorious as 'the gay band'. In time, other bands in Stafford referred to us as 'Pretty Shitty'.

After our debut show supporting Rachel Stamp, the lead singer offered to produce an EP for us. It felt like we were famous; we were interviewed in the *Stafford Newsletter* and played live on BBC Radio Stoke. We were far more flamboyant and interesting than the other crusty Stafford rock bands. We were in a league of our own – nobody else locally had the guts to do what we did and get away with it. Indeed, it was our onstage look that drew all the attention and which we flaunted as much as we could. We soon developed a queer following around the Midlands, with glam girls and boys coming all the way from exotic Wolverhampton to watch us perform live. Considering this was the pre-internet era I don't know how we managed to attract so many groupies. Perhaps it's because we were truly being ourselves. Individually we were all outsiders but collectively we were pretty and united. And there was something magnetic about this.

The band allowed me to channel my desire to cross-dress. At seventeen I was very happy being a femme boy, and for the first time in my life I felt comfortable in an identity. I loved being able to smudge glitter all over my eyes and wear exactly what I wanted. By this point I had shoulder-length black hair, and was wearing tight T-shirts and flared jeans. It felt like a great time to be a teenager—it was a great time to be me. The music I was writing and performing live was also drastically shaping my lifestyle and by turns my hopes for the future. The boys who used to call me 'faggot' or 'poofter' at school were now trying desperately to sell me Ecstasy outside the Zanzibar nightclub in Stafford. I couldn't help but marvel at how the tables had turned.

In 1998 I discovered transsexuals, thanks to Dana International winning the *Eurovision Song Contest* and the character of Jackie appearing in my favourite TV show, *Paddington Green*. Of course, I'd heard of men transforming into women through scandalous front-page tabloid headlines, which mocked, rather than celebrated, their transformations. Now I was witnessing something different, something real. The visibility of these trans women was not reduced to a horror story. Instead they were winning prizes and appearing on TV.

At this stage my own thoughts about becoming a girl were still abstract to me – I wasn't able to pinpoint how it was ever going to manifest in my own life. Many people would often say to me, 'You're such a girl,' while I was at college. It wasn't derogatory, it was simply an observation – and I agreed with them. I remember vaguely thinking, 'Maybe, one day I will be.' In many ways, cross-dressing for my band's gigs and wearing make-up to art college was enough for me at this point. To a degree I felt satisfied and I didn't feel the need to explore my femininity beyond this.

College marked my sexual awakening, if you could call it that. Julie was my first girlfriend and the person who I lost my virginity to. While we were at my friend's house party we decided to go and 'do it' in the bathroom. It wasn't a beautiful or romantic first experience as we crammed our bodies between the bathroom sink and the U-bend of the toilet. Every two minutes somebody would bang on the door and demand to come in. Days later I was lying on Julie's bed listening to King Crimson and she wanted to have sex again. She told me that all of her previous boyfriends wanted to have sex all the time and she didn't understand why I was so frigid. This unnerved me. I hated the comparison to other boys, something I felt that I'd been subjected to my whole life, and I told her I couldn't see her any more.

At art college I became mesmerised by a girl I spotted walking around. Her arms were adorned in plastic bangles, her hair was dyed bright red and she had the most incredible sparkling green eyes. Her name was Jet and she was studying fashion. My jaw dropped whenever she walked into the room; I thought she looked incredible. Within the month she was my girlfriend and we paraded ourselves around art college together, connected by dog collars and chains. At weekends I would go to her house to hang out. Her bedroom wall was covered in hand-drawn fashion illustrations, scarves were hung over lamps and she had a collection of dolls. It was my dream bedroom. Jet was smart, a kindred spirit who I knew also dreamed of bigger and better environments than where we found ourselves at that moment in time. Jet knew about fashion designers like Jean Paul Gaultier and Vivienne Westwood – she believed in the importance of culture. Our relationship was based on creativity. We took 'arty' photos in the woods, each taking turns to lie on abandoned sofas, jumping through small fires we made out of newspaper.

One time, while straddled on top of me, Jet said, 'You're different, I think there's something you're not telling me.' She was right; there was something that I was holding back, that I didn't know how to voice yet. I wasn't even sure exactly what it was. Soon Jet felt unfulfilled, bored of my procrastination and lack of sexual desire towards her. One day she phoned me and ended the relationship, saying that an ex-boyfriend wanted to see her again. I understood – in all honesty I didn't want to have an intimate relationship with her. In reality I had wanted to mirror her. I loved her company and her appearance. I wanted to be her.

I hadn't explicitly said I was gay at this point, I didn't think I needed to. I enjoyed the company of these girls and they enjoyed me. Being homosexual was gradually becoming a possibility but because I hadn't seen anyone like me who was gay, I couldn't identify completely with the label. In the Nineties, the 'gay' scene being depicted felt very mainstream and commercial, rather than alternative or queer. I was born and raised in a village in which people openly condemned gay as being wrong. No wonder I didn't feel able to voice a desire for men – my voice was being suffocated by other people's prejudice.

Although identifying as gay felt like an option, I knew it wasn't the full story. I was happy wearing make-up and femme clothes and these explicit actions led to others demanding to know what my sexuality was. In the end I decided to claim that I was bisexual (which looking back was actually the truth). This way I could suggest that I liked men, but it didn't seem like such a crime – although I only admitted this to my closest friends. With hindsight I was just trying to figure things out. This was the start of some degree of honesty and identification – it was a baby step. At this stage I didn't know that gender identity and sexuality are two very different things.

The next big step forward in my life was going to university. Although I wasn't ready to make this decision alone. I was torn – I was having fun with the band and I didn't want to leave them behind. I voiced this to my lecturers who immediately all turned around and said, 'Ryan, you need to go to university now. You can't stay here!' I didn't understand it back then – I thought the band would become the next Radiohead – but their advice was priceless. I needed to explore the possibility of more growth in my life.

After deciding to pursue university I knew that I wanted to leave the village and move to a city so I narrowed it down to three universities: London, Brighton and Manchester. I applied to study jewellery design at Middlesex in north London and applied arts at Brighton. I'd never been to London or Brighton so I was taking a punt and happily throwing myself into the unknown. When my friends and I went to visit the Cat Hill campus at Middlesex University, I decided there and then that London was my destiny. I knew right away that I wanted to be inside this thriving metropolis of culture and crime even though I'd never stepped foot inside Zone One before.

Weeks later I stood on the platform at Stafford station with my mum. We were waiting for the train to London Euston to arrive and I was smoking a roll-up and carrying my portfolio under my arm. The draught blowing through the station was cold and we wondered what the weather would be like in London. I was extremely nervous – this was an important day that would decide my fate. If I were successful at today's university interview then I would be moving to London in four months' time. My tutors at college explained that the jewellery course at Middlesex was difficult to get on to, but they assured me that my work was well suited. I hoped they were right.

Once my mum and I arrived at Euston we were like fish out of water. I was that person you see at tube stations, completely lost and one step behind everyone else. My portfolio kept bashing into passers-by as we tried to negotiate the Piccadilly line towards Cockfosters.

We took a detour and went for a walk around Finsbury Park because we were two hours early for the interview. We thought it would be lovely and green and that we could get something to eat. We weren't prepared for what we found. We emerged from Finsbury Park tube station onto a noisy road full of people and traffic. We had no idea what the area was actually like and we failed to find the park.

At the Cat Hill campus we joined the queue of teenagers all patiently waiting for their interviews, filled with nerves and worry and avoiding eye contact with each other.

Thankfully, my interview went well – the lecturers seemed to like me and my work. I was chatty, friendly and felt comfortable in their presence. They liked my ideas and encouraged me to go and explore London while I was there. Mum and I jumped back on the tube and ventured into central London.

'Are you a sinner or a winner?' boomed the man with a Scouse accent at the top of the steps as we climbed out of Oxford Circus tube station. Square yellow signs advertising a 'Golf Sale' littered the view of the huge branch of Topshop. A young boy played an accordion in the street, busking for his supper. We trotted down the length of Oxford Street and back again, looking at the Union Jack umbrellas and the Big Ben key rings. We felt like tourists because we were tourists. It was all new to us, a far cry from the sleepy village we would be returning to later that night. Those brief hours spent in the city ignited my desire even more. I was hopeful this world would become my permanent new reality.

Back at college we were rapidly running out of time as the end of year show approached. It was the only thing on our minds during our many fag and coffee breaks in the refectory. For my final show I designed a codpiece, an idea spun from Henry VIII. It was a beautiful but ugly sculpture, an aesthetic I loved to play around with, and teamed with my attitude and work over the year I won a prize. I was awarded £1,000 and named 'Student of the Year'. It was an honour to be acknowledged for all the hard work I'd put in over the last two years. I had done everything I could to learn and absorb every art form and technique and it had paid off.

One sunny morning later that month the post came through the door. I could see an envelope with the Middlesex logo emblazoned in the top corner. My heart skipped a beat; this was the moment I'd been waiting for. I opened the letter and read: 'We are offering you an unconditional place on the BA (Hons) Jewellery Design course at Middlesex University.' On the first read I was confused, not understanding what it meant. I called my friend Julia who explained, 'It means it doesn't matter what exact grades you have from college as long as you pass. They are offering you a place regardless, or something like that.'

I was ecstatic. I knew that everything was about to change.

Chapter 3

THE BIG SMOKE

Up until the age of eighteen I'd never ordered a soy flat white, eaten an avocado or surfed the internet. I'd lived a rural, sheltered life, cocooned within privet hedges and net curtains. I arrived in London with a beautiful naïvety, without any experiences of fast-paced city life. I was a fresh-faced boy who would need to become streetwise very quickly.

I loaded my entire bedroom into the back of my mum's car, and we drove down to the London borough of Enfield ready to start my new life. I didn't know what to expect when I turned up at my new halls of residence in Ponders End. When we arrived we were surprised to see a horse standing in the middle of the car park and a cockerel sitting on a wall. It turned out that one of the neighbours kept a variety of animals in his back garden, many of which escaped, to our amusement.

I wasn't alone, and soon after I arrived my Stafford chum

Lucy popped her head around my door. She had been given the room three doors down from me. Having Lucy around made the transition from rural hell to paradise city easier for both of us. Within hours, more and more students arrived with their parents, unloading cars stuffed with TVs, videos, stereos, CDs and clothes. We introduced ourselves and began decorating, transforming our mundane dorm rooms into places we were comfortable calling home for the next year. I immediately covered my walls with pictures of Courtney Love and hung up reams of fairy lights. The halls of residence felt new and clean, and we all bounced off the walls, excited to be in a new city. That night our whole block went to a local pub to get to know each other. I was thankful to meet Anna and Blossom, two girls who were also studying jewellery design. Alongside them I met Jen, Susie and Erin. Straight away I'd found a group of girls within my halls that I felt comfortable around. It was already starting to feel like home.

We slowly began acclimatising to life in Ponders End. It should've been named 'World's End' because it didn't feel like much was going on. It was miles away from anywhere interesting or fun. Ponders End was a run-down area, and it took some time to get used to the abandoned mattresses and fried chicken boxes littering the pavement. This was a new kind of 'gritty' I'd have to come to terms with. I stuck out as a mincing cash machine with privilege and although

I never came across any violence, I did sense the ominous city energy exuding the possibility of danger.

To support me through university I was given a student loan, which at the age of eighteen I was delighted with. For the next four years, £4,000 a year would be drip-fed into my account. Aside from paying for my accommodation, food and other mundane necessities the rest was mine to spend however I wanted. It was time to have fun! I'd made friends with a redhead girl who lived on the floor above me. Amy liked the same bands as me and wore black clothes. She invited me to go to a nightclub called Heaven with her. On Monday nights the second floor played alternative music and the drinks were dirt cheap. In Stafford I'd rarely gone out clubbing or to late-night bars. Adrienne from art college was always desperate for me to dance at Prop's wine bar with the gang but I'd always decline with a silly excuse like, 'I'm cleaning out my goldfish tank tonight.' There was part of me that was really afraid of social interaction. I didn't like the thought of being surrounded by so many drunken people, especially where there was the possibility of running into the men who bullied me. It scared me to be around male aggression – a fear directly related to my childhood. Instead of the clubbing scene I preferred getting drunk with friends in fields, parks or the safety of our bedrooms.

But London was a whole other kettle of fish and on a chilly Monday night while listening to Le Tigre and drinking cheap white wine I got dressed to go to Heaven. In 2000 my hair was dyed raven black and cut into a choppy bob with a fringe. I was still wearing flared jeans and sparkly home-made T-shirts. In my usual style I smudged glitter around my eyes, added a choker to my slightly Goth look and trotted to the train station. Amy had said very little about what Heaven was like, so I didn't know where it was or what to expect. While on the Northern line she let it drop: 'Heaven is a gay club.' I was confused, and not just about my gender identity. Shocked, I exclaimed, 'What? It's a GAY CLUB? And they play Marilyn Manson?' I couldn't comprehend it. It sounded like nothing I'd experienced before, nothing I thought possible.

In the queue outside Heaven, I saw my very first drag queen standing by the door of the club. I was immediately intimidated and in awe of this seven-foot, flame-haired dragon breathing smoke into my face. She flicked her hair and looked at me. 'One,' I said.

'One what?' she retorted.

'One entry,' I replied.

'Child, do I look like I'm working?' rasped the queen back to me in between drags on her cigarette. Amy laughed at me and said, 'Ignore him, he's new to London.' Indeed, I was as new as they come but over the moon to be there.

Once safely inside Heaven, the lights flashed to the excruciatingly loud sound of Suede's 'Beautiful Ones'. Girls and boys wearing plastic bangles and spiky dog collars girated towards each other under the hue of ultraviolet light. Alcoholic drinks glowed green, glitter highlighted revellers' cheekbones and I stumbled to the bar and ordered two pints of snakebite and black. The dance floor erupted to the sound of gender-blending, glam-stomping, alternative classics. I couldn't believe that an army of queer people were interested in rock music, I couldn't believe so many of them were here. It was the first time I'd ever seen men lip-syncing the words to David Bowie's 'Rebel Rebel' while posing like shop mannequins. I even saw a man wearing high-heeled shoes.

As I stood on the dancefloor utterly entranced, Amy whispered into my ear, 'I knew you'd like it!' In fact it was a complete revelation to me. While shopping in WH Smith's back home I'd often glanced curiously at the front cover of the gay magazine *Attitude*, but I wouldn't have been caught dead reading it. I still deemed the consequences too high. And yet here I was inside the beating heart of queer London. No wonder it was called Heaven.

I'll also never forget the first time I went to Camden Market. Historically, Camden Market is the alternative centre of north London and I was keen to lose myself there. For somebody who had just established a brand-new identity in London and recently discovered clubbing, I could buy whatever I needed there. It was the perfect place to start blowing my student loan on tat. Just like most other tourists or freshers discovering London, I happily snatched up as many studded belts, Dr Martens and second-hand blouses as I could carry. One of my biggest regrets in life is not buying a second-hand pair of white cowboy boots that fitted perfectly and were only £15. I shied away from the boots because I felt ashamed and embarrassed, another hangover I was yet to shake off. I often stopped myself from buying things I wanted for fear of being ridiculed or laughed at. I would have been fashion forward in 2000 wearing those beauties but totally on point now. I'll live and learn.

In the early years of university we haunted Camden. The Electric Ballroom, Purple Turtle and the Underworld clubs became popular destinations to get smashed and loaded. Camden Market with its street food and 'shrooms' were staples of our student survival. The bunch of eclectic punks that stood outside the tube station with orange mohawks, drinking from cans of Skol lager, and the crowds milling around Camden Lock were postcard images brought into hyper-reality every week. Waiting in the rain for the number 29 bus – the infamous 'party bus' – heralded the end of a good night.

I didn't realise it at the time, but I dug my new surroundings because I was anonymous. In this new city, I knew no one and no one knew me. I felt at home walking down the cracked, concrete-paved streets of Ponders End with its messy overgrown gardens and burnt-out cars. I didn't spy any net curtains twitching as I strolled past the endless rows of houses. I didn't hear any gossip in the corner shop. I didn't care about my neighbours and seemingly they didn't care about me. It was a release from the chastity of small village life, a welcome change from its parochial nature. I was discovering myself while discovering this epic new city.

One day I decided that instead of getting the tube everywhere, I would walk. I strolled past the familiar sites of the Astoria club and the Central St Martin's art school on Charing Cross Road. Carrying on, I wandered into China Town and saw row upon row of terracotta-coloured ducks hanging in restaurant windows, waiting to be devoured. I'd never eaten duck and I couldn't imagine how the greasy carcass could be seen as a delicacy. Eventually I wound up in Trafalgar Square and I remember sitting on the edge of a fountain and texting my mum: 'Hi Mum. Just found Trafalgar Square. Miss you but love it here. ;-) X'

There were so many 'Oh my GOD!' moments as I discovered new areas and stumbled across buildings I had seen in films. Trafalgar Square was one of the locations I'd only ever seen on the TV and suddenly it was right before me. Another time, my teenage self felt very cool as I travelled to Brixton while humming the song 'Guns of Brixton' by the Clash. With new eyes and little responsibility I was in awe of London's beauty. Bit by bit, I memorised the warren of streets above ground, while hopping on and off tubes underground. The city was a magnificent maze and I finally felt at home.

Back at university I loved my jewellery class, mainly because it was a predominantly female environment. Aside from myself, there was only one other male on the course. We learned the basics of jewellery construction, from soldering to polishing. I didn't like working with metals as I had a habit of overheating the silver, which would melt and become redundant. At our individual workstations we each had a gas torch to heat the metals. Every now and again you'd smell burning hair and turn around to see smoke rising from a student's head while the rest of us pissed ourselves laughing. Long hair and naked flames weren't good friends, however funny we found it.

The jewellery course at Middlesex was broad, which is why I liked it. The focus was 'body adornment' rather than designing traditional jewellery that you might find in Elizabeth Duke. I liked this approach and the freedom it allowed us. I was happy playing in the studio, constructing pieces out of scrap clothes and fabrics, and using dance, photography and mirrors to alter the body. This was the beginning of me using my creative practice to think about changing my body. I didn't worry about the wearability of my creations – it was about distortion and pushing the boundaries. I wanted to blur the lines and interrogate the conventional. I once stuck two colourful beads up my nose during an assessment with my lecturer. I was willing to try anything.

We shared the Cat Hill campus with the various fashion

courses. In the canteen we got to know who the fashion students were very quickly. In they would strut, in packs of three or four, adorned with oversized bags, fur stoles, white sports socks and asymmetrical haircuts. Without saying a word they'd scream, 'I'm in Fashion. Attention please. Me. Now!' And that was just the boys. They looked like they'd stepped right out from the pages of *The Face* magazine. I was green with envy while I ate my chips and beans. I knew I had to up my game.

In July 2001, the Strokes released their debut album *Is This It*, heralding a new style that I was more than ready to embrace. For those who were movers and shakers this was the beginning of a new musical era, which in turn influenced the style of the time. Skinny jeans, leather jackets, Converse trainers, messy hair and blazers became fashionable once again. I went to a nightclub called Popstarz at the Scala in King's Cross. When the DJ dropped anything by the Libertines, the Hives, the White Stripes (or any band beginning with 'the'), the crowd thrust cans of Red Stripe into the air and sang along. These were the anthems for the youth of the new millennium. If you were under thirty years old, this was an incredibly exciting emerging subculture. For everyone else, it was just a pastiche of the Seventies garage rock all over again.

I tried out this 'look' by modelling myself on the lead singer of the Vines, although I secretly wanted to be Karen O from the Yeah Yeah Yeahs. I fixed my hair in a shaggy, unbrushed style, wore less glitter and generally dressed down or up (depending which way you looked at it). For those couple of years, spending hours getting ready to look like you'd just crawled out of bed became the thing.

One assignment at university was visiting the Geffrye Museum in Shoreditch to research a project on interiors. I had no idea where Shoreditch was and it was confusing trying to work out how to get there. I had my trusted A–Z of London tucked inside my over-the-shoulder burgundy Adidas bag to help me. Once I arrived, I was on my guard – it felt rough and dirty.

I travelled by tube to Old Street and walked down the road towards Hoxton. I took in street art by Banksy, depicting John Travolta and Samuel L. Jackson holding bananas instead of guns, an iconic scene from the film *Pulp Fiction*. I walked past several abandoned warehouses and a club called 333. I knew this was a trendy place – I'd overheard the fashion lot talk about it while having a ciggy outside the uni bar. This was my first experience of Hoxton and the London borough of Hackney. There wasn't much fuss around it then. At this stage I didn't know about the Hoxton Square gallery scene or The Bricklayers Arms – venues that would soon become my go-to destinations. I didn't see people who looked like hipsters, or any 'Hoxton Fin' haircuts (a trendy hairstyle I was one year away from having). But some years later this would

become my stomping ground as I criss-crossed this small tri-
angle of east London from one after-party to another.

In my second year of university I moved with three girls
into a semi-detached house in Bounds Green. It was more
expensive than the halls of residence and further away
from college but it finally felt like we were living in the
heart of London. The tube rattled noisily past the house,
making it vibrate in typical *EastEnders* style. Our second
year was like one long house party. Every weekend somebody was having a party. Either the fashion house, the fine
art house or the graphics boys' house. They were typically
the same affair week in, week out. Lots of alcohol, silly
dancing and vomit. I notoriously choreographed a dance
routine to 'Bootylicious' by Destiny's Child. At every
party the girls and I would dance to it, clutching an invisible hat and lip-syncing along to Beyoncé.

Within my circle of friends in London, I eventually came
out as a gay man. After I'd visited Heaven and many other
'alternative' clubs, for the first time I saw people that I could
relate to. I finally shook off the constant name calling from
my childhood, which had left me timid, shy and uncomfortable. With this new freedom and the opportunity of finding
romance in every nightclub in Zone One, I happily basked
underneath the LGBTQ rainbow trying to find the hidden
pots of gold. Boys were bountiful as I relaxed into my identity, and I was delighted to find other gays who liked glitter,

spice and all things nice. I made friends with people who openly rejected gender binaries, referring to themselves as 'genderqueer' and 'transdrogynous'. I was no longer alone.

I discovered I didn't need to feel any shame around my sexuality. It was a revelation to me that liking men wasn't a bad thing. I'd grown up suffocated by the mentality that if you took it up the bum you were disgusting and revolting. I heard people call Julian Clary out for being effeminate, saying horrible things about his mincing physique. Where I was from, being camp was a crime and flamboyance was frowned upon. It was only when celebrities like Will Young, Stephen Gately and H from Steps frequented the front covers of magazines owning their sexuality that people in my village finally got the gist that being a gay person was OK. These stars portrayed a version of homosexuality that was digestible to my sorry hometown peers as they dipped their white bread sandwiches into lukewarm tea.

'Coming out' is a monumental moment in most queer people's lives. I'd grown up hearing horrific stories about families disowning children and the many street queers rejected from their families who have nowhere to go. This petrified me. I didn't think my family would go as far as to disown me but I didn't know what the consequences would be. It was a daunting time.

I told my mother that I was gay on the night of my sister's eighteenth birthday. I was twenty and had been living in London for two years, so I was no stranger to the scene. At this point in my life I was comfortable being queer; I felt I'd found an identity that I could wear well. While drowning myself in Bacardi rum I began to brag to my sister's mates about my queer life in the big smoke. I knew in my heart that I should have told my mum before one of the little tipsy seventeen-year-olds got there first. Gossip spread like wildfire through the village.

Once home and sucking heavily on a Marlboro Light (my heart was beating so fast I thought I might have a heart attack), I said, 'Mum, I've got something to tell you . . . Erm, I'm gay!' This was a pivotal moment in my life and the first time I had to 'out' myself to my mum. Being honest and truthful was a huge weight off my shoulders. I felt an instant release at no longer hiding my identity or behaviour; I immediately relaxed. To my relief, her response was 'I bloody knew it!' which made me laugh. It was fantastic to come out and admit my sexual preference after so many years of confusion and shame. My mum and I became much closer as a result. Some years later my sister told me that she identified as a lesbian and had started a relationship with a woman. Several years after that, I had another 'coming out' ceremony all over again.

In the early Noughties I was the happiest I'd ever been. Living in London turned out to be the best thing for me – I was geographically and emotionally miles away from everything that had caused me distress and it showed. Although I did experiment with my 'presentation', this period was definitely the most 'masculine' of mine in recent years and I was comfortable with that. I still dyed my hair different colours and at one point I had a bleached Hoxton Fin, similar to David Beckham at the time – but we all make mistakes!

I can vividly remember the day two aeroplanes crashed into the World Trade Center in New York. My housemates and I should have been at university but we decided to stay at home and eat cheese toasties instead. We were watching an episode of the American talk show *Sally* and gossiping about the guests when an announcement appeared on the TV. We immediately turned over and watched the events unfold. In shock we talked about the end of the world, wondering what would happen next and if London would be at the mercy of an attack. We were petrified it was the beginning of World War III.

It was one evening around the time of the terrifying attacks when we decided to dress up and photograph ourselves doing stupid things. We were bored and looking for cheap ways to amuse ourselves. My outfit consisted of a long pink wig and a trilby hat, and several layers of lipstick. Jen photographed me lying on the sofa, in a casual but slightly feminine catalogue-style pose. Although we were messing around and taking the piss out of each other, this female presentation ignited something that had been lying dormant inside me for a long time. I felt fantastic, I felt like me. Feelings clicked into place and I found myself saying to myself, 'Yes, you should have long hair. Yes, you should wear make-up. This feels really good!' Dressing in a femme presentation seemed deeply natural to me. Suddenly – and surprisingly – I was being honest with myself about how I truly felt underneath the costume of a boy.

As I stood there all dressed up in front of my friends, I felt vulnerable exposing this part of myself. To them it was just a game – not a life-defining, revelatory moment like it was for me. I loved playing with my identity and I used every possible opportunity to dress up in masks and make disguises. This moment wasn't supposed to be serious – how could it be, I looked ridiculous. I doubt my friends realised the impact it had and how the experience stayed with me. Despite being deeply affected, I didn't harbour any thoughts or hopes that I could transition, although I did acknowledge that a sense of 'otherness' was lurking, slowly oozing out of my pores. I just didn't know when or how 'she' would materialise.

During the summer of 2002, I moved to an area called Clapton. No one had ever heard of Clapton back then – it was the arse end of Hackney and not a place you'd desire to live. In those days you had to catch the crammed Silverlink train if you wanted to travel to east London. Hackney, Homerton, Dalston, Hackney Wick and Clapton weren't for the faint-hearted, but they were deliciously cheap. For the grand sum of £240 a month I lived in a huge three-storey townhouse with four others. It was rough around the edges and the area was in decline, but at that bargain price we definitely weren't complaining. At this time there was a derelict building on Lower Clapton Road that had a blue neon sign on its front façade. It read 'EVERYTHING IS GOING TO BE ALRIGHT'. I clocked the electric slogan as I

*Pink wigs and trilbies, a casual 'dressing up' night
in Bounds Green (2002)*

witnessed two young boys setting off a firework in the direction of an old lady walking down the street. I wondered if everything really was all right in this part of town. I didn't know then that the neon sign was by the artist Martin Creed.

Hackney had a bad reputation; it was a gangland. We lived with the soundtrack of sirens day and night. Every time I said I lived in Clapton, people would shudder and reply, 'Ooh, Murder Mile!' I didn't know where this mile began or ended, but apparently I was slap bang in the middle of it. After several months things became rather shady. The house next door but one was being squatted in and the occupants had frequent loud parties with lots of people coming and going all through the night. We would watch them all from our kitchen window, drinking in their back garden at 8 a.m. One night on my way home I noticed a prostitute standing on the corner of Chatsworth and Millfields Roads. She had straightened long blonde hair and was wearing black PVC knee-high boots. I noted how her body language changed the instant a car drove past – selling herself and thrusting her tits into the air. I saw her regularly for a couple of weeks and then she disappeared into thin air. It struck me one day, as I walked past the squatted house, that it was a place to buy drugs. I'd heard the description 'crack house' used on TV, but now I was seeing it for real. I began to avoid walking past, instead walking around the block, especially at night when there'd be odd characters sitting on the steps, 'watching'. There was an uncomfortable energy on that corner and we all felt it.

It was a crisp autumnal evening when two of my housemates, Carolyn and Mike, and I decided to go to the local pub for a pint. As we left our house and walked down the steps, I noticed two men leaving the shady house. We continued our short journey through the nearby estate, which was the route we always took. As we turned around the corner we saw the two men standing there. They looked at us, we looked at them and we carried on walking. As we passed them, they grabbed Mike, pushing him against the wall. Carolyn and I stopped dead in our tracks before they shoved us against the brick wall too. One of the men had a gun concealed inside the sleeve of his jacket and he thrust the end of the gun into my leg.

'Give me your wallet,' he said. But I didn't have my wallet on me; all I had was £10 in my jeans pocket. I hadn't even brought my phone out because I didn't think I'd need it. I handed over my £10 and they moved on to Carolyn. Carolyn had cleverly hidden her phone inside her bra during the kerfuffle and denied having anything else on her. Next they moved on to Mike, who was holding a carrier bag containing a DVD of *Julian Donkey-Boy* and a portable CD player. He was reluctant to hand it over, wanting to keep the DVD. The muggers asked, 'Is that porn?' Mike very smugly informed them, 'It's an art film by Harmony Korine.' But under Carolyn's insistence he handed over his swag and the two men walked off. It was a surreal three minutes, like a scene from a movie. Immediately after it happened, we just stood there for a while, shocked and confused. I couldn't believe we'd been held up at gunpoint. Oddly enough it wasn't all that scary, violent or threatening. It was very matter-of-fact and it felt like a dream.

Once we'd jerked back to life again we walked to the police station in Hackney and reported the incident. The police immediately bundled us inside a squad car and drove us around the streets trying to find the two men. I told the police I knew exactly where we could find them, but they didn't listen. Instead we were driven around under a blue flashing light, a beacon to everyone else, but not much help to us. We never found the two men and Mike never got his swag back. Early one morning a week or so later the police raided the house. Woken up by the commotion, I saw several people being marched down the path, handcuffed, and stuffed inside a police van. The house was immediately boarded up and we didn't hear another peep from it again. Months later it was bought and renovated into a nice family home. Not a squatter in sight.

I've lived in Hackney for fifteen years. It is a place that I can call home. Happily, being mugged at gunpoint is the only time I've been on the receiving end of violence in the area. Chatsworth Road has changed dramatically over the past twenty years – it's almost unrecognisable. Pre-Olympics, I used to go to the car boot sale in the disused greyhound stadium in Hackney Wick. I bought pirate copies of David Bowie CDs and anything to make jewellery with. It was a random market, with all sorts of East End types selling their wares. Hackney Wick was made up of lots of factories and warehouses, with raves happening every weekend. I liked Hackney because you could jump on the bus and get right into town. In my early days the Routemasters seemed to whisk you down to Tottenham Court Road in no time. After two years of living in London, I didn't relate to the country boy any longer.

A turban on the beach in Crete (2004)

Chapter 4

THE CLUB KID IS BORN

As soon as my second year at university ended I set to work as part of my placement year. I began working for Paul Seville, who makes leather accessories. It was a brilliant first placement and it clarified my love of London and my love of designing. It was a thrill running around town assisting a designer, seeking out stockists all over the city and purchasing materials.

After my initial placement I started working for a small company on Brick Lane called Tatty Devine. I was immediately struck by their designs – I hadn't seen anything like them. They were daring and out there and I felt an instant kinship with them. I couldn't wait to be part of their colourful world. I began assisting on the production of jewellery. It was a close-knit group – we'd sit around a large table, eating bagels and gossiping while we attached guitar plectrums to safety pins and glued brooch backs onto two-dimensional wooden budgies. I found Rosie and Harriet – who run Tatty Devine – very inspiring. I loved how they would arrive dressed for work. Harriet wore boiler suits and bright pink Converse, while Rosie wore berets and styled her hair like a 1920s silent movie star. They wore their passions and eccentricities with pride. We happily worked away while listening to bands such as Belle and Sebastian, Stereolab, Huggy Bear and Chicks on Speed. I really believe that certain people arrive in your life as catalysts, to help you grow and move forward. My time working with Harriet and Rosie was just that, and they helped mould me greatly. They nourished me very generously with their time and energy.

In 2003, Tatty Devine contributed to 'Fashion East' – an edgy offshoot of London Fashion Week. I was very fortunate to play a part in the concept from drawing board to catwalk show. Everyone – including Harriet's mum – contributed to the production of that show. The models wore pixie ears for the runway and I was delighted to be given my own set of ears. I wore them all day and all night, reluctant to take them off. I loved their sweet, playful and humorous aesthetic.

I stayed with Tatty Devine for the rest of my placement year, working as the 'Saturday girl' in the Brick Lane store. Through my Tatty connections I also secured a job at Hoxton Boutique and met stylists from the ultra-cool

Dazed and Confused and *i-D* magazines. It dawned on me that I was enveloped in everything I'd dreamed of when I was sixteen years old.

It was during my placement year that I began to realise the currency in nightclubbing. I noticed very early who the 'movers' were in the club world. If anything I sought them out because I longed to be part of that world too. I'm talking about the individuals who'd get picked out of the queue and walked straight to the front while looking down their noses as they strutted past you. The characters who wore funny clothes, dressed up like clowns and jesters, and the recurring faces propping up the bar. I knew I could join that gang; it was only a matter of time.

On Monday nights, Trash in Soho was the place to be seen, and I was there. I got there so early that often I was the first person in the queue – a foolproof plan to avoid getting turned away. I slowly got to know the 'door whores', as they were affectionately known. If you looked familiar and turned up week after week, it drastically improved your chances of getting into the club – although this method couldn't always be relied on. The door whores had all the power and I wanted it too.

Clubs were absolutely pivotal in shaping my identity. I remember dancing in a club called Area in Vauxhall and turning around to look at the DJ. They were powdering their face in a compact mirror and pulling cute little poses to the music. The DJ was called Tasty Tim and I was instantly fascinated. Tasty Tim was wearing a face full of beautifully applied make-up, with extra-long eyelashes and gorgeous pouty lips. Tasty's hair was a shocking mop top of blue and green feathered spikes that trailed down the back. Tasty was exquisite – a perfect example of someone rejecting gender entering my consciousness and having an impact.

I started to embrace clubbing and partying. There was a scene growing around me, which I thought I could easily become a part of. It contained kindred spirits: art and fashion students, photographers, dancers, queers and locals from the estates. Budding young wannabes, singers, MCs and DJs also frequented the mix. Larger than life personalities appeared overnight with no intention of disappearing into the shadows of Soho.

The 'THE' movement rattled, rolled and burnt out. The Libertines broke up and checked into rehab. Kids didn't know where to go next as their idols crashed and burned. By this point I'd found a new tribe of edgy social climbers, colourful creatures and catwalkers. It all started way back in 2001. Back then I read about it in the *NME* but I was still tucked away inside a jewellery studio in north London. I read articles about a band from New York called Fischerspooner who'd released a single called 'Emerge'. The sound was given the name 'electroclash' by the DJ Larry Tee. I liked this movement more than the 'THE' movement. This style was neon, modern and queer all rolled into one. I saw photos of Fischerspooner and instantly loved them. They exuded drama – mixing camp, cabaret and art. They used make-up, hair pieces and clothes to dramatic effect. All of a sudden many other dazzling artists were smeared all over the media. You couldn't escape the Scissor Sisters' and Peaches' similar aesthetic. I was crazy for this new sound and style, which seemed to give me a free pass to explore my own femininity.

The course of my life was about to change as I strutted aboard a boat moored on the River Thames called the *Tattershall Castle* with my new bessie Hanna Hanra. The boat was home to a new club night called Kashpoint. This club, together with the people I met there, would be important in my life for the next ten years. Show woman Bishi and MC Matthew Glamorre held court on this damp Thursday night as day-glo gender delinquents swaggered around the dance floor to the sound of 'Train' by Goldfrapp. Inspired by the modernist sounds of electroclash, clubbers introduced a new razor sharp style into the grubby early Noughties aesthetic. Kashpoint was a prime example of the many new clubs that littered London at that time. Nag, Nag, Nag, The Cock, Computer Blue and

Golf Sale all held weekly parties, which anyone who was anyone made sure they were seen at.

I'd studied the likes of Ziggy Stardust, Brian Molko and Marilyn Manson. I knew how to apply make-up and I knew how to style my hair. I was primed for this emerging style and fully embraced it. Up until this point I'd kept the boy who liked to wear make-up hidden safely in his bedroom, frustrated and unable to find an outlet. The scenes of Glam rock, the New Romantics and Romo had been and gone and were only to be found in reference books at the library. I was yet to find a scene that embraced femme, camp and colourful boys that wasn't mainstream. When electroclash arrived I'd found my calling. I started wearing expressive, crazy outfits and drawing the attention of many. Once I went out wearing a floor-length fur coat and dunce's hat to a nightclub in Shoreditch called Candy Is Dandy, But Liquor Is Quicker. Here I caught the eye of Kashpoint promoter Matthew Glamorre, who asked if I wanted to start working on the door for the legendary 'Alternative Miss World' competition. A week later I was dressed as a 'black hole' and stuffed behind the counter of the Hippodrome nightclub ticking Pete Doherty and Amy Winehouse off the guest list. Amy was so thrilled that I'd let her in for free that minutes later she came back with a whiskey and Coke for me.

To keep up with my club commitments I had to source

garish and strange items of clothes. I'd religiously travel to car boot fairs to buy cheap oversized accessories, odd children's toys and anything I could customise into a 'look'. A lady at the Battersea boot fair was selling lots of old stock from her clothes shop, which had recently closed down. I bought bags full of Eighties cocktail dresses, harem-style trousers and printed leggings. My bedroom was beginning to resemble a church jumble sale with exotic-looking things stuffed in boxes or hanging from the ceiling. I collected a

I'm a Club Kid at Kashpoint (2004)

lot of clobber, with the odd exciting designer item thrown in for good measure to balance out the tat. My outrageous creations were strictly night-time garments – I wouldn't have dared to do my weekly shop wearing stilettos in broad daylight. During the day I wore scruffy clothes, not bothering to spend time considering outfits for 'Ryan'. I was far more preoccupied with creating fantasy creatures and ripping off the latest Dior catwalk looks with my student budget. At night my desired identity came alive.

Clubbing opened up many doors for me and widened my eyes to other possibilities. Trans women started to appear in my life, especially on the nightclub scene. At first I was envious of the women that I spoke to; I was jealous of their beautiful and calm demeanour. I saw elements of myself reflected back to me, but I knew they had gone through a process of transformation and I was intrigued. At the same time, I resented them for having the courage to fulfil their desires. I hadn't considered transitioning but my eyes were finally being opened to the possibility of it, although I was still years away from being able to accept it within myself. My gender identity was slowly piecing itself together, bit by bit – one polka-dot polyester blouse at a time.

I didn't communicate these feelings to anyone. Instead I used dressing up as a way of expression, resonating how I was feeling. Over time I lost my night-time look of wacky clown drag in favour of a presentation that looked more feminine, because that was the presentation in which I felt most at ease. I wanted to be seen by others as a woman and began adjusting my wardrobe accordingly. Most of the time I borrowed clothes from my female flatmates, incorporating wigs from Dalston and high heels from Primark. In the dark, shadowy crevasses of a nightclub, I might have got away with it if you were partially sighted, and this pleased me. However, my make-up was very heavy and far too over the top for a natural aesthetic. When I tried to achieve something which was feminine and failed, it really angered me. I spent hours trying to perfect a clean flick using liquid eyeliner. When it smudged I would draw black lines all over my face in frustration and go out like that. I didn't always want to look like a club freak but I hadn't figured out how to be feminine yet, so I just rolled with it.

Towards the end of that placement year I took a holiday to New York, which was a milestone of growth in my life. Just like London, New York had an energy that enthralled me. I was left to my own devices in a new city for ten days – it was magical! Everything and everyone in New York entertained me. I visited a club run by Larry Tee called Berliniamsberg. This was the first time I encountered the celebrity transsexual Amanda Lepore and the throngs of brightly coloured creatures of the night, known as the club kids. I was well on the way to becoming a club kid myself, a vocation I happily immersed myself in.

The summer of 2003 was scorching. I remember sitting on the steps of Hoxton Boutique. There were no customers to attend to – anyone with any sense was sunbathing in Hoxton Square or drinking in London Fields. I was wrapping up my placement year and dreading the return to university. I didn't want to stop partying or working at Tatty Devine – I was leading a very comfortable exist-ence. University seemed a lifetime away because of my jam-packed, clubbing routine. A club kid's week looked like this:

Sunday night – George & Dragon/Golf Sale
Monday night – Trash/Heaven
Tuesday night – Stay in
Wednesday night – Trash Palace/Nag, Nag, Nag (if you were lucky enough to get in)
Thursday night – Kashpoint
Friday night – The Cock/Popstarz
Saturday – Stay in

It was a wonder we had time to do anything else. To most this routine would have seemed excessive and I'm sure my liver would have agreed. But to myself and many other club kids, this whirlwind contained the forging of new identities and new friends.

Being in my early twenties on the club scene was really

exciting because you never knew what could happen or who you would meet on a night out. I remember once wearing an Elizabethan-inspired ruff made from black tutu material, a glittery bowler hat and black high heels. A woman came up to me and said, 'You look amazing!' In my dry Midlands accent I managed to exhale 'I know!' and walked off. The next day I was told the woman who spoke to me was the singer Björk.

There was an unwritten rule between us club kids: our outfits needed to get bigger, wilder and more daring every time. The more ridiculous, the more everyone applauded. You couldn't be seen wearing the same thing twice, and if you couldn't afford a new wig you wore a handbag on your head. By day we made our outfits and at night we came alive. My tribe and I wore OTT make-up, high heels and cardboard boxes. We called ourselves art.

I once made an outfit out of four large yellow rubber rings and the striped cushion of a sun lounger. It wasn't my greatest moment, especially when I returned home and couldn't find my house keys. It looked like a human Cheese String was trying to break the door down.

My creativity and design skills definitely came in handy for my many outfits. I used pom-poms, papier-mâché and foam (particularly car sponges) to create headwear which I adorned with sequins and Indian decorations. My house-mate Carolyn drew my attention to an artist called Leigh

Bowery in a biography of him subtitled *The Life and Times of an Icon* by Sue Tilley. This book became my bible – I was hooked on the stories of cheap decadence in 1980s London. I was inspired by Leigh, who went to such uncomfortable lengths to transform his body into different forms. He was often referenced in popular culture in the early Noughties, with John Galliano dedicating his spring/summer 2003 show to his old friend. Occasionally people would approach me in nightclubs and say, 'Great look, very Leigh!' It was a lovely accolade, but I also wanted to be praised for my own merits. I wanted to generate my own style – to feel like me.

The more visible you became, the more praise you received. If you bagged the job of doing the door at the newest hotspot, you were considered someone to 'know'. A close friend of mine, Jeanette, outdid us all when he was appointed as the door whore at a hot new club called Family, somehow blagging a new Gareth Pugh designer outfit each week.

Using my real name of Ryan Wagg just didn't seem to fit with my burgeoning career as a successful scenester. The people surrounding me were called Jim Warboy, Molaroid and the Disco Wizard. I wanted to separate myself from the village boy and fully embrace my new night-time persona, so I decided to change my surname from Wagg to Styles. As well as being in keeping with my new eccentric

style, it was also a pun on the successful American come-
dian Ryan Stiles. It was done. 'Ryan Styles' was born, the
new flamboyant persona of Ryan Wagg. It was a decision
that took just two minutes – I think I may have briefly
discussed it with my fellow door whore Scottee while
standing outside Kashpoint one cold Thursday night. I
didn't know then that this new name would stay with me
for a long time to come.

With 'Ryan Styles' appearing frequently on club flyers,
and now my official MySpace profile, I was gaining a reputation for being something of an 'it' boy. I'd transcended
from being a regular clubber to nightclubbing royalty
within months. I secured jobs working on the doors of all
the hottest clubs, getting to know hundreds of people who
turned up week after week looking for love, oblivion and
connections in London's nightclubs. I partied with A-list
celebrities and enjoyed turning away *Big Brother* reality
TV stars who grovelled at the desk trying to get in for free.
But beyond the sequins and false eyelashes lay a different,
deeper need. It wasn't just about free booze and photos
splashed across magazines. This chapter of my life was a
voyage of discovery that I needed to embark upon, freeing
my inner desire to experiment with my image and my gender. At this point I still didn't explicitly identify as a trans
woman. This process was taking years to work through in
my head. Instead I was a club kid, drag queen and a freak.

I was extremely happy with how far I'd come and how I was living my life.

All this nocturnal activity spilled over into my final year of university. During an assessment with my tutor, hungover from the night before and the night before that, I told her, 'I just want to make necklaces out of tennis balls!' The costumes of my night-time were bleeding into my daytime. Although I'd already spent four months working on my final project, I'd hit a wall. The endless hangovers left me confused about what direction I wanted to take with my art. I was being forced to re-evaluate who I was in the harsh light of day when I stripped away my after-dark identity. My final show consisted of large masks made from brightly coloured vacuum-formed foam, accompanied by photographs of myself wearing the pieces illuminated in large lightboxes. I called the collection 'Approaching Anonymity' because the head adornments disguised and disfigured my features. This work blended my two personas of 'clubber' and 'maker'. I was tentatively exploring the possibility of leaving 'Ryan' behind because I wanted to escape him and explore the potential of something or someone new.

I graduated university with a successful 2.1. My dissertation on 'Gender Exploration: Bowie, David Beckham and the Kashpoint Clubbers' received a first. It was an accomplishment to be proud of – I'd completed the course

I'd moved to London for. Our degree show was installed in Brick Lane's Truman Brewery and the Oxo Tower in the summer of 2004. Our technician helped me through many agonising moments, trying to attach heavy light-boxes onto concrete walls and making them level. I often wondered about the tennis ball necklaces, and how much easier they would have been to display.

Once the never-ending degree shows and parties were out of the way, the big question was, 'What are we going to do next?' I thought about applying for a Masters at the Royal College of Art but worried about how I was going to afford it. I also knew that I was enjoying the nightclubs and that they could potentially be a source of revenue in the future. In the end, Tatty Devine came to my aid, with a newly opened boutique in Soho. I began working in the shop on a part-time basis, which allowed me to pursue my art on my days off. I loved travelling into Soho every day, getting to know the other sales assistants in the area. I often witnessed dodgy dealings in the nearby courtyard as fake sex workers ripped off willing punters and tourists. I'd often be in cahoots with the many scallywags and ped-dlers, exchanging pleasantries on the street. I liked that you could witness the seedy side of Soho if you looked beyond the façade of fancy restaurants.

In Soho my mind would race as gender identities were regularly played with on its streets. I saw a tall transgender woman with long red hair weaving down Berwick Street buying fruit from the market. I even witnessed the transition of a traffic warden whose hair grew longer and whose appearance slowly became more feminine. Although I had many questions I wanted to ask them it didn't seem appropriate to stop them in the street. But I gained a wider knowledge of a transition timeline just by observing everything over the two years I worked at the Soho boutique. Something was sparked in me.

Another bonus was that the shop was in an ideal location for getting dressed up to go clubbing. When I closed the boutique at 7 p.m. I'd walk to Old Compton Street to grab a falafel wrap and then meet people in the Friendly Society bar for a drink. An hour or so later I'd be back at the shop to put on my high heels and lip gloss, ready to strut down the streets of Soho and into Madame Jojo's, Trash Palace or the Ghetto nightclubs. At first, every step I took generated an internal 'Ouch!' as my feet adjusted to the court shoe heels and a new pace of walking. Tourists would stop me in the street and ask for a picture, to which I'd hiss, 'That'll be a fiver!' and carry on walking. Curious men occasionally wolf-whistled as I passed them standing outside the old man pubs but the majority of people didn't bat an eyelid. There was a mentality in central London and Soho that anything goes. The unexpected is expected and largely accepted.

After two years of working at Tatty Devine, I felt it was time to pursue my dreams of becoming a self-employed artist. I'd secured enough club work to provide a healthy weekly income and I wanted to branch out. I liked the idea of becoming a performer, devising work with other companies and acquaintances. The reality of standing on the door of a club until 2 a.m. before heading home and getting up for work at 8 a.m. was also taking its toll. It would have been easier to sleep in the Tatty boutique rather than slogging back to Hackney on the night bus most nights. With a constant hangover as company, my days were getting shorter and I found it difficult to be productive, staying in bed for as long as possible. My art was beginning to stall.

Getting paid to dress up and play around with my identity was a dream job. I lavishly created a multitude of personas and key 'looks'. One of my favourite adornments was a huge Mohawk headdress I created using raven and peacock feathers. One night I'd teamed the headgear with a black dress and a journalist from a style magazine in L. A. approached me outside a club and asked, 'Where is that dress from? It's amazing!' I told her it was a Dior dress that I'd customised and practically destroyed. The journalist looked visibly shocked and saddened by my cheeky tale. The reality was I'd bought the dress from a charity shop in Peckham and couldn't have paid more than £3 for

it. Like they say, it's not what you wear, but how you wear
it. The fashion designer Gareth Pugh said I looked great
that night, which was a high accolade and made the pain of
the Mohawk glued to my head all the more worth it. My
outfits were becoming increasingly painful and cumbersome. If the club didn't have a changing room it meant
hailing a taxi into town. It could often feel glamorous
whizzing past the sights of London all dolled up and giddy
about making my grand entrance into the club. But more
often than not I was battling away in the back seat with
fifteen helium balloons attached to my outfit, trying to
figure out how get out of the car stylishly for any awaiting
paparazzi.

Before I moved to London I'd seen London Fashion
Week parties depicted on *Absolutely Fabulous*. They
looked like bitchy, smoky, champagne-fuelled riots. Obviously, I couldn't wait to join in. True to form, I found
fashion parties to be wild. At one notable party, my two
friends Russella and La John Joseph accompanied me. At
this point I was regularly starstruck when I saw pop stars
or actresses I admired. This particular party was overflowing with grade A celebrities and I was wide-eyed. I
drunkenly chatted to Róisín Murphy and art dealer Jay
Jopling (I have no idea what about) while Russella blagged
himself into Kate Moss' private cupboard, and was subse-
quently swiftly ejected.

Fashion parties equal free alcohol. Every fashionista knows this. That's why there would always be a queue at the bar while we tried to fill up every glass we could find. If you're wearing five-inch stiletto platforms, four wigs and three waist cinchers, you need alcohol. It's medicinal, trust me.

Towards the tail end of the Noughties I'd become slightly redundant as a 'club kid'. A new subculture had emerged from the spikes of electroclash called 'Nu-Rave', epitomised by geometric neon prints and sound-tracked by the band Klaxons. Although many of my friends crossed over and embraced this new genre, I couldn't. Rather, I'd found a tribe of cavorting, bearded trannies to run around with so I could indulge in my cross-dressing exploits all night long. I was yet to consider my own transition, but at this stage I did begin to identify as a tranny. We used the word 'tranny' because it was a label that fitted who we were. Labelling ourselves as 'drag queens' didn't seem appropriate; it felt dated. The term 'female impersonator' also felt ingrained with a different connotation. We weren't trying to impersonate anyone – we expressed the feminine, masculine and otherness found within everyone. A tranny didn't necessarily mean you had to be in drag – it's a more fluid term. As trannies, we explored flamboyant, sexualised presentations of ourselves to queer and corrode heteronormative structures.

Within our world, there were many variations of trannies. It wasn't exclusively boys wanting to be girls – I knew women with vaginas who called themselves trannies. East London adopted and reappropriated the word, creating a space where we all felt safe. We took ownership of the term, and used the word with love, not hate. I do need to define that a tranny is different to a transsexual or transgendered person. The word should never be used to address others. Beyond our own use it is offensive, derogatory and causes upset. We used the word proudly in the Noughties, but it's doubtful I would use it now.

From the outside, it may have seemed that my glittering friends and I were just going out and partying till all hours and there was nothing more to it than that. While it's true that there was an element of euphoria and hedonism in our activities, I like to think we were also influencing culture. We were cultural catalysts. We created the parties, created the events and created a scene. This whirlwind of parties, guest lists and VIP areas was a fantasy life I loved, but eventually the glitter would wash away. However many layers of lipstick, tiers of wigs and pairs of fake eyelashes I wore, at the end of the night I always went to bed naked. It was in those dark moments between reality and dream state that loneliness, despair and frustration ravaged my mind. Over time I found that going out dressed as a boy completely lost its appeal. I no longer had fun or felt comfortable. It felt like I wasn't presenting the best version of myself – I knew there was more to reveal, more layers to unpeel. I wanted to experiment even more with my identity and push it to the furthest limits imaginable.

I needed to refocus. The pain of living with who I hadn't become was unbearable. I felt confused. I felt like I was treading water and putting off the inevitable. The pain was so intense that I did everything I could to forget about it. It was easier to pretend it didn't exist than to face the possibility of a transition. What often stopped me from totally drowning in this crippling uncertainty was my newfound desire to become a performer. I'd witnessed the start of the cabaret scene in the early Noughties, and I knew I wanted to become a part of it. This scene was exciting and electric. I saw lots of people experimenting with personas and characters. I hoped I'd be able to combine my artistic background with my cross-dressing desires to create performances that would resonate with people.

Looking in from the outside, the performers I witnessed were clowns, strippers, tattooed ladies, freaks, transvestites, show girls and show-offs. I so desperately wanted to join this gang. Suddenly it made absolute sense why I changed my name . . .

'Ryan Styles' was the perfect pseudonym for a decadent cabaret ego.

Chapter 5

LIFE IS A STAGE

No need for words now . . . I'm a mime artist (2005)

I soon learned that a cabaret performer wasn't the decadent career choice I thought it was. The glamour is saved for the stage, but plenty of drama goes on behind the scenes. Public toilets and pub kitchens are often used as changing rooms, without any mirrors to assist with applying your make-up. In these scenarios you'd have to come equipped for any and every possibility. I'd do my make-up looking into the back of a CD while ten performers and I were squeezed into a disabled loo, squabbling over the warm white wine found on the backstage rider. The backstage rider is a glorious thing – one of the only comforts if you're changing in a freezing cold tent in the middle of a field at 2 a.m. That's the other thing about cabaret: it's often the graveyard shift. In the beginning I wouldn't expect to perform much earlier than 11 p.m. Quite often I'd be on the 38 Routemaster bus, half asleep with make-up smudged around my face, hoping not to catch the eyes of fellow passengers on my way home at 4 a.m.

True to my hopes, performing was an outlet for my desire to explore further possibilities when it came to my identity. I enjoyed creating a carousel of characters to bring alive on stage. These characters were often just me in a new wig, but even so, the difference between a short crop and a luxurious, shoulder-length layered wig brought out an alternate woman in me every time. Slowly, this is exactly how I began to view myself: as a woman. I wasn't cross-dressing for sexual kicks; I didn't get an erotic thrill when I wore female clothes. Rather, instinctively I wanted to look like a woman – an inner desire I'd harboured my whole life. Performing as a woman enabled me to satisfy these desires. It allowed me to escape the reality of being a boy. I felt comfortable when I appeared like this. I felt at home within my own body. When I saw myself as a woman the effect was tremendous – I was instantly happier. I started to think about what this meant, and the serious implications of transitioning. If appearing as a woman made me feel this content, I knew it was a way forward.

During my performance career there were many times when I portrayed a male character. I wore striped vintage male bathing suits and adopted a Pierrot aesthetic. There was a brief period when I even grew a moustache. (I'll explain that one a bit later!) To my surprise, I enjoyed playing up to these roles and acting out these typically 'male' cabaret characters. They felt like costumes, an act, and further away from how I truly felt than my feminine portrayals. I could distinguish the difference: these male roles were cabaret characters and not the real thing.

I never trained in theatre – my younger self hadn't known that the stage would be such a therapeutic outlet. My performance education was purely punk rock. It came from seeing musicians throw themselves around on stage, smashing their guitars over stacked amplifiers and diving into mosh pits wearing babydoll slips. It was only by moving to London, maturing and meeting other artists that I slowly began to hone my interests and branch out from my teenage fantasies.

My first solo performance was in a new venue called Bistrotheque as part of a show called 'Hanky Panky Cabaret'. I'd recently been inspired by two performers I discovered on YouTube called Marcel Marceau and Lindsay Kemp. Instead of talking to express ideas, they danced and moved gracefully to translate the narrative. This appealed to me as I was terrified of speaking on stage – I'd only ever used my voice singing backing vocals in Pretty Kitty. But I knew that I could move, and I could definitely make a costume that moved with me too. This felt like the best solution and I began searching for ways to make this happen. I had a concept, a costume and a soundtrack, so next I thought about the physical aspect of the performance. I spent hours in my bedroom trying things out in front of the mirror. I didn't know how you made up acts, so I just looked at the reflection of what I was doing and when the movement felt right, I used it. I realised my instinct was going to get me through it.

I concocted a strange plan. My idea was to stick a balloon inside oversized white pyjamas and pretend to give birth to it. Once the birthing was over I would take a puff on a large fake cigarette I had cunningly disguised down my long johns and then, perfectly timed to the music, I would pop the big white balloon to release the small red heart balloons hidden inside. Once these were revealed I would take the heart balloons and offer them out to the audience before walking off stage. This act seemingly came from nowhere, although I suspect a trip to a party shop in Dalston had something to do with my props. It was simple and naïve, and my make-up reflected this too; a simple white clown face with expressive black eyebrows. I didn't want to look female or male for this performance – I liked the idea of being androgynous. The performance wasn't directly addressing gender dysphoria because I wasn't clear on the condition in relation to myself – I still hadn't computed that I was suffering from it. Rather, the performance was simply the beginnings of expressing something 'other'. It was playful.

My first show was a hit. Members of the audience approached me afterwards saying how much they enjoyed the theme and wanted to see more. I went home feeling happy with what I had performed on stage that night. I knew this was the beginning of something special and I was raring for more. Luckily for me, I didn't need to wait long before being asked to perform again.

At the epicenter of this new alternative cabaret movement was a man named Jonny Woo. Woo is well known for his performances in Shoreditch and he was on the lookout for contestants to appear in Bistrotheque's new competition, 'Trannie Talent'. I didn't have a traditional talent to speak of but I knew that I could create a bizarre performance-art piece that would hopefully win an audience over.

It was the very first time I'd entered a talent competition and I had no idea what to expect. My plan was to create a big mess, which involved suggestively eating bananas, standing on a stack of dinner plates and squirting milk all over my waitress costume. It was a euphoric feeling, looking femme yet drenched in milk. At the end of the competition, it was the crowd that decided who was the winner. When the audience entered the cabaret room they were given two 'trannie dollars'. When the time came I leapt around the audience in my black high heels trying to collect as many dollars as possible in a pint glass. My popularity with the crowd shone through and I won the heat that evening. The validation from the audience deeply satisfied me. I automatically got entered into the final, which was in four weeks' time. I honestly didn't expect to get that far but I was thrilled.

The final was full of established performers. This time, instead of using 'trannie dollars' to decide the winner, two celebrity judges, DJ and club queen Princess Julia and fashion designer Giles Deacon, were on hand to cast their eye over the performances and determine the results. I breezed through the performance and made even more of a mess than the first time – I realised that the crowd enjoyed the chaos on stage. I had gained confidence since winning the first heat and was building my performance skills, much to the audience's delight.

For this show, my housemate Carolyn helped me with my

make-up. Carolyn taught me about primer, foundation and powder. 'When in doubt,' she said, 'always add more!' With her magic skills she lovingly created a face that was soft and feminine. I also wore a long curly blonde wig, which made me look like Madonna (a dream finally come true!). I felt fantastic.

Once each performer had showcased their 'talent', everyone lined up on stage to await the judges' decision. Third place was announced, and it wasn't me. Second place was announced and it still wasn't me. By this point I wasn't sure if I'd won, but being in front of the audience I kept smiling and nervously ground my heel into the stage. Jonny began the build-up: 'The winner of Bistrotheque's Trannie Talent Competition 2005 is . . . [very long pause] . . . Ryan Styles!'

The audience went wild as I raised my glass of Prosecco to the crowd. I was shaking, I was so thrilled. I couldn't believe I had actually won. It took minutes before it sank in; I was in total shock. My housemates ran up to me and gave me a hug, congratulating me. It was a good few minutes before I realised what had happened. Not only had I won the title, but also a £250 cash prize and a Sony Play-Station. However, this win would signify so much more to me than just the money and the PlayStation (which I sold immediately to a friend of a friend – it definitely wasn't my bag, not after the horrors of Subbuteo). That night I walked home carrying my drag bag over my shoulder with a big smile on my face. The event received great publicity and featured in scene magazines *Boyz* and *QX*. Word of mouth spread and I was springboarded onto the London cabaret scene. I had finally made it.

Bistrotheque became a very significant space for me. It was here that I grew and developed my own style of performance. After the success of the 'Trannie Talent' and the 'Transvestite Lip-Synchronicity' competitions, Bistrotheque owners Pablo Flack and David Waddington decided to get all the winners and popular contestants together to create a cabaret supergroup called The LipSinkers. If I was looking for an education in performance then The Lip-Sinkers was it. I made every mistake possible and honed my stagecraft during my stint with the group.

To The LipSinkers, cross-dressing was what mattered, and we were the first group of its kind in east London. I adored our work and being able to wear lacy bodices from Peacocks every Friday and Saturday night. The dressing room at Bistrotheque became known as the 'Trannie Tank'. This consisted of three toilet cubicles, a cleaner's cupboard containing hazardous chemicals, and a small surface with a mirror and a strip light. During the summer it was baking hot and in the winter it was stuffed full of props for The LipSinkers' Christmas show. With four, five or more performers crammed into the bogs, tempers would occasionally rise and silly cat-fights would break out. Quite often you'd find your wig on the floor, having been knocked over accidently, or your blusher in someone else's make-up bag.

I have many fond memories of the hilarious occurrences in our shows and on tour. It was often like living in a *Carry On* movie. We trundled back and forth, up and down the country, transporting cardboard cauldrons, blow-up dolls and suitcases of rags. Costumes often disappeared without a trace and we would always make do with a mop when we needed a broomstick.

What held The LipSinkers together was our friendship. During all the turbulence and mishaps, we behaved like professionals and the show kept rolling. I performed with The LipSinkers for seven years in total. Throughout my time in the troupe, babies were born, performers rotated and I transitioned from male to female. We worked so closely together for so long that they saw me right through my transition. As individuals they were amazing and adjusted very quickly to my new name and pronouns. I remember talking about my transition for hours with Richardette, as we drove through London to and from rehearsals. It's fitting that I turned to Richardette, who is known as 'Moth' within the group, which is short for 'Mother'. Every step of the way I felt supported by their friendships. We were like a family and everyone's emotional stability mattered.

I can't sum up why The LipSinkers were so special because I'm far too attached. I'm still emotionally inside

Photograph © William Baker

the madness as opposed to observing it from the outside. During my wonderful years with the group we received five star reviews, celebrity endorsements and gallons of free Prosecco. Every performance with The LipSinkers was utterly unique; no show ever felt the same.

This quote from *Time Out* London by cabaret critic Ben Walters perfectly sums it up:

The sensibility is utterly leftfield: the looks are brilliantly bonkers, the routines are tightly choreographed, despite

often giving the impression of on-the-hoof vamping; the
lip-synching itself is technically spot on; the acts are sexy
without really being erotic; and the chemistry between the
charismatic performers – Lisa Lee, Richardette, Rhyannon
Styles and Blanche Dubois – is affectionate and assured.

Things soon stepped up a gear for me. In December 2006, I
was invited to perform at the Guggenheim Museum in New
York. The event was officially called 'Solomon R. Guggenheim
Museum's Young Collectors Council' and was sponsored
that year by Armani. Aside from performing at the Guggenheim, I was also booked to perform at 'Distortion Disko' – an
infamous club-kid hangout run by night-life legends Kenny
Kenny and DJ Larry Tee. That was such a buzz! Instead of
visiting Larry's night, I was performing at it.

As I hit New York, it was absolutely freezing. I had to
dodge the ice walking around Central Park, the East Village and Brooklyn. I lapped up the city, visiting the
MOMA, Coney Island, Trash and Vaudeville, and peeked
through the windows of the recently closed CBGB music
club. I strolled to Patricia Field's and bought sequinned
berets while listening to Blondie. I ate 'Whoopie Pies'
from Ellen's Stardust Diner in Times Square as I read
Courtney Love's newly released diaries, *Dirty Blonde*. I
don't think New York could ever be boring. It always feels
like you're walking around a film set. As I trotted down

the avenues drinking coffee and smoking cigarettes, I day-dreamed about being Carrie Bradshaw from *Sex and the City*. Even though I was still Ryan, this reality didn't feel very far away. I could easily picture myself as a female col-umnist one day. (And here I am, today!) I thought about how far I'd come since my first trip to New York City. It struck me how much had changed in my personal life – I'd grown so much as a person and I felt independent and con-fident. Yet I knew I was still in a state of flux – I sensed there was more change looming on the horizon for me.

While in New York I felt more comfortable going into shops looking for female clothes – something about the anonymity of being a tourist swept away any feelings of shame around cross-dressing. And if anyone asked I could easily quip, 'It's for my performance at the Guggenheim, don't ya know!'

On the night of my performance I had no idea what to expect. I wanted to be prepared and decided to do my make-up in my hotel room. I didn't know what the dressing-room situation would be like and I wanted to look perfect. I felt slightly uncomfortable and comical leaving the hotel and hailing a yellow cab with my face painted white, exaggerated features drawn on and wearing a red fez hat to add to the craziness. But I reminded myself I was in New York and the cab drivers had probably seen it all before.

Arriving at the Guggenheim, I saw the red carpet rolled

outside and a long line of paparazzi on the sidelines. I had no idea it would be such a star-studded event. I was driven around the back to meet Susanne Bartsch – the well-known NYC nightlife doyenne. Susanne had heard about my performances through scenester Kenny Kenny and booked me for the show. I was in awe that I was on these stars' radars! I was shown to my dressing room, which was in the bowels of the museum, and left to wait. It felt strange being on my own, knowing a party was happening upstairs. I changed into my costume and prepared for my show, patiently waiting for my call. After a short while I was led upstairs and told to wait some more. Then, 3, 2, 1 . . . Large double doors swung open to reveal the ground floor of the museum, which was packed to the rafters. As I took in the vast crowd my heart skipped a beat and I wanted to run away. The bright lights turned blue as I heard the intro of my show music. I began to walk slowly to the stage at the side of the room. It was a surreal moment.

My show was finished in under four minutes. The time flew past. I left a small collection of red heart balloons on the stage, my performance legacy, and headed back towards the dressing rooms feeling on top of the world. It was only later when I scoured the internet for documentation of the show that I discovered the event was attended by celebrities such as Kim Cattrall, Mary J. Blige and Ivanka Trump, to name a few. I felt honoured to perform at such a

star-studded event and it was incredible to perform the
first show I ever created in a building world-renowned for
its grandeur, status and architecture. I was over the moon
with how my career had surged forward in the short year
since I'd won the Bistrotheque competition.

In the mid Noughties another important east London
venue championing the cabaret scene was the Bethnal
Green Working Men's Club – a kooky, detached venue on
Pollard Row. The BGWMC is actually still a functioning
working men's social club. Downstairs you find darts
tournaments while upstairs girls and boys twirl their tas-
sels. It was here that I made many new performance
friends, including the wonderful Paloma Faith. In 2006
Paloma drove me to the Big Chill Festival. We were both
shaking our bits to pay the rent and had been booked to
perform in the cabaret tent. Paloma was performing a
show which involved a fake belly stuffed with dead fish,
while I, dressed as the Virgin Mary and painted white,
cracked raw eggs over my head. Once our eccentric shows
were over, we were messy and desperately needed to wash.
We walked all the way to the other side of the festival in
search of the showers. After plodding through the mud
and past drunken punters we finally encountered a sign
saying: 'Due to water restrictions, the showers have been
turned off. Please come back at 9 a.m.' Our hearts sank.

We had to trudge back to the dressing rooms and use every baby wipe in sight to try and remove the white make-up and lingering smell of fish before we could shower in the morning. I told you performing isn't glamorous!

Paloma and I shared a love of the macabre. She introduced me to the music of Maria Callas and the Russian clowns in 'Slava's Snowshow'. We wanted to make a piece of performance art together, involving all the elements we loved. As a result we conceived a ten-minute spectacle called 'Love Will Tear Us Apart'. In 2007, we debuted the show at Bistrotheque's new cabaret night, UnderConstruction, programmed by the performer Lisa Lee. Paloma and I appeared as a mangled mess of hair, dressed in nude body suits which were sewn together down the side. The concept was that we were conjoined twins seeking to separate and become individuals. At the end of the show I choose glamour and fame instead of my twin. It's no coincidence: this was an analogy of how I felt at the time, desiring freedom and the need to finally be myself. As such, some of my performance work indirectly dealt with the themes of release and rebirth. For this performance I literally cut myself free using scissors while bursting several blood bags disguised in the costume. I crawled forward destined for a future wearing a pair of sequinned silver stilettos. As I separated myself from my conjoined twin she dramatically died as a result. It was a heavy concept but Paloma and I brought relief with our love of spectacle, camp and drama.

With my love of spectacle comes my love of music festivals. I first shimmied to Glastonbury Festival in 1999 at the age of seventeen. I made the pilgrimage to go and watch my favourite band Hole play on the Pyramid Stage. In music magazines I'd seen pictures of hippies wading through fields of mud – it didn't look appealing; it looked cold and wet. I imagined you'd get food poisoning from not washing your hands. But nonetheless I was intrigued because I loved bands and I was beginning to become aware that there was more to life outside my small village. At Glastonbury I spotted other festival-goers with blue hair, tattoos and piercings. Hungover, I brought fried-egg butties for 50p from ladies with dreadlocks out of a small Volkswagen campervan. I sampled 'space cake' from a man smoking a pipe with no teeth and dirty fingernails. I ate cold baked beans out of a tin for breakfast at 1 p.m. I didn't shower for three days. It was incredible.

My purple nail varnish glittered beneath the midsummer sun. I glued sequins and silver stars to my face using Vaseline. I wore 1970s women's polyester blouses that I bought from vintage stalls. I circled my eyes with black pencil and my wrists were adorned with plastic bangles. I wrapped myself in a feather boa as I watched Patti Smith, REM and the Manic Street Preachers. I smoked Marlboro Lights and drank Thunderbird wine straight from the bottle. I savoured every last drop of this magical universe. It's hard to believe it was nearly twenty years ago.

At Glastonbury I stepped into a different reality. The fourth dimension became home. At times I was on a different planet entirely. I was free to experiment and be myself without fear of anyone hurling abuse or mocking me. I saw so many others who were louder, wackier and more colourful than me, that I felt comfortable in my identity and expression. I can't reiterate enough how much of a relief it was. It felt thrilling, like the Wild West; cowboys were replaced by gangs of scallies with Scouse accents. Children walked around wearing fancy dress and women painted their bare breasts gold. Back in 1999 I caught a glimpse of myself, a small sliver of my future reflected back to me. I didn't know it at the time but it set off a powerful train of thought that would manifest itself eight years later under very different circumstances.

If I thought my first experience of Glastonbury Festival was cosmic then nothing prepared me for what was going to happen next. It's taken for granted now that you'll see drag queens at festivals, but before 2007, queer culture was almost completely absent from English festivals. Even cabaret and burlesque didn't have the strong presence it does today. In 2007, everything changed. That year, I rocked up with a small group of London cabaret artists and circus performers destined for 'Trash City'.

Trash City was a new field in Glastonbury, the brainchild of Joe Rush from the Mutoid Waste Company performance arts group, performer Ruby Blues and set designers Block9. I'd never seen anything like it; I felt like I was stepping straight into an apocalyptic dream. It was the future of civilisation haunted by the past. Scattered around the field were smashed-up cars with giant skulls attached to their roofs, ex-Royal Navy helicopters covered in graffiti, giant cranes shaped like mechanical arms with robots dancing at their feet, the body of a crashed aeroplane lying in the mud. This was my playground for the next five days. Its crowning glory was a nightclub called the NYC Downlow.

In my teenage naïvety I hadn't realised that after-hours Glastonbury existed. I thought that when the bands finished you went back to your tent and carried on drinking for a bit before going to sleep. I knew nothing about trekking to the Stone Circle field and watching the sunrise. I didn't realise that fields came alive as people took drugs and partied till 6 a.m.

The cinematic exterior of the NYC Downlow resembled a ruined New York City tenement building, which cleverly disguised the marquee behind it. It was beyond wild. It was a level of euphoria that I'd never experienced before. When the clock struck midnight, Trash City was only just waking up. Jets of fire shot out of destroyed buildings, acrobats hung from hoops and silks attached to cranes high in the sky. A pimped-out dystopian truck churned through the mud driven by a man with one eye as bejewelled drag queens held on for dear life in the back seat. This became our nightly ritual as people left the main stages in search of more.

The field became a swamp – it had rained heavily since we arrived. All the performers were walking around wearing fluoro wigs, sequinned leotards and wellies. We used the façade of the Downlow as a stage. We slipped on our heels and danced around the exposed rooms, entertaining the revellers in the queue. We hung out of the pretend open windows, heckling the crowd with dodgy American accents. Our motto became, 'What happens in the Downlow, stays in the Downlow, OK!' I was part of a dance troupe called 'Maude Adams and all their Children', which entertained the masses crammed inside the tent. We performed choreographed dance routines to Abba's 'The Visitors'. We held 'Vogue Balls' in tribute to the film *Paris Is Burning*, in which performers dressed up hoping to win the category of 'festival realness'. Every night the stage was invaded. Neon lights flashed as the DJs from Horse Meat Disco kept everyone dancing until dawn. We discovered, in the small crevasses of the club, people having sex wearing stuck-on moustaches, as our final dance routine to 'Ring Them Bells' by Liza Minnelli boomed out into the last shadows of darkness.

Behind the Downlow was our dressing room. For the first year the dressing room was a small marquee that we all squashed into. The following years we used a shipping container where we still felt like sardines, but at least it had a floor. The dressing room was the place where all the action really happened. Drag dramas unfolded as shoes were lost, costumes were covered in mud and we each returned every ten minutes to raid the pile of booze. Other performers from the festival dropped in to witness the explosion of colour, drama and drags. This routine felt wonderful to begin with. I started work around 11 p.m. and I didn't stop dancing until 7 a.m. I was able to indulge my cross-dressing desires all night long. It felt like my performance identity and my gender identity were more entwined than ever and it was a wonderful feeling.

After the NYC Downlow closed, we went to one of the many after-parties or to the Stone Circle. It had become near impossible to get around. We were knee deep in mud. The daily slog to the Stone Circle or back to our campsite – which we renamed 'Camp Bitch' – took hours, or maybe it just felt like it. To alleviate the torture we made the journey more fun by sniffing poppers. Anyone who witnessed the gaggle of performers stuck in the mud wearing Eighties cocktail dresses, oversized sunglasses and sniffing poppers should have filmed it. It must have been pure entertainment. We roared with laughter and fell over multiple times as the damp morning engulfed us.

That first year I only ventured out of 'Trash City' once. We all made a special trip to go and watch Dame Shirley Bassey perform on the Pyramid stage on Sunday afternoon.

I'm not a Shirley fan but we knew it would be a glittering spectacle. Dame Shirley didn't disappoint, wearing diamante pink wellies and singing 'Big Spender' twice. By Sunday I was exhausted – the nights were long and they took their toll. Most of my costumes were stained with festival gunge and covered in glitter. Our stiletto heels had giant balls of mud and grass stuck to the bottom. The drag slowly dishevelled, as did my mind.

When I returned to London it took me a week to feel any sense of normality again. I lay in bed for days watching the highlights of Glastonbury on the TV, trying to find some evidence of the fun I'd had. I wept into my bed sheets as my body convulsed, replaying Shirley Bassey singing 'The Living Tree'. I couldn't face opening my drag bag – I didn't want to unleash the horrors lurking inside. I didn't want to accept that it was over. I longed to return to that world – a world of no limits, no boundaries, where anything goes. I felt depressed that the colourful, carefree festival existence was over. I missed my gang and our daily escapades. I missed being able to dress how I liked and perform what I wanted. I missed living out my desires night after night. I wasn't ready to return to life as Ryan.

Luckily, my festival days were far from over. The next time I spectacularly crash-landed back into Trash City was as a vampire! Burlesque performer Ruby Blues had a vision. She wanted to create a performance and club space in Trash City which resembled the 'Titty Twister' bar from the film *From Dusk till Dawn*. Thrown in were other references from the movies *The Lost Boys* and *Tank Girl*. It was a surreal vampiric blood fest featuring podium dancers, trapeze artists and nudity. Ruby asked me to devise a new performance for the show. We all decamped to Bristol for a few days while we explored the concept, workshopped ideas and chose songs to dance to. I adored the theme – I had a penchant for Eighties 'hair metal' bands and Nineties rock anthems so I couldn't wait to have a big barnet, slashed jeans and extreme make-up. I loved that it took the campness of Prince and the aggression of Guns 'N' Roses to another level.

As part of the performance, I was told that I could fly. And who doesn't want to fly? But I didn't have any circus training or upper body strength so I wasn't sure how it was going to work. It turned out that I would be strapped into a harness and pulled through the air on a rope by a rigger some twenty metres above in the top of the tent. Next we needed to choose the music. I've always enjoyed the spooky drama of Alice Cooper and his anthemic song 'Poison'. It was the only song I wanted to lip-sync to while flying through the air.

I thought my first two experiences of Glastonbury were completely out of this world. Could it get any weirder? I was about to find out it could. Flash forward to Friday night at 9 p.m. in Trash City, with ten people getting into 'vampire drag' backstage. We were due on the back of a truck circling around the field in an hour – or so. (The only thing set in stone at Glastonbury is the Stone Circle.) My 'vampire drag' costume consisted of three big curly blonde wigs stuck together to make a helmet-style wig that Mozart would have been jealous of. It was so huge that I had to glue it onto my head to stop it falling off. I bought some cheap white jeans from the local market which I severed into trashy-looking ribbons. I'd returned to Camden to buy white stiletto knee-high boots which were perfect for prancing around in. I wore a ripped black T-shirt with a panther airbrushed onto it. My face was powdered white with dramatic orange blush and striking black lips. I brought to life all this drama, darkness and horror. I twisted it together to represent a gender-free fluid creature. It was totally me. This job was a dream come true. In my past I had fantasised about becoming a rock star, glued to MTV, studying my idols. Now was the time to imitate them.

The stage was a long catwalk protruding into the swell of hungry audience members. I strutted down the runway, spraying hairspray onto my bouffant wig, and awaited being lifted into the air. The audience didn't know what was about to hit them and when I started rising, my legs dangling off the edge of the stage, they went wild.

Intoxicated by hairspray fumes, pure adrenaline and vampire blood, I felt like I could take over the world. It was a glorious sensation.

Chapter 6

THE BUSINESS OF SHOW

My Glastonbury adventures opened doors to many new experiences in the performance-art world. One of the Trash City performers was an acrobatic aerialist called Empress Stah. In 2007, Stah asked if I'd like to perform in her new show 'The Very Best of Empress Stah', which would run at the former strip club Soho Revue Bar. By this point I had created a repertoire of five short cabaret acts – a combination of mime, drag, lip-syncing and performance art. For Stah's show I performed four pieces, in various locations around the venue and in between Stah's acts. 'The Very Best of Empress Stah' sold out consecutive performances and received positive reviews that led to our profile exploding. We were thrilled to take our show on the road.

Our next stop was on the other side of the world. In 2008 we headlined the 'Umbrella Revolution', a huge circus tent parked in the Garden of Unearthly Delights at the Adelaide Fringe Festival in Australia.

As well as Stah and myself, we brought along an artist called Le Gateau Chocolat. Le Gateau Chocolat is a baritone opera singer who wears figure-hugging Lycra body suits and sings songs from *The Lion King*. He fitted into our crew perfectly.

The Adelaide festival was a month long. At this point in my career I'd never performed night after night for such a long stretch. It was a great way of discovering new dimensions to my acts and occasionally experimenting with a different face or hand gesture. I grew in confidence too – we weren't performing to our friends in London any more. We had a paying audience of people who had never heard of us. We needed to win them over in an instant.

I had literally run away and joined the circus – it was an incredible chapter of my life. The atmosphere in the Garden of Unearthly Delights was never the same on any given night, filled as it was with a mixture of burlesque artists, comedians, drag queens and boys wearing sequinned Converse. It was a dry, arid and dusty parkland. Colourful spotlights lit up the trees as fruit bats caught their dinner suspended in the emerald sky. I was in a happy place performing my cabaret act every night and hanging out with newfound friends during the day. We partied on our nights off and had barbecues with other cabaret performers, which felt deliciously Australian. Whilst in Adelaide my gender euphoria exploded. I felt comfortable in my appearance on stage night after night. The drag costumes and the performances deeply satisfied my desire to present as female.

Sadly, beyond the safety of the carnival campness I witnessed occasional homophobia. Every night Le Gateau Chocolat and I walked around the park handing out flyers. One evening before the show someone threw a plastic ashtray at Gateau's head, but luckily his big fluffy wig took most of the impact. After that incident, every time we went out flyering we had secret security guards following us around.

We were the last performance in the 'Umbrella Revolution' and once we'd finished the roadies came in and started tearing it all down. The show was over. I didn't have any plans for where to go next. Gateau was returning to the UK and Empress Stah was travelling to Melbourne to stay with a friend, so I asked if I could accompany her. For the next four months I criss-crossed Australia, travelling backwards and forwards between Melbourne, Sydney and Brisbane. I was living out of a suitcase and staying with friends I'd made at the Adelaide festival or in backpackers' hostels. It was easy to connect with others on social media sites like MySpace and Facebook. I would seek out the creative people in every city. Artists, performers, club kids, promoters and photographers all became vital pillars that I could lean on. We formed a sort of motley family, helping each other out and belonging to one another. I had my 'drag bag' and could pick up work in cabaret venues, burlesque nights and drag clubs.

During the Adelaide show a lady from Cirque Du Soleil handed me her business card. She told me she thought I was a very good clown and could work well in their productions. Other performers would also comment, 'Your clowning is great!' and follow up with the dreaded question, 'Where did you train?' The truth was, I hadn't. Not in theatre, dance or anything related to the performing arts. I'd simply made it all up myself. I did what felt natural to me and followed my instincts, and it seemed to work. I didn't consider myself a clown, although I did dress like one. I loved the iconic look of the 'Pierrot', but my clown-like costume was purely a stylistic choice. I frequently used white balloons in my shows and often painted my face white, but again this was for aesthetic reasons.

One particular teacher and clown school was repeatedly mentioned to me. Philippe Gaulier is a French master clown, pedagogue, and professor of theatre. He is the founder of École Philippe Gaulier, a prestigious French clown school just outside Paris. While in Sydney I found out his next semester started in July. The school didn't require an audition, you simply paid the fees and turned up to class. It felt like the right time to leave Australia behind – I couldn't see a future for me there. I'd tasted the salty sea and had experienced far too many cockroaches crawling around me. I immediately signed up for the course and made arrangements to return to London.

Back home I was thrilled to tell my friends that I was moving to Paris to train at a theatre school. But for the time being I was homeless, with all of my belongings locked away in storage. I stayed on friends' sofas wherever I could, floating from house to house. I spent most of my time with my ex-boyfriend. In July 2008 I was on the Eurostar destined for Paris. It was a relief to be moving forward with my life again. London had begun to feel stagnant and I felt like I was losing myself, confused and disorientated once more about my identity. A new city felt like the best place to explore my sense of self again. The course wasn't really about becoming a clown; I just wanted to find myself. I hoped that Paris might hold some answers for me.

In Paris I'd arranged to stay with a friend of a friend's. A very kind woman called Jessica Ogden let me stay on her sofa and cat-sit while she was away. Her apartment was my only stable base in Paris. Everything else was in a state of flux.

School didn't get off to a good start – I hated it from day one. I was out of my comfort zone and surrounded by people I didn't know. Looking back, I know it wasn't the school, it was me. My state of mind and lack of a grasp on my identity rendered me miserable. I was terrified of standing up in front of my class and improvising. I'd never improvised in my life. My performance was about spectacle, costume manipulation and props. I didn't enjoy wearing a red nose and trying to be funny. I felt extremely vulnerable and I retreated into myself, becoming incredibly shy. My previous performances were a cathartic process for myself, steps on my journey of self-discovery. This felt very different; I felt exposed.

I had a little posse of girls from the course who I'd hang out with. At night, when it was still warm, we'd sit on the grass bank next to the Sacré-Cœur and drink red wine. We watched circus performers play with fire as North African men tried to sell us embroidered friendship bracelets. In Paris I smoked Gauloise cigarettes, a brand I favoured because David Bowie smoked them.

After the first week of clown school, Philippe Gaulier gave everyone a character and told us to return on Monday with a costume. I was ordered to be a Scottish man. The only silver lining in this was that I found a kilt which I fashioned into a knee-length skirt. I thought having a costume to wear and the guise of a character would give me more confidence, but it did the opposite. It felt like my performance language wasn't going to translate in this environment. I would sit at the back of the class, hiding, excusing myself from the dreaded 'show and tell' at the end of the day. No one in the class would cross-dress – all the roles were strictly male and female. This felt alien to me and as a result I felt less like myself than ever.

Gaulier would bang his drum and stroke his beard while saying to me in a thick French accent: 'You are a mime or some kind of bizarre, but you are definitely not a clown.' I liked the idea of being a 'bizarre'. I didn't know quite what that meant but it sounded good. It was non-descriptive and fluid, refusing to be categorised or labelled. I liked the fact that I'd never heard anyone else being described as a bizarre before. I decided there and then to embrace it.

In common with most of the other students in my class, I endured daily embarrassment and ridicule from Philippe Gaulier – in some ways it reminded me of being back at high school. Gaulier's technique is designed to break you down before building you back up again. I witnessed classmates standing in the middle of the dance studio crying so much that they nearly passed out. They would beg to be allowed to stop and sit down, but Gaulier would play with us, keep poking us until we were exhausted. It could be incredibly funny for those of us watching, and our bellies hurt from laughing so much. It was a momentary relief from the discomfort and awkwardness I was feeling within myself.

Although I didn't find my inner clown while I was under Gaulier's gaze, it did make me a better performer. After we so-called clowns paraded for one last time, I quietly tucked my red nose into my sporran, hoping never to have to use it again. It's such a shame that I couldn't appreciate its worth because I was completely clouded by feeling uncomfortable in the environment and uncomfortable within myself.

When I started performing in London again my focus was different. Though my journey had been gruelling and tough I now had inner confidence in my core abilities as a performer. I decided to push forward with work which some might label as 'bizarre' because that's who I felt I was. I felt like I was being true to myself. The first performance I created as a bizarre was called 'Fuji Yama Mama: The World's Only Lip-syncing Volcano'. Its timing was perfect – it was the summer that aeroplanes were grounded due to volcanic ash clouds. I sensed an eruption of creativity and identity.

My shows with fellow performer Scottee caused quite a scene. Scottee and I met when we both worked as door whores for the club night Kashpoint. Every Thursday we stood together in the doorway of the venue Moonlighting on Soho's Dean Street, clipboards in hand and completely freezing. Each week we had a stand-off, competing to create the craziest outfit. We were loud, enthusiastic and hungry to be noticed. I'd found my equal and I loved him for it. In fact, it was me who gave Scottee his first pair of heels and willed him on when the pain of wearing them became too much. Our mutual love of showing off cemented our bond and it wasn't long before we started performing together.

In 2005, Scottee and I created 'Dough', the moniker we would use whenever we performed together. Scottee would come and visit me when I worked at Tatty Devine in Soho. At night when the store was closed we practised our routines. The back wall of the shop was covered with a large mirror – the perfect space to prance around in our high heels. We wrapped bandages around our heads in the vein of someone who'd had a face-lift and we smudged red lipstick around our mouths. We paraded around in black oversized sunglasses, long grey coats and cheap wigs worn backwards. Looking back, I don't know what we were thinking, but it was the beauty of being in your twenties and not caring.

While performing at the Edinburgh Festival, we caused havoc. I know from experience that it's really hard to walk up and down the cobbled streets of Edinburgh wearing six-inch stiletto heels. It's almost impossible at 7 a.m. if you haven't been to bed yet. We must have woken up so many people with our cackling and screaming in agony as we crawled home kitted out in our drag from the night before.

Scottee and I had a certain 'femistry' when we were together, egging each other on and pushing ourselves further. I remember when we both wanted to shave off all our hair and eyebrows – which seemed incredibly scary and daring at the time. We were in my bathroom using clippers to shave our heads when the battery dramatically ran out. We had the bright idea to go to the shop and buy some razor blades to finish the job. It was a disaster because we couldn't get an even result. Eventually we gave in and went to the local Vietnamese barbers who laughed at us. When we got home we completed the look by shaving off our eyebrows.

There was no doubt about it, at first we looked strange and we reverted to wearing hats and hoods. Having literally no hair was weird. Out of context, beyond the nightclubs, it must have looked odd. However, it felt great. We liked it because it gave us a blank canvas to paint our entire heads with make-up. Our bodies became our art. You didn't need to be limited by eyebrows when you didn't have any – the possibilities were endless. During this time I felt less like Ryan and it was the beginning of exploring the possibility of something other. I enjoyed sticking random things to my head like plastic beetles, glow-in-the-dark stars and Mr Kipling's French Fancies. Though there came a point when I unfortunately had to grow my hair back because it was becoming increasingly difficult to attract potential partners. And when it rained, without eyebrows to hold back the water, the rain would run directly into my eyes. It felt like I was forever crying.

It was with Scottee that I first performed at Duckie. Duckie produce large-scale events, parties and spectacular theatre shows. In 2010, I was asked by Duckie producer Simon

Casson to perform in a new show called 'The Readers Wifes Fan Club'. The show was born from Simon's experience in a New York gay bar. Stylistically it echoed an episode of *Top of the Pops* circa 1987 meets a teenage mix tape brought to life. Snippets from TV adverts, counter-culture films, pop videos and game show voiceovers were used in the show. It celebrated LGBTQ culture and heritage. We explored stardom and fandom with the stage transforming from a teenager's bedsit to a rock concert stadium in a matter of seconds.

My favourite part of the show was our homage to Venus Xtravaganza. Venus was a transgender woman who lived in New York during the 1980s. She starred in Jennie Livingston's iconic documentary *Paris Is Burning* and was tragically murdered in 1988. Her body was found in a New York City hotel room. She was my favourite character within the documentary – I was delighted by her visibility at a time when transgender wasn't as mainstream as it is today. And I hoped she would have been pleased with her name check in our show.

For the performance I created a short dance, which celebrated the life and influence of Venus – it was a tribute to her revolutionary voice, visibility and legacy. Although I didn't know it at the time, two years later I would embark on my own transition, so it was incredibly important and poignant for me to celebrate the transgender women who had come before me. In the dressing room the other performers and I often discussed transsexuals because of the nature of the show but I didn't feel able to freely express how I was feeling. I was close, but not there just yet.

Since starring in the 'Hanky Panky Cabaret' in Bistrotheque I'd become firm friends with a musician and producer called Xavior. We bonded over countless cups of Earl Grey tea while chatting about Courtney Love, New York's club culture and the occult. Xavior hatched a plan to form a band of boys dressed as girls. He wanted to create a cross-dressing rock band that carried the anger, venom and DIY punk aesthetic championed by the Nineties underground feminist movement Riot Grrrl. The band would be called Ladynoise and Xavior wanted me to front it. I'd always longed to be a frontwoman so the opportunity seemed ideal. He'd already written four songs and had recorded the instrumental parts, so all that was needed was vocals. The songs were called 'Chop It Off', 'I Look Good in Her Dress', 'They Found Her Dead' and 'He's Just Not That into You'. The lyrics and titles reflected the themes of cross-dressing and gender identity.

When we initially formed Ladynoise I wasn't planning to transition, but I was cross-dressing more overtly in my performances. For the band I created an alter ego called 'The Brass'. I wore a long black wig, a bright blue leather pencil skirt, a padded bra and damaged silver sequinned heels which were so broken that my toes stuck out of the bottom. I loved this trashy aesthetic and it quickly became the 'Ladynoise' look. I printed slogans on vest tops that read 'Chop It Off', 'Bucket' and 'Twat', which were directly inspired by Vivienne Westwood's early punk career. We wanted to destroy glamour and conventional ideals of beauty. Over the course of two years my look evolved and by the end I wore a long copper-coloured wig – something very similar to the colour of my hair today. Was this a prediction of the future?

Xavior decided we needed two more glam-influenced boys with a punky edge to join me on stage. We discovered Hermes and Nicholas by trawling through Facebook. It didn't matter that they hadn't sung or performed on stage before – it was all about the look. Xavior's vision was to create a band that didn't need to play live. How many bands went into a live music venue with the intention of not playing? I'd never witnessed it before and I was struck by the idea. In the beginning we always mimed at gigs. We pretended to play the guitars, shouting over the CD playback and creating an atmosphere. Ladynoise upset those who came to watch us expecting a typical rock show. We deliberately set out to disturb preconceived notions of a performance. Our sound was loud, our attitude was aggressive and we flung ourselves around the stage, pulling off our wigs and ripping our clothes. It was painful but joyous. After a Ladynoise gig I'd lose my voice for several days and have bruises colouring my legs. We caused a scene wherever we went and word of mouth soon spread. It wasn't long before we were interviewed by the music press and photographed for *Dazed and Confused* magazine by Nick Knight, as well as being offered more gig opportunities.

As time went on, performing in Ladynoise became difficult. Maintaining that level of intensity and energy during every show was hard and I would be in pain for days afterwards. I was damaging my body and I needed to soften the edges. I needed to learn to respect myself. In hindsight, it's clear that I had such hatred for my physical body that I wanted to destroy it. I just didn't care any more; I had given up. I wanted so badly for things to change, but the notion of a change from the perspective of loving myself didn't occur to me. I was too caught up in hatred. I was like those butterflies I kept in jam jars as a child – desperate to be released.

As time went on, we decided to add an element of live performance to the show. I would play the guitar, which stopped me from throwing myself on the floor. We adapted our songs for live performances and created a new vision for Ladynoise. We began to be seen as a 'real' band, much to our amusement. Ladynoise was an art-rock project; it wasn't about being the best musicians or singers in the world. We were all about developing the performance and its ritualistic qualities. That's why we never released or sold our music. We wanted Ladynoise to be seen on stage amidst the drama and aesthetics, not listened to at home.

In our live performances, the audience heard something different every time. It was the evolution and, eventually, the hiatus of the band. Ladynoise had transformed into something different – distorted and not as dynamic as we once were. It became a burden lugging the drum kits, guitars and wigs from venue to venue. We laid Ladynoise to rest while we were still riding the crest of a potential gender riot. These days people occasionally mention Ladynoise to me and I like to remind them that we started out performing under a railway arch in Bethnal Green and ended

Photograph © Nick Knight/Trunk Archive

up supported by Adam and the Ants for our last show. We certainly finished with a bang.

'*Chop It Off*', *by Xavior*

I don't need a doc dictate when I'm a woman
Don't you know the gender revolution's comin'
I don't need your fascist medical approval
I can be a girl without a cock removal.

We didn't know it back then but the transgender tipping point was right around the corner. Xavior and I laugh about it now, how his prophetic lyrics came true. At every show I screamed those words about transvestism, transsexuals and gender. Four years later I decided it was the right time for me to transition. We really were on the cusp of a gender revolution – and I would be playing a central role.

Lots of people in the performance industry have been central figures in my transition. One such is Marisa Carnesky. Marisa's brilliant showcase 'Carnesky's Ghost Train' was set on a fairground ride. When I first witnessed the performance it was installed in the car park of east London's Truman Brewery during the summer of 2004. I'd heard that the ghost train was home to live performers instead of animatronic puppets. I managed to ride the ghost train on the last day, just before it closed, and I was thrilled to experience the cabaret skits crafted by an all-female cast. It left a lasting impression on me that creating a performance on such a huge scale was possible. That anything is achievable. I hoped that one day in my career I, too, would be able to star in something equally as inspiring.

A few years later in 2008 my wishes came true. As my profile as a performer grew, fate would have it that I became friends with Marisa. And I couldn't believe my luck when she invited me to play the part of one of the ghosts. Carnesky's Ghost Train was due to reopen in Blackpool for the winter season.

That September I found myself at Euston station waiting for the train to Preston with a cast of female performers. We relocated to Blackpool for the winter while we worked on the ghost train and snuggled up together in a cosy B&B. It was magical being in Blackpool while the days grew shorter and the air became crisper. Blackpool out of summer season is quite like a ghost town itself, and there we were playing the spirits of women in a ghost train tucked inside the Winter Gardens. I was the first male to be included in the ghost train cast, and I usually played the role of the old lady. Sometimes an audience member would notice and I'd hear them mutter things like, 'That's a man!' Comments like this have plagued me my whole life whenever I presented as female and it hurt when the public reacted like this.

Outside of the show we soaked up Blackpool's tacky

aesthetic. We frequented the drag show *Funny Girls* until we knew all the lines off by heart. When Christmas came, the town sparkled with 1970s tinsel Christmas trees. Northern women and men infiltrated the town on stag and hen weekend benders, obliterating themselves wearing Santa hats and foam boobies. To amuse ourselves we visited the fortune-tellers who had curious little shops along the sea front. After several sessions of palm readings and gazing into crystal balls, the outcome was always disappointingly the same. They never predicted that I would transition; it felt like poppycock. I'd secretly hoped for a shining prophecy of how things would turn out, something to move towards. This wasn't it.

Blackpool's spiritual churches also drew me in. It was here a clairvoyant on stage picked out Marisa and said to her, 'A transvestite needs your help.' I wasn't wearing any foam boobies inside the church but I was sitting right next to Marisa, who was wearing a big theatrical fur coat which could have possibly drawn the psychic's attention towards us. I would have loved to believe that the psychic – who was wearing a sequinned red jumper, chandelier-esque earrings and clasping a pack of B&H Super Kings – knew all about my gender dysphoria and desire to be female but I couldn't believe it. Even so, when I heard her words it gave me a glimmer of hope. Deep down I knew that transitioning was my destiny, but I remained very conflicted. So instead I just sat back and enjoyed the spectacle.

The next time I worked with Marisa I had already started my transition. 'Carnesky's Tarot Drome' was an immersive theatrical spectacular. The concept for this show was to bring the major arcana from tarot cards to life. I was going to play the role of 'The Chariot'. This was the first production where I would be directly address-ing my gender change. It was a pivotal moment in my performance life, reflecting the monumental changes in my private life. In the tradition of tarot, The Chariot represents conquest, victory, spiritual change and success in pursuing your goals. It was the perfect casting by Marisa.

My contribution to the show involved turning the Char-iot into a celebrated figure. While stood on a red carpet behind a VIP rope I invited members of the audience to join me on my pedestal to have our photo taken. Twice each per-formance I would make a speech about transcending gender. Not dissimilar from a motivational life coach, I corralled the audience with my story. I explained that anything is possible, that I'd once had a dream and had now achieved it. I was working towards being the woman that I'd always wanted to be. Through the process of various presentations and guises of femininity I finally felt comfortable within myself and began to embrace it. I started to love myself and this acceptance of who I was and who I would become was key to the evolution of Rhyannon.

Going public about my transition in this performance was daunting. At this point nobody outside my inner circle of friends knew about my decision. I was in the embryonic stages of navigating the world as Rhyannon. I felt quite vulnerable and young. In many ways I'd just been born. But despite my nerves, it felt liberating to unleash Rhyannon to the world.

Marisa announced that she wanted the finale of the Tarot Drome to be a choreographed skating piece. I was thrilled. I've been roller-skating since I was seven years old and I was in my element skating with a group of girls on stage wearing a gold sequinned bikini. This was a pivotal turning point where I could feel my life starting to come together. I was onstage being perceived as a woman (possibly!), performing explicitly and directly as a transgender female. Every night after the show I had a big smile on my face. I was achieving everything I had dreamed of since I was young. I felt accepted and I knew I belonged. To this day, I continue to discover who I am and to shape my gender identity through performance.

Throughout my life women have supported and encouraged me, taking me under their wings or leading me astray (in the best possible way). The notorious performer Penny Arcade is one such woman. I first met Penny at the Royal

Vauxhall Tavern way back in 2011 (pre-transition). She didn't need to introduce herself to me – I knew exactly who she was and I was thrilled to be performing with her. Our meeting went like this:

'What do you do?' she asked me.

'I'm an artist,' I replied.

'Don't ever call yourself an artist!'

'What should I call myself then?'

'Say you're a person who makes art! So, let's start over. What do you do?'

'I do mime.'

'Don't ever say you "do mime", people will want to kill themselves!'

'How do you describe yourself, Penny?'

'I'm a performer who makes art. So, what's your name?'

'Ryan Styles.'

'Maybe you should call yourself an art stylist. That's it, you're an Art Stylist!'

I spotted Penny watching me from the side of the stage that night. I had performed a piece called 'Old Age'. Afterwards she told me she very much enjoyed it, which delighted me. 'Old Age' was based on my experiences of working in a retirement home as a teenager. It was my first job when I left school and I needed money to buy art supplies and the bus fare to college. I cleaned dirty toilets, dusted china ornaments and discovered old stockings hanging in the laundry. Chain-smoking pensioners recounted tales of their youth, while TVs in suffocatingly overheated bedrooms blared out *This Morning* in the background. Every day was a repeat of the day before. I'd find Ivy sitting on her bed with her suitcases packed, waiting for her son to come and take her home. 'Am I going home yet?' she would ask. It was very sad. My 'Old Age' performance celebrated these women and the bonds I forged with them. I created a character honouring their presence in my past, and bringing to life the joyful anecdotes they shared with me.

At the start of my transition in 2012, I auditioned to be a dancer in Penny's show 'Bitch!Dyke!FagHag!Whore!' I wasn't a trained dancer, but I had attitude and sass in abundance. Despite my lack of a traditional background, I knew I could express myself in front of an audience in the medium of dance. I brought my identity and a trans element to the forefront. Plus, I really wanted to strut around wearing high heels and skimpy outfits. I had only recently changed my name to Rhyannon and begun dressing as a girl every day. I wasn't yet taking hormones to aid my physical development and I was still in the process of working out my look as Rhyannon, so this was a daunting task. I had to be brave.

It was interesting expressing my newly exposed 'female' self during this production. I needed to wear a padded bra to give the impression of breasts and I carefully selected leotards that disguised the breast area with a piece of mesh.

Under the glare of the stage lights and from a distance, they may have even looked real. It was harder disguising my penis dancing in such figure-hugging clothes. I wore what's called a 'dance belt' in the trade. This is a specialised undergarment commonly worn by male ballet dancers to support their genitals. Most are similar in design to thong underwear. Now for the scientific bit – I needed to push my testicles up inside my body and then pull my penis between my legs (a trick commonly used by drag queens called 'tucking') to achieve a smooth, flat appearance on the front of my body. It was difficult to maintain when dancing around and some-times my penis would slip forward or my testicles would fall out. In the beginning it felt painful and odd. I would be quite paranoid about it during the show, afraid to kick as high as the others. The splits were completely out of the question.

It was the first time that I had to explain myself to stran-gers. The cast often asked intimate and personal questions. In the beginning, 'Are you male or female?' was a popular one. 'Are you getting tits?' and 'Are you having the opera-tion?' also cropped up. I didn't mind though, and over the course of the summer we all became friends. The other female dancers gave me make-up tips and advice on every-thing from clothes to dating. These conversations allowed me the space to publicly think about what I wanted, and I made small, tentative steps towards my new identity.

*

The year 2012 held more surprises for me than I could have ever imagined. At the start of the year I would never have dreamed that I was about to become a fully fledged pub quiz hostess. In April I received a phone call from an acquaintance called Lee, who is now the landlord of a pub called the Kennington in south London. Lee asked me if I'd like to host a regular Sunday-night pub quiz. I immediately thought it was a naff idea. I wasn't a stand-up performer who had a repertoire of one-liners – I was a 'bizarre'. I hadn't actually spoken in any of my performances – it wasn't something that interested me at that point. I used other mediums to translate the meaning and narrative of my work. Going to work in a pub every week, entertaining and engaging with drunk people also sounded like a nightmare. But Lee insisted that he had seen 'something' in me when I was performing in The LipSinkers. He thought I'd be confident and entertaining hosting the quiz.

I told Lee I would think about his offer and call him back in a couple of days. If I was honest with myself I could have done with the regular work. Being a freelance artist meant the money wasn't always rolling in, so I had to take work whenever it cropped up. I was also conveniently always free on Sunday evenings, having recently split up from my boyfriend. But I was worried. In January I had made the decision to begin my transition and journey to becoming Rhyannon. I was concerned about starting a pub quiz, knowing that my appearance was going to change over the course of it. I was also troubled by the thought of being surrounded by people drinking alcohol – drunk people aren't always known for being restrained or polite. But I talked it through with my housemates and came to the decision that I should at least try it for a couple of months. Two advantages I did have were that I could DJ (I had a good stack of CDs) and I had a killer wardrobe (I'd based my entire career on costume and creating 'looks'). All I would need to do was compile the questions from sources on the internet. So I rang Lee back and happily accepted his offer.

My first quiz didn't quite go to plan. It was an alien environment and managing a rowdy pub was a completely new experience. The quiz was too long and complicated for people on a Sunday night. Luckily my music went down really well, as did my outfit. But I needed to work on the questions and my banter if the quiz was going to be a success. Within a month I'd turned it around and I was taking real pleasure in this new outlet for my performance. It was like being on stage all over again. The audience seemed to enjoy my presence every week and looked forward to seeing what outfit I would turn up in. I also soon realised that the easier you make a quiz, the sooner you'll make friends. Nobody likes to feel alienated because they don't know the answers to the questions. I wanted my quiz to be inclusive instead of exclusive – just like my performances.

The quiz became a weekly job for me and the Sundays started rolling past at an alarming pace. It grew from strength to strength and most weeks all of the tables were reserved. The crowd particularly enjoyed the half-time ritual of 'Elvira's Deep-Fried Delights'. The 'Deep-Fried Delights' were all the bits of food the pub hadn't sold during the day. Yorkshire puddings, roast potatoes and a side of gravy were offered on platters to anyone playing the quiz. I think people often just came to be fed.

In the summer of 2012 I was making the first steps presenting as female and living every day as Rhyannon. My closest friends knew about my transition but it wasn't public knowledge yet. Three months after starting the quiz it became difficult to hide it. I couldn't keep travelling to the pub every Sunday wearing boys' clothes and then getting changed into drag for the quiz. At home during the week I was wearing girls' clothes and padded bras, so it didn't add up. I felt like I was still pretending to be Ryan for one day a week and this was an uncomfortable sensation. But I was scared about telling Lee and his partner Steve about my transition because I didn't know them very well. The fact that I was so visible in such a public environment also made me fearful. I soon realised that I wasn't doing anyone any favours by pretending to be someone I wasn't.

I didn't officially tell my quiz regulars or people in the

pub, instead I slowly introduced my female wardrobe – even adding a padded bra into the mix, which definitely raised a few eyebrows. My drag became less theatrical and more natural as the lines between performer and person became blurred. Thankfully I had the microphone, which equalled power. When I introduced myself by saying, 'My name is Rhyannon, welcome to the quiz!' I was already dressed as a woman so it didn't matter.

Time and patience paid off. I ended up presenting the quiz every Sunday for two years – quite an achievement considering I'd originally thought the idea was naff. Over the two years I gained a cult following and many of my 'quizzers' became very loyal, returning every week. In that time I changed dramatically. As well as my hair growing longer and my style becoming more feminine, I had also started taking hormones and was changing the pitch of my voice through voice therapy. I was transitioning very pub-licly and openly. I had to be strong to deflect any negativity, so my confidence as Rhyannon grew. I was discovering who I was and establishing my new self inside a pub on a Sunday night, tweaking and expanding my identity so as to allow Rhyannon into the spotlight. By the end I felt so comfortable in myself that performing was a joy. If I could present a quiz to a rowdy pub as a trans woman, I could do anything! I was very grateful for that opportunity and the sense of self I found along the way. With more confidence, comfort and assurance in my identity I decided it was time to tell my story. It was time for my debut one-woman show.

Enter 'Styles' Saturn Returns', my first ever one-woman performance. Styles' Saturn Returns touched upon the emotional, physical and political aspects of transitioning, cobbled from diary extracts, songs I'd written and previous performance work. 'SSR' was my story, the story of growing up as Ryan and transitioning into Rhyannon. Aside from the autobiographical angle, the show was also my response to recent comments made by the journalist Julie Burchill. Burchill's comments in defence of fellow journalist and friend Suzanne Moore were published in the *Observer*. Burchill labelled people like me 'bedwetters in bad wigs', 'dicks in chicks' clothing', 'she-males', 'shims' and 'big white blokes who have cut their cocks off'. I'm none of these things and I wanted to invite people into the process of transitioning to allow them to make up their own minds. I felt my narrative needed to be told in defiance of her toxic opinion.

We scratched the show (theatre lingo for 'presented some new ideas') to a busy audience at Camden People's Theatre. The director and I were pleased with the response. It felt like the first time I was directly saying: 'Here I am. I'm transgender. My name is Rhyannon' and this was empowering. For the first time I wasn't hiding behind a mask of white face make-up. I wasn't playing a character or buried underneath a tier of wigs. I'd stripped away the costumes, props and stage sets. I'd arrived on stage with no need to reinvent myself. I'd finally got there, eight years after I began performing. I'd found myself.

I embraced my trans identity at the same time as the band Arcade Fire released a song called 'We Exist'. The accompanying video featured the actor Andrew Garfield playing a character discovering their trans identity. I'd met David Wilson, the director of the video, some years before. David had used images of me as inspiration for storyboarding the music video, and we planned a meeting with Andrew Garfield to discuss its sensitive nature. In 2014, Arcade Fire were touring the world and were looking for LGBTQ dancers and performers in every city to recreate the 'We Exist' choreography on stage at their shows. David wanted to know if I'd like to assemble a group of performers and to dance myself with Arcade Fire at their Earls Court shows later that week. I jumped at the chance. I'd really enjoyed the video David made for 'We Exist' and I knew this was an incredible opportunity. I wanted to play a part in bringing trans issues to the consciousness of the public.

I'd never been to Earls Court before and I wasn't aware of the scale of the venue. The musicians I liked tended to play in more intimate spaces, so I was blown away by the sheer size of Earls Court. Originally I thought that we were going to be dancing with the band on stage or tucked away at the back. But it transpired that we had our own stage in the middle of the venue, which rose some twenty feet into the air. The production was wonderfully theatrical – American-style trash cans in the corners of the stage flowed dramatically with dry ice. It reminded me of the old ITV show *Stars in their Eyes*.

It was an insane experience. The catering provided was like a banquet. Multiple tables were laid out with copious amounts of cake, cheese and fruit. One night I had three puddings because I couldn't decide which cake looked the tastiest. The wardrobe department resembled an east London fashion boutique with stylists and make-up artists on hand to help assemble the band. The sheer number of people required for a show of this scale was a revelation. Hundreds were needed to ensure it ran smoothly.

I'd never performed in front of so many people before. We danced for two consecutive nights to a crowd of 20,000. It was such a rush being surrounded by that many faces looking straight back at you. I felt completely in my element. The band dedicated the song 'We Exist' every night to anyone on the LGBTQ spectrum who had suffered in their lives. I could relate to this stirring dedication and it was incredibly emotional. Dancing on the hydraulic stage high above people's heads, I was grateful and proud to include myself within the LGBTQ rainbow.

I was conquering my fears about transitioning one by one but one thing I'd never done in a performance was get butt nakcd. This was the last defence in revealing my true self. I'd stripped away everything else – could I expose one of the remaining things that signified my sex to the rest of the world? As someone who identifies as trans I use tools typically associated with women to portray a female identity. Everything from the clothes I choose to wear, the way I do my make-up and how I style my hair is considered. It's my way of saying to the world 'I'm female'. And when I am recognised as such it makes me feel *great*. Could I achieve this europhic feeling if I was totally naked?

In autumn 2015, a friend forwarded mc an email from the Barbican Gallery. They were auditioning roller-skaters and dancers to perform in a new exhibition by the artist Eddie Peake. Not only did you need roller-skating skills, the perfect fit for me, but the job also required nudity. I wasn't sure how I felt about this. I'd worn a swimming costume and a figure-hugging body stocking on stage, but I'd never performed completely naked. The costume for Peake's exhibition consisted of a sheer, see-through onesie with nothing underneath. Onlookers would be able to see everything.

At the audition, Eddie asked if I was OK with being naked. The fear of exposing myself was a deep-rooted one, which I had so far been unable to shake off. But I said yes. I wanted the job and I wanted the challenge. I didn't know if Eddie knew that I was transgender and I wondered if I should say anything.

On the first day of rehearsals the other roller-skaters and dancers stripped their clothes off for the first time. The dancers were completely nude except for the white Reebok trainers they'd all be wearing. As I removed my clothes I felt shy and intimidated. I was peeling off my desired identity and baring my body for all to see. At this stage I was taking hormones so my upper body had started developing. What would the other dancers, skaters and gallery staff think when they saw somebody with breasts and a penis? I was paranoid. I wondered if people would relate to me differently – or worse, see me as a man. I couldn't bear this thought. During this moment of heightened anxiety I forgot that everyone else was naked too. It struck me that perhaps they were just as uncomfortable as I was. This was a reassuring thought.

There I was in a public art gallery, revealing my body for all to see. My sheer transparent costume didn't hide a thing. I could still wear make-up, nail varnish and style my hair as I wished, but my body was fully exposed. There was no turning back now. For the first week or so I criticised my body and compared myself to the other performers. Such niggling thoughts hung around for a while and I was plagued with anxiety. But the more I was naked the more it occurred to me: I needed to embrace the body that I had. There was, and is, nothing wrong with it. Absolutely no one came into that gallery space and pointed at me. In fact, I enjoyed being naked around other women, appreciating our different, unique and beautiful bodies. I decided I needed to leave my ego and insecurities in the dressing room from there on in.

Once I was in the gallery, skating around gracefully and fully taking ownership of my body, I was finally free. Within five minutes I forgot I was naked. It didn't matter that the world could see my genitalia. It didn't matter that I was revealed as being transgender. I stopped worrying about the physicality of my body and enjoyed being part of the spectacle. My shifts in the gallery were five hours long, so I was free to skate around the curved gallery space showing off my skills. I interacted with the sculptures, art pieces and the dancers, avoiding crashing into any member of the public.

It was interesting observing the reactions to my body. I aroused a response and I could see people visibly trying to understand what they were being faced with. When a heterosexual couple left the exhibition I heard the man say, 'He's a good skater!' His partner immediately corrected him, saying, 'You mean, *she's* a good skater!' This delighted me. I loved it when people looked me up and down. I could see them look at my face, look at my breasts and then . . . their eyes would pop out as they saw my genitalia. I got used to people staring at me and whispering to their friends, 'Have you seen the skater?'

Another time, a group of young art students came and sat in the gallery for hours, drawing in their sketchbooks. On

Facebook I found a thread from their tutor saying that the biggest discussion point when the group returned to college was, 'Was the roller-skater female or male?' I was very happy about that. I was glad to be raising important discussions about gender among the future artists of this country. This is why I decided to apply for the job. I wanted to provide the public with the option of viewing a different reality. The purveyors of the exhibition may have passed me on the street, unaware of my trans status. But in the gallery I was visible – they were confronted with the possibility of something beyond the binaries of 'female' and 'male'. It felt great because I had the power. It was my choice to be in the gallery and my choice to present my body for the world to see. And the odd comment or glance could never take this away from me.

Performing in 'The Forever Loop' allowed me to embrace and harness the amazing, powerful body I have. As I revealed my true self my self-esteem and confidence rose dramatically. It was completely the right time in my transition to shed the final layer.

This wonderful note I received afterwards from the artist, Eddie Peake, sums it up perfectly:

It is a magnificent and fortuitous coincidence that you were involved in The Forever Loop during such a significant moment in your life. It was brilliant for the world to be able to engage with you in that moment, and your confidence and exuberance is something that we can all learn from and enjoy. I am very grateful for your participation.

I forget that I was once a boy who grew up in a small rural village. It's hard to imagine that there was a time when I wasn't who I am today. Performing allowed me to develop and expand my identity beyond the realms of imagination. Ryan bowed out and Rhyannon bravely stepped onto the stage and into the spotlight.

Beyond the theatrical façade and trans visibility, however, there is a side to my experiences that I have left out until now. Another story, another identity, another long battle which I needed to overcome.

The year 2012 was significant in more ways than one.

Chapter 7

THE B-SIDE

As with all of my favourite classic records, there is always a B-side. Turn over the black disc and you find a different selection of songs. Darker, broodier or less commercial, perhaps. Demo versions, home recordings and unreleased tracks – these paint a different picture of the artist and allow the listener a passage into a parallel existence. This alternative chapter makes up the whole story. This is my flipside.

'Growing Pains' by Ryan Styles

I've got growing pains
I'm watching repeats again
I lie naked
Disregard for everything

I feel it in my bones
From my head to my toes
It's like nobody knows

I spend my days
Staring at the walls
Trying to find a cure
For reasons which I'm not sure

I feel it in my bones
From my head to my toes
It's like nobody knows

I'm turning thirty
I can't think clearly
I'm turning thirty
I want to die early
(repeat)

My lyrics perfectly sum up my mood and outlook in 2011. I felt defeated. Soon I'd be turning thirty and I wanted to die. What began several years earlier as an experimental psychedelic voyage of discovery slowly disintegrated into sleazy shenanigans soaked in Prosecco and caked in Class As. For a couple of years there was a silver lining – having a partner who kept me above water. But lurking underneath the shallow muddy pool were deeper feelings that dragged me down and whenever I could, I obliterated myself.

The momentum had been building for years. I was no stranger to packing sunglasses in my handbag because I knew I'd still be out partying when the sun rose over the Hackney gas works. I loved being out of control, out of my mind and out of the house. I sought oblivion, a state of consciousness where I could exist within my reality without actually being present. I didn't want to feel anything and the only outlet for this negativity brooding inside me involved behaviour that put my life in danger.

Alcohol was medicinal – the more I drank, the better I felt. I used this substance and many others to escape the discomfort I was feeling inside. I constantly felt isolated, separate from and different to others. I felt like I only had the confidence to do what I wanted and be who I was when I was drunk or high. I only felt comfortable around people if I could be somebody else. I was plagued with fear and insecurity. I wasn't alone in this respect. The 2012 Trans Mental Health Review reported that 62 per cent of trans people suffer from alcohol dependency or abuse issues. Perhaps I wouldn't have felt so alone if I was aware of this shocking statistic.

I suffered my first alcohol blackout when I was fourteen years old. My friend Pippa and I shared a two-litre bottle of cider behind the Fox and Hound pub's car park and proceeded to get blind drunk. Naturally my body rejected this excess of sour alcohol and I was sick everywhere. I don't remember a thing except waking up on Pippa's sofa next to a bucket with her mum looking on angrily at me. I was in trouble but I didn't know what had happened. The last thing I remembered was sitting in the long grass with a group of friends. Then it went black. I couldn't retrace my steps and I had to rely on Pippa to fill in the blanks.

After moving to London, opportunities were handed to me accompanied by treats and pleasures to which I couldn't say no. If anything, I sought them out. Pills peppered my playtime. Alcohol distilled the darkness. With such escapades came many of these blank episodes, blackouts, blurred memories and warped versions of the truth.

As a performer, I travelled all around the world, a perk of the job that I thoroughly enjoyed. As nightclubs became my place of work, boundaries began to blur. I couldn't separate when I was working or when I was partying – the two became one all too easily. My warm-up routine involved drinking as much of the alcohol on the backstage rider as possible. Even throughout a show, I'd figure out when to have a sneaky drink in between acts. It wasn't a great idea, especially downing red wine before running out on stage. Sometimes I ended up with bright red stains around my mouth and on my costume – it was a dead giveaway.

One time, Jonny Woo, Russella and I performed a dance routine inside the garden of a nightclub in King's Cross. For one part of the show we covered ourselves with squirty cream. That weekend I stayed out partying for a long time. I originally performed on the Saturday night but was still inside the club on Sunday afternoon. I loved an after-party. That particular weekend I took an Ecstasy tablet that was dipped in LSD. When I went to the dressing room to change my wig I discovered an ironing board was changing shape and I started to talk to it because it looked like a pair of lips. Several days later, when I eventually unpacked my costumes, I discovered the squirty cream had slowly fermented in my bag and turned to soft cheese.

I never wanted the night to end. I tried my hardest to avoid going home after a night out, always wanting to keep the party going. After my performance at the Guggenheim in New York, I'd drunk all the red wine in the dressing room and wanted to find more fun so I decided to head out. On the social media grapevine I'd heard amazing things about a club called Mr Black in SoHo, where New York's iconic club kids often attended. I headed straight there. I didn't care that I was on my own – I was in New York and I knew they loved an Englishman.

The club was small and crammed with flamboyantly dressed people sitting at leather seats. The waitress was a drag queen on rollerskates wearing a costume that looked like a pink poodle. I befriended a small group of people who were enjoying partying, buying round after round of drinks. After the club closed I was invited back to one of my new friends' apartments to carry on the party. The apartment was in a very exclusive tower block which had a concierge. I remember we all had to act like we were sober as we entered the reception to take the elevator. Imagine four club kids smothered in make-up and glitter greeting you at 4 a.m. But the concierge behaved like he'd seen it all before.

I had no idea who these people were or where I was in Manhattan. While the party carried on in the bedroom I snuck off towards the lounge. I looked out of the large glass windows, which stretched from floor to ceiling. The sun was just rising further down the avenue between the skyscrapers. It was the start of rush hour and steam rose from the road's subway vents in that typical New York way. Women wrapped in scarves and wearing fur hats chatted on the sidewalk, heading off to work. I closed my eyes as the sunshine penetrated the curtains and warmed my face. Around me I heard the sounds of the city starting a new day. But I was still in the middle of yesterday's party.

It was becoming increasingly common for me to go out for as long as my body could endure it. If I could suspend myself and float within these exotic voids, hours lost to madness and hedonism, I would drift further away from the reality of being me. The epitome of this was an experience at Trash City, when I became a semi-immortal vampiric version of myself that never wanted to sleep. I have sewn together these fragments of memory from the very little I remember.

Our new show debuted when the clock chimed midnight. People flooded into the venue as the theme tune from *The Lost Boys* rang out and vampires flew down from the rafters, picking out their prey. As I got ready to fly I dropped an E. It seemed logical to me that I'd want to be high while flying above people's heads lip-syncing to Alice Cooper. After my spectacular show and with the drugs, drag and adrenaline pumping through my body, I wanted to celebrate. I shimmied next door to hang out at the NYC Downlow and when the club finally spat out the remaining stragglers I joined the throng of glittering fairies making the pilgrimage to the Stone Circle to watch the sun rise – a ritual for many and a Glastonbury tradition. Some hours later at the Stone Circle, people were slowly welcoming back a sense of reality. But I didn't want reality – I was doing my hardest to escape mine – so I decided to take more drugs. I often mixed drugs in my quest for oblivion – I remember my friend Sam calling to ask where I was when I was lost one time. I was making no sense on the phone so he asked, 'What drugs have you taken?' I replied, 'Ecstasy, cocaine, MDMA, weed, ketamine and I licked someone's finger who'd been making acid.' Sam's reaction was to tell me that I could die, which was secretly what I was hoping for.

I ended up back at the campsite with some friends who also hadn't been to sleep yet. It was 10 a.m. and I still had the big wig glued to my head and the straggling remnants of my make-up on. I decided to entertain people by singing 'Poison' and running around the tents and up and down the ramps attached to caravans. I woke up somebody by unzipping their tent and screaming, 'I'm going to fuck your brains out!' It was light-hearted fun really, and my new friend Willy didn't mind. Time passed by, and we smoked cigarettes and drank wine. Before I'd been to bed, changed clothes or even had a wash it was time to start getting ready for the next show. I'd literally been awake and entertaining people all day.

The next few days at Glastonbury are somewhat of a blur. The lights were on but nobody was home. I was totally out of it and unaware of what I was doing, but I remember the odd fragment here and there. I managed to perform in the next vampire show, though God knows how. I think I took more drugs in order to get back on stage. I stupidly ran down the catwalk and jumped off the end, causing the rigger to spring into action and stop me from falling flat on my face. Luckily he pulled me up just in time, saving me from a broken nose or worse. The drugs had loosened my inhibitions as well as my grip on reality. After the performance I was firmly told off. I'm sure it looked great to the audience but I had learned my lesson. Don't take drugs and fly.

Undeterred and with the wig still glued to my head, I ran back to the Stone Circle. At some point that morning I needed to go to the toilet. Off I wandered to find the nearest 'long-drop'. But the moment I sat down I immediately fell asleep – by this point I must have been awake for over twenty-four hours. Thankfully two angels called Lyall and Lisa who had watched me skip off half an hour previously came to my rescue, waking me up by shouting my name. It's not a good look, passed out in a toilet at Glastonbury. In my semi-conscious haze I could hear my friend John Sizzle's voice echoing around the Stone Circle shouting, 'Taxi for Lulu!' It was a jovial catch-phrase of his when somebody really needed to call it a night.

Once back within the safety of the stones I nodded off again. I'd been awake for so long that my body needed to shut down. In my head I felt fabulous but my face must have told a different story, with layers upon layers of smeared, mashed-up make-up slowly eroding. The sun was fierce and I was melting away like the witch in *The Wizard of Oz*. When I woke up from the heat some hours later I noticed that my legs were sunburnt. I was still wearing the shredded white jeans so I ended up with bright pink stripes criss-crossing my legs. It was now Sunday morning. I hadn't removed the wig from my head that I'd glued on at 9 p.m. on Friday night. I felt disgusting. I'd become a complete hot mess!

This was my life. Without a day job and with no routine I was free to decide when I worked, when I partied and how long I stayed out. I had nothing else to do. I didn't know if I was wearing the drag or the drag was wearing me. Without structure to my days I had too much free time on my hands and I couldn't enjoy it.

During my time in Sydney I went swimming in the outdoor pools, hung out with the cockatoos in the Botanical Gardens and hopped waves at Bondi Beach. It was a paradise, but I felt a complete lack of enjoyment and connection. Although I'd made friends, I felt isolated during the days when everyone went to work. I pretended to skip from coffee shop to deli with a spring in my stride, but this self-employed, soy-flat-white, artisan-bread lifestyle was wearing thin. I didn't have any plans for the future or know where I was going to go next and I felt completely alienated as a result.

Weds 8 May

PR party at a mansion. Took a cab to Tamarama near
  Bondi.

Blaggers, surfers, rodents, blonde hair.

One valium later and it all disappears . . .

I am so fucked.

Dying.

Poisoned.

Smoked too many fags last night.

Talked too much crap.

Party was crap.

Why have I started chasing substances so much? Booze &
  drugs. Need to give it up.

Club was shit. After-party was shit, we had no alcohol.

The guy I slept with the night before sits next to me. I
  dressed a little crazy. We don't speak. Jared tells me he is
  a tramp and has a boyfriend. That is so fine by me.

Ugh.

Reading back through my diaries it's clear that I was
rapidly slipping into a downward spiral. I was treading
water. I couldn't get it together to make anything more
than a handful of club performances work. I'd become
unproductive, simply not making the most of the opportunities life threw at me.

Moving to Paris and starting clown school felt like the

perfect chance for a new beginning. Little did I know I was carrying the same baggage with me. I thought a geographical move could restore my faith, but it was little more than a fragile band-aid. The mess of my life imploded as soon as I opened my suitcase.

While I was in Paris, I became quite detached from myself. I felt restless, discontented and sad. I was pre-occupied with my negative thoughts, which told me I was worthless and useless. I couldn't escape the dark cloud hanging over me.

I was frustrated and angry but it wasn't clear why. I walked around the muggy boulevards, getting lost and hoping that the nightmare would come to an end. I was lost both internally and externally. I carried on living as Ryan because the consequences of facing my transition felt much too difficult. I hung around the Père Lachaise Cemetery visiting Jim Morrison's and Oscar Wilde's graves with no shoes on. I don't know why; I was making decisions that were quite out of character. In the evenings when I was on my own, I would somehow gravitate towards the Metro stations. I didn't know how I got there but I would suddenly come out of the dreamlike state and find myself sitting on a platform. I listened to 'The Rip' by Portishead on repeat and willed myself to jump in front of the next train.

One sticky evening I was walking down a Metro

platform staring at the floor when I heard a voice in front of me say, 'Hey! Nice T-shirt!' I was wearing a top by one of my favourite bands, Sonic Youth. As I looked up I saw it was Thurston Moore, the singer and guitarist from Sonic Youth, who was speaking to me. Wide-eyed, I replied, 'Hey! Thanks!' and we both carried on walking. For me, that was a sign from the universe. I was saved that day by Thurston. His brief interaction with my world stopped me from killing myself that afternoon. I wasn't supposed to die that day.

During my mid-twenties, I fantasised about killing myself on my twenty-seventh birthday. I wanted to join the mythologised '27 Club'. Kurt Cobain, Amy Winehouse, Jimi Hendrix – they all died at the age of twenty-seven. It's also worth mentioning that many others of my icons didn't. But I wanted my life to be over. I was so miserable and I couldn't foresee my situation improving in any way. This unhealthy fixation failed to bring me any closer to a solution and I was willing to try anything to make the pain go away. I wanted to die because it felt like the only way of escaping my feelings. I wasn't alone in contemplating suicide. According to the 2009 Trans Mental Health Review, 84 per cent of trans people have considered ending their lives at some stage, which is a truly disturbing statistic, but one that I can relate to.

I'd planned the whole thing out. I wanted to take an

overdose of painkillers and wash them down with Prosecco, lying on my bed surrounded by beautiful flowers. I
was lost and was using fantasy to escape. Talking about
suicide isn't easy and thinking about this period of my life
is distressing. It's such a far cry from the person I am today.
But sadly, this was the dark place where my thoughts took
me. I believed I was unworthy, unloveable and that the
world would be a better place without me. Thankfully I
didn't go through with it because I was in a relationship by
the time my twenty-seventh birthday came around – I
didn't feel so alone any more and ultimately this saved me.
But the relationship and love of another only went so far. I
still couldn't find the love within myself that I desperately
needed.

At the time I couldn't decipher where the unease within
myself came from. In its most simplistic form, I hated my
life and I hated myself. The thought of going to therapy
didn't occur to me – I was blinded, unable to think straight.
I tried my hardest to figure out what was wrong with me
but I would come up empty every time. I didn't know if it
was related to my gender or not. I concluded that I was
suffering from depression – but this wasn't the whole story.
I wasn't aware of the crippling effects of my gender dysphoria and how damaging it was.

With clowns for company I carried on running around
Paris until we took our final bows. Once the final curtain

came down I returned to London. I've renamed the summer of 2009 as my 'Summer of Love'. I spent three months touring festivals, gigging and partying. I stayed awake for two days at a time more and more frequently. I sought out the characters who were happy to do the same and the places that facilitated us. Together we encouraged and accelerated our hedonistic lifestyles. At the time I was living on my own in a flat near Old Street. One Monday lunchtime, after returning home from a weekend bender, I called the local pizza joint to satisfy my intense hunger. When they heard my voice they declined my order. Apparently, I'd ordered several times in the past but had always passed out by the time they delivered the pizza, never answering the door. They weren't going to take the chance on me any more.

Throughout this madness I did have some semblance of discipline. The four days of the week where I was awake and not numbing myself, I created art and made projects happen. It would be unfair to completely write off these times. Many experiences enriched me and satisfied my desires, certain relationships developed and blossomed. All the while I was present within my life, but not in my own head.

Towards the end of 2009, I started a relationship which in many ways pressed pause on this destructive behaviour. I discovered that I would rather be in bed at 3 a.m.

snuggled up to Gus than numbing myself with alcohol or scoring mind-bending substances. But when my relationship with Gus came to an end three years later, it didn't take long before old habits resurfaced and the wild child was back. The release from the relationship, not having anyone to answer to, and the desire to further explore my gender presentation landed me in my darkest scenario yet.

There comes a point when drinking and taking drugs recreationally becomes destructive. When you find yourself in dangerous situations, you've got to admit that you've gone too far and crossed the line. Once your health and safety is not your primary concern it's game over.

Black.

I came to, slumped on a sofa in an obscure room. A rope light dazzled in the corner, illuminating a vague outline of a bed. Black PVC coated the walls, reflecting the empty space. A strobe light flickered in a faraway room, keeping time with 4:4 beats of incessant techno. My head crunched as I blinked my eyes open, trying to familiarise myself with the environment. Faces around me warped, like I was looking into a house of mirrors at the fairground. I couldn't make out anyone I knew. I didn't know how I'd got there, or who I'd come with. I sat very still, trying to gather my thoughts, wondering what to do. I was given a drink by the person sitting next to me. Moments later, I slipped back into the abyss.

Black.

I was standing on the pavement, shrouded by the glowing amber of a street light and the rising sun. My black pencil skirt was ripped, the split revealing my torn tights. I was missing a shoe. A white fur coat was draped over my left arm. I stumbled forward, trying to get into a stranger's car. I shouted at the person in the driving seat, demanding a lift home. The young lad locked the door and told me to fuck off. I staggered towards the next vehicle.

Black.

I was sitting in the back of a taxi, staring at the red light of the LED meter and watching the numbers slowly rise. Out of the window I saw the Hackney Empire flashing past. I realised, thankfully, that I was on my way home. I avoided my housemates in the kitchen making breakfast, quietly sneaking off to my bedroom. In the safety of my room I scraped my hair into a top-knot and looked in the mirror. A caricature reflected itself back at me. Lipstick was smudged around my mouth, my foundation resembled the cracked surface of the moon and my eyes were bright red and bloodshot.

Pass out.

I don't know what happened to me that night. I can

loosely join the dots but there are huge blanks in my memory. When I had left the house the previous evening it definitely hadn't been my intention to end up in such a dangerous situation. I'm thankful that I came to no harm, as I know the outcome could have been far worse. But I felt like I was living in a nightmare.

Why did I feel the need to reduce my existence to this? My gender dysphoria confused me, causing me to feel incredibly insecure. My behaviour was a direct result of the voice inside my head, which constantly told me, 'You're not enough.' My lack of self-worth resulted from the shame I was carrying about who I was – or rather, who I wasn't.

I didn't know about mental health back then. I didn't know that mine was shot to pieces. I often spoke to my partner at the time about the darkness. About how I felt like I was being suffocated by the destructive thought patterns of my mind. I'd be crippled by negative thoughts as soon as I opened my eyes each morning and plagued by them throughout the day. My brain churned out endless reams of rubbish. 'You're not good enough, you never have been . . . Everything you do is shit . . . You're a waste of time . . . Your boyfriend is cheating on you . . . You'll never be loved,' and so on. My mind liked to self-harm with such words. I longed to lower their volume or turn them off permanently. I tried to press the escape button. I wanted out – out of my life and out of my body.

On 21 March 2012, I woke up with a pounding headache. I felt disgusting. I was totally hungover and ran to the bathroom to be sick. The night before I'd been DJing at the George and Dragon pub in Shoreditch. Taking full advantage of my free drink tokens, I'd necked far too many gin and tonics on an empty stomach. It had got to the stage that every time I went out I pushed myself to extreme limits. I had nothing left in me. I was drained. My time was up – I needed to step off my toxic orbit and find salvation in a new one.

This was to be the second biggest decision of my life. I decided to change my lifestyle and become clean and sober. I'd recently begun to identify as a woman and knew I wanted to start the process of transitioning to female. I was aware that this wouldn't be possible if I was continually destroying myself with an unhealthy attachment to alcohol, drugs, food, sex and people. I knew I would require a healthy body and positive mindset if I were going to embark on the biggest journey of self-discovery yet. I'd relished my identity as a performer and wore the label 'wild child' like a badge of honour. But I told myself that this was the old me. I wouldn't be able to move forward with any grace if my destructive behaviour continued. I needed to go cold turkey and discover who I was, who the real me was, with clarity.

I was handed an olive branch. One of my good friends invited me to join him at a twelve-step recovery meeting.

Initially I was hesitant. The meetings were often held in church buildings and they weren't the glamorous after-party I so desperately sought. I felt ashamed, embarrassed and full of fear. My ego felt deflated and I couldn't accept it. At the first meeting I didn't identify with what I heard from the other attendees and I was put off by the fact that I didn't see another trans person. I still felt isolated and I was looking for ways to write it off. I was sceptical to say the least and to top it off, I didn't think it was cool. Pride, ego and insecurity were trying to sabotage my wellness.

At the time I didn't regard myself as a heavy drinker or drug user. After all, I wasn't drinking every day. I'd often go for days without a drink and I rarely shared a bottle of wine over dinner with my partner. I didn't think of alcohol as something to savour or enjoy – I was enticed by its other purpose. My problem was the binges, the lost three-day weekends, forty-eight hours of not sleeping and the festival shenanigans. Once I was in party mode I didn't want to stop. This lifestyle was so normalised that I never questioned it. It had simply become a way of life for me.

If I looked even closer, there were other alarming signs in my behaviour. I didn't have the ability to stop. I could never have just one piece of cake. If I had a slice, then I wanted to eat the whole thing. A desire would be triggered inside me, an obsession set off. If I bought a pack of

Viennetta ice cream, planning to save it in the freezer, I was deluding myself. I'd eat it all the very same night. I came to the realisation that I acted out and binged in areas beyond alcohol and drugs. My motto had always been 'all or nothing' – I always wanted more. More money, more drugs, more booze, more cake, more love, more sex. I would never be happy or satisfied. The hole inside me was never filled and my life felt totally unmanageable.

I sought solace in an LGBTQ recovery group and I eventually met other trans people with similar experiences to me. It was so refreshing to realise that I wasn't alone any more. The truth was, I never had been. I began to piece together my life, examining my way of thinking and the reasons why I behaved the way I did. I worked through the twelve steps and my life changed dramatically.

After a month clean I felt amazing. I had energy, clarity and enthusiasm. In that clichéd way I started to practise yoga, meditation and Pilates and I discovered I could actually enjoy these activities without a hangover or a comedown. Going to the gym became my new obsession – I had an arse to die for. My mental health rapidly improved, and although my life still felt unmanageable, I was beginning to feel less hollow, one day at a time. I spent less time sulking in bed wondering 'what if', 'poor me' and 'if only I were somebody else'. I felt more engaged, dedicated to making a change to my lifestyle. I achieved the new perspective that I'd been looking for and to my surprise, self-control felt sexy. I breezed through the first month, floating on a cloud of self-assurance. I couldn't have done this alone and I'm immensely thankful to those who reached out and helped me.

I decided to continue with my new, improved lifestyle. Nothing would get in my way. I was about to embark upon a process that would require me to honour the desires and dreams of the little boy I once was. I couldn't let him down . . .

. . . 'Her' time had come.

Chapter 8

TRANSCENDENCE: THE BEGINNING

The world was supposed to end in 2012, but for me it had only just begun. For years I'd been wading through reservoirs of denial, shame and guilt. I'd shaped, modelled and formed multiple identities. But the finished product was always a poor imitation of what came before it, so I would start all over again. Throughout the suffocating expanse of black I was searching for the feminine. The reality was that I had to wait for the femme to find me. Ever since I was a child I'd launched countless wishes into the universe that one day I'd be a woman. But I had never allowed my desires to come into being – because of fear. In the end, I had become so low, so unfathomably unhappy that something had to give. I couldn't deny myself any longer. I needed to confront who I was and I wondered what it was going to take to find the strength to do so.

A year earlier, in 2011, Channel Four screened *My*

Transsexual Summer – a documentary series that followed seven trans people at various stages of their transition. It was incredible viewing. For the first time ever I saw people who I related to, living their lives identifying as trans. It was positive, contemporary and groundbreaking. It had a huge impact on my life. Watching it I realised that it was possible – that I could transition too. Coming out to myself as trans was a defining moment for me – it was accepting who I truly was after years of denial. It was embracing who I was after years of confusion and disconnection in a male role.

Before *My Transsexual Summer* beamed into my living room, my only other references for trans women on TV were Jackie from *Paddington Green* and Nadia from *Big Brother*.

When I encountered these trans women I was still too young. I wasn't ready to believe that I could make the transition. Now it was different – I knew, in my heart of hearts, that I was transgender. For the first time in my life I needed to start thinking about it seriously. I had to find out if I felt comfortable in a female presentation and if this new way of life would make me feel happier about myself. These were gigantic ifs.

My boyfriend Gus had suggested that I seek out private psychotherapy in 2011, to talk to someone about the constant, crushing negativity inside my head. I finally followed his advice, attending sessions with a local Hackney

The end or the beginning? Or somewhere
between the two? Ryan in 2011

therapist once a week. Over the course of a year's therapy,
we discussed everything that was happening in my life in
great depth. My therapist heard about my decision to transition, my abuse of substances, the break-up of my
relationship, getting sober, changing my name and becoming Rhyannon. It was hugely beneficial to have someone to

talk to who wasn't close to me – who was objective and non-judgemental. These meetings proved very painful, stirring up difficult emotions that I tried hard to repress. Often I didn't want to go because the sessions were so emotionally gruelling, but I forced myself to return every time. I had run away from my truth for long enough. Therapy was absolutely key to my journey – at the start of our sessions I was dressing as Ryan and by the end I was presenting as female and called Rhyannon. Once I had pinpointed the root of my problems, reaching a stage where I felt happier within myself, I was faced with a dilemma. How do you tell people that you're going to transition?

In January 2012, a few months before I'd made my decision to finally get sober, my sister Danielle returned to the UK with her girlfriend. Danielle wanted all the family together – it was the first time she'd returned home since travelling around Australia, so I visited her in the village we had grown up in. I planned to tell my sister about my decision to transition first, summoning the courage to open up to her. The fact that she worked as a nurse comforted me – I imagined that she might have encountered trans people before. That we had both come out to each other in the past as queer also really helped with my nerves. I hoped that she'd understand after the initial shock wore off. In her eyes, I was still her brother Ryan – she didn't know what was about to hit her.

While Danielle was driving us around the village, I turned the car stereo down. I knew I should just come out with it rather than prolong the agony. I said, 'Sis, I've got something to tell you. I've always known that I might not be a boy. Perhaps it wasn't always as clear as it is today. But I've decided I'm going to transition and make it happen. I'm going to become a transgender woman.' I was amazed at how smoothly it rolled off my tongue.

Danielle didn't slam the brakes or crash the car. After a moment of agonising silence, her response was, 'Oh my God!' I didn't blame her; I knew it would be a shock. She went on to say, 'I'm not surprised, you've always been different.' Relieved, I asked her what she meant by 'different'. Danielle explained that as a child I was always playing with girls and had generally been more 'girly' than most boys. But like everyone else she had assumed that this was simply because I was gay. I reiterated that I had known I was transgender since I was young – but that I wasn't able to accept it or even understand it. I was heartened to hear that she agreed that it made sense.

Her next question was, 'Are you going to tell Mum and the rest of the family?' I explained that in time I would, although it was very early days. So I asked her to keep it a secret. Years ago I'd asked her to keep my sexuality a secret but she didn't manage it – this time she assured me she wouldn't let me down. After telling my sister I felt a huge weight lift off my shoulders. I knew it was important to have someone within the family to whom I could talk about it, especially in the early stages. I was relieved at her reaction and understanding. It was wonderful to finally open up about who I was and it initiated a year-long process of coming out as transgender to the world.

Months later, Danielle admitted to me that she was finding my shift of identity hard to process. The news hit her harder when she returned to Australia – I think it must have finally sunk in then. She confessed that she missed her brother. I was gutted to hear that she wasn't feeling great about my news but I explained that I was still her sibling. I would always love her and I hadn't changed. I had always been trans – the only difference was that it was now visible. The only difference was that she now knew.

Next I needed to tackle my friends. My friend H Plewis was top of my hit list and one afternoon that February I told her that I needed to talk to her about something. She came over to mine and I awkwardly skirted around the issue for quite some time, sipping herbal tea and staring at my fish tank. I felt scared, fearful and vulnerable. It was incredibly daunting telling someone the 'secret' I had kept hidden my whole life. I started to cry, unable to suppress the emotion flooding me. Somehow, through the tears, I managed to tell her that I was trans. In response, H looked at me sympathetically but there was also confusion written on her face. She was completely shocked. She nodded and managed to respond with 'Hmmm'.

H had lots of questions for me. One of her main concerns involved my relationship. She wanted to know how I was going to tell my partner Gus and what it would mean for us. She warned, 'You will break his heart; he loves you. He's a nice guy and you don't find many of those.' In all honesty I hadn't got that far yet. I had only just faced up to the fact that I was going to transition and I was still trying to get my head around it. I hadn't yet factored in my relationship, and this threw me. H was right. I had to ask myself if I wanted to continue in a relationship that was based upon a partnership of two men. I wondered if together we would be able to adapt to my change of identity. I loved him dearly and I cherished the intimate relationship we'd nurtured but I had to face up to the fact that it might spell the end of us. Telling H had seemed like a monumental step – I didn't know how I was going to tell Gus and I didn't know if I was prepared for the consequences.

Despite the difficulty of our conversation it was a relief to get my news off my chest and into the open after so many years of burying it deep. I'd opened a door, which I thought would be locked forever. I'd stepped through into a new life and I felt incredible. But I knew that my next hurdle was telling my partner. Days later I sat down with Gus and told him. I honestly can't remember what I said – the intense emotion of the conversation has blurred it all. We both had tears rolling down our faces as the news reverberated around the lounge, followed by an ominous silence.

I was utterly conflicted. I didn't want to leave him, but I thought I needed to be with someone who saw me as a woman. I needed to be in a relationship where I could be the person I'd neglected for so long. The truth was, we had begun the relationship as two men. Gus was a homosexual man, attracted to people who identify as male. As painful as it was, and as much as it broke my heart, I told him I thought it would be beneficial if I were single while I worked everything out. I needed to focus all of my energies on discovering who I was as a person, and I had to do it alone. Gus, whose nature is kind and gentle, was very supportive and I was incredibly grateful for this. Not many would have reacted so graciously.

Following this, there was a period of time when it was unclear if we were in a relationship or not – it wasn't like a typical break-up, and we weren't sure how to behave. We carried on sleeping in the same bed until we realised that it would be healthier emotionally if we had separate rooms. Over time we gradually detached from one another – it was a slow process. We continued to live together for the next four months, cherishing our friendship, and it was amazing to have his support as I began the process of transitioning. It was a difficult time for both of us – it was all so new and happening so fast.

Having finally come to the conclusion that I was transgender I knew that my next step was to reach out to people who were trans. I hoped to gain some much-needed guidance by asking them the questions that nobody else was able to answer. I was lucky to be in the position of having several friends who had transitioned since I'd first met them and others who had transitioned years before. This was invaluable for me.

Back in 2009, when my friend Amber told me she was going to start living as a woman full-time, I couldn't help feeling jealous. I was envious that she had finally made the leap and got there before me. I sent her a message congratulating her bravery, but secretly I was sulking and resentful inside.

Amber was like a sister to me. We'd known each other since 2005, having frequented the same clubs and partied together late into the night. We were partners in crime and our behaviour drew us together. She would say to me, 'I thought I was wild until I met you.' With so much history between us I knew that Amber deserved to be one of the first to hear my news.

Amber had completely transformed herself from stocky northern lad to a slim, healthy and attractive woman. It was incredible. I knew that her new presentation indicated she was happier and taking care of herself. She was proud of her body, seeing this spurred me on.

Amber kindly shared her experience of transitioning with me, telling me what she had gone through at the early stages. It was a lot of information to take in – I didn't know where to start. It was clear that transitioning from a man into a woman wasn't as simple as flicking on a light switch. It was going to take time, determination, money, patience, frustration and tears. This was a daunting realisation.

Amber advised that the first thing I needed to do was to book an appointment with my GP. I needed to tell my doctor that I was transgender and I wanted to transition, and to request a referral to the Gender Identity Clinic at Charing Cross Hospital because of my gender dysphoria. This sounded completely terrifying – I didn't want to tell a stranger all about how I was feeling, I had only just faced up to it myself. What if they didn't believe me? I was also terrified by the thought that this would be it: the start of my transition. My dream might finally become a reality and that was an overwhelming feeling. I felt sick. Everything was very real all of a sudden.

When I visited Amber to tell her my news I was dressed as Ryan or, let's say, 'in a male presentation'. In early 2012, my hair was shoulder-length, curly and my natural mousy brown colour. I was dressed in scruffy jeans, Vans trainers and a grungy jumper. I wasn't wearing any make-up or anything feminine at all. I had completely given up on myself – I wasn't interested in clothes or style. I was depressed and I just didn't care any more. I asked Amber what small changes I could make while I waited for my doctor's appointment. Amber asked me about my facial hair – what was I going to do? Luckily I didn't have much. I had grown a moustache the year before in a desperate attempt to try and adopt some masculinity during the dark times but aside from that I was pretty hairless all over my body. She recommended a clinic for laser hair removal, phoning them up and haggling me a good price for a six-session course. It was going to cost £300. Amber reminded me that it was a good idea to start saving, as I would need some extra cash for this life-changing journey. She also recommended having my eyebrows threaded so that the arch was softer and more feminine.

I'll always remember the sparkle in Amber's eyes as she whispered, 'Baby girl, what's your new name gonna be?' She advised me that the sooner I changed my name and began living as a woman, the sooner I would be able to start treatment at the Gender Identity Clinic. I was warned, 'You're gonna have to be patient, it's a long wait!' I wasn't sure if I was ready for a new name yet – it seemed like such a gigantic step – but her comment got the ball rolling. As I was leaving she kindly gave me two dresses and a pair of heels – her way of showing support. When I got home I tried them on straight away, striking a pose in the mirror and sending her a picture. Her reply was, 'Beautiful, baby girl!' Although it wasn't the first time I had worn a dress, this was different. It was a fantastic feeling having come out to my closest trans friend, and someone who had inspired me.

Slowly I began taking small steps towards my new identity. On one occasion I decided to turn up to a cabaret show by Bourgeois and Maurice wearing a padded bra underneath my Pam Hogg T-shirt, which I'd teamed with black skinny jeans. I was nervous about revealing myself in this way, but I knew that it had to be done. I used a padded bra, a Primark staple, stuffed with bags of rice from my LipSinkers performances. I certainly caused a reaction. Jonny Woo stared at my chest and asked, 'Is this performance art?' while the bartender came right out with, 'Are you going to become a woman?' I answered all of their questions proudly, telling everyone my plan. The cat was out the bag and tongues started wagging.

It was evident that people were surprised and shocked. These were friends I'd known for over five years and I'd never breathed a word about how I felt. They were confused and some even felt betrayed. One friend said to me, 'All the time we've been drunk and shared secrets, how come you never thought about telling me?' I explained that I couldn't face up to the reality. That I wasn't ready then, I was still running. I'd been trying to escape from the truth for years.

It was now time to face the music and talk to the professionals. As well as being the time when I decided to clean up my life and get sober, March 2012 also marked my first doctor's appointment. I remember sitting anxiously in the surgery with my friend Maria, making polite small talk with each other. I was waiting for Dr Ashrafi, a doctor I'd never met before, which made me even more nervous. I didn't know what to expect and I felt scared; my stomach was in knots. Before I knew it, Dr Ashrafi appeared, calling 'Ryan Wagg'. Maria and I looked at each other – Dr Ashrafi was hot!

Inside his office, I sat down on the green plastic chair and looked at the skeleton standing in the corner. 'How can I help?' he asked. I told him everything that I had rehearsed – asking for a referral to the GIC, and saying that I wanted to transition and start taking female hormones. I was firm and to the point, which made me feel confident and assured. I was totally honest, explaining how long I'd felt like this, and that I'd been cross-dressing ever since I was a child. I said that after years of bearing the burden on my own, I was keen to start talking to professionals. To my surprise, Dr Ashrafi wanted to know how I was feeling mentally. Was I suffering from low mood and anxiety? Had I been coping? I confessed that emotionally and psychologically I felt much better after making the choice to transition, and that I'd recently begun weekly therapy sessions. I told Dr Ashrafi it felt good making a decision which had been haunting me for years.

Dr Ashrafi reassured me that he had referred patients to the GIC before and he could do the same for me. But he warned, 'It's a long waiting list to be seen,' and it could take up to six months. Compared to a lifetime of feeling displaced, six months didn't sound all that long to me. I felt a rush of happiness wash over me – I had initiated the journey on the medical side of things. It was really going to happen.

Four days later, it was my thirtieth birthday. I'd arranged a big house party and invited all my friends. I have lots of small groups of friends, isolated from each other due to my various vocations in life and all the different things I've done. I decided I was going to dress in a female presentation for my party – it would be my way of showing everyone who I was all at once. I'd started buying dresses online so I could experiment cheaply. It felt much safer than using the dreaded gendered changing rooms. Plus, if a dress didn't fit my masculine body it didn't matter, especially if it only cost £4.

The night of my party I wore a figure-hugging black dress, a padded bra, and a face full of make-up. My hair had recently been dyed a darker red rinse. I felt good, although I kept touching my padded bra – it felt too big and cumbersome. Gus made fresh sushi rolls and my housemates brought alcohol and nibbles. My friends started arriving in small groups as I heavily knocked back the Prosecco – this was just days before I got sober. When I opened the door to greet them they laughed and told me I looked 'fit'. They thought it was one of my performance characters. But one friend pulled me aside and asked, 'Is there something you need to tell me?' One by one, I told them all about my desire to transition. It's not like I could hide it any longer, especially considering how I was dressed. I felt a mixture of emotions as I told them all – nervous, scared, vulnerable and excited. I was beaming with happiness that I'd had the strength to uncover Rhyannon but I was worried about their reactions. Luckily, fate was on my side that night. As it was my birthday my friends couldn't say much there and then, except 'Cheers!' and 'Nice one!' Mind you, I was so drunk I'd have never known.

By the end of March, my life had transformed in many ways. As well as being newly sober I needed a new name. Changing my name felt like such a leap, but there was no escaping it – it was essential. It would mark a whole new me so I decided to embrace it. I knew that I didn't want to stray too far away from Ryan so a name beginning with R was a good start. It would be helpful to my friends and family, and all-round easier to remember. But my middle name 'Edward' was definitely going to go! Girls' names beginning with R which I liked included Roxy, Rio, Randy and Rachel. I had often used Rachel to take ownership of the homophobic abuse I received when I was young. It was my way of sticking two fingers up at the bullies of my past.

As a late birthday treat I went to dinner with my friend

Rhyannon Styles photographed by David Bailey © 2017

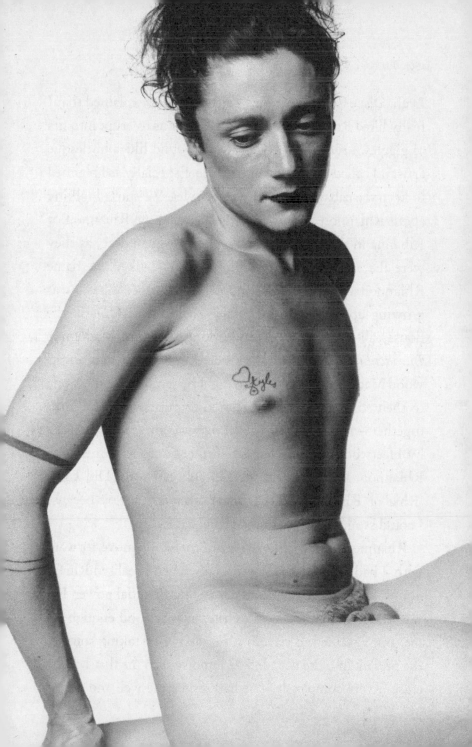

Lyall. Discussing names was on the menu. I explained that I really liked Roxy and Rio, which caused us to erupt into fits of giggles. I realised I would always sound like a burlesque artist if I called myself either of those. Especially as I planned to keep the cabaret-style surname Styles. We started talking about Rhiannon. Many people had called me Rhiannon or Rihanna in the past, especially when I was in drag, as they were the easiest ways to feminise Ryan. I liked the name Rhiannon as it had other connotations for me. When I was growing up, my mum only had a handful of CDs in the house, all Greatest Hits collections. We had Madonna's *Immaculate Collection* alongside Eurythmics and Fleetwood Mac – who I grew up loving. I remember singing along to their song 'Rhiannon'. I started to put the musical links together – my idol Courtney Love was massively inspired by Fleetwood Mac, so I was definitely onto a winner with Rhiannon. Lyall and I discussed abbreviations. Did I like 'Rhia' or 'Rhi-Rhi'? I liked them both, even more so because I could steal Rihanna's thunder one day.

Rhiannon seemed like a natural name to move forward with. I had always liked it, especially when I realised Rhiannon was a Celtic goddess and a lady of influential power. If it was good enough for folklore then it was good enough for me. But I wanted to refresh it somehow, by taking some of the present into the new. It was important to me that I didn't erase 'Ryan' completely – he had served me well and would help me grow into the woman I longed to be. I wouldn't be Rhiannon without Ryan. It was then that I decided to change the 'i' into a 'y'. 'Rhyannon' allowed me to roll my future and past all into one.

Having chosen a name it was time to apply to change it by deed poll. In keeping with my new female identity I planned to go from 'Mr' to 'Miss'. I signed up online and anxiously waited for the forms to arrive. Although I was more than ready to change my pronouns from 'he' to 'she' and from 'Mr' to 'Miss', for many it is not this simple. It's not uncommon for trans people to reject traditional pronouns for more ambiguous terms such as 'they', or 'Mx'. If you're ever unsure when referring to a trans person, don't be afraid to ask what their preference is.

At the start of April it was time to begin a three-year process of removing my facial hair. I visited the clinic where Amber had negotiated me a deal, requiring a patch test on my face to see how I would react to the laser. I turned up wearing boys' clothes and using the name Ryan. I wasn't yet presenting as female twenty-four/seven, instead slowly introducing Rhyannon into the mix. There was also the reality of not being able to afford a whole new wardrobe. At the clinic, the beautician asked what areas I wanted to treat and why. I said I needed to remove my facial hair because I wanted a smoother face when I was doing drag. I couldn't quite stomach admitting the truth there and then. At the time I felt like the only person in the world who had been there while in transition (even though Amber had been there herself!). I know that thousands of people have laser hair removal; it isn't a taboo cosmetic procedure at all. But for me it was monumental. It marked the beginning of my physical transition.

Once my face was cleaned and I was wearing protective goggles, the beautician fired three lasers onto my chin and neck. It made a tick-tick sound every time she fired the trigger, a small shock that was over in a second. It wasn't painful – I'd had tattoos that had taken hours so I knew all about pain. Before leaving the clinic I made my appointment for the first proper session. Provided I didn't have a reaction to the patch test, it would be in four days' time. I regarded this as the start date of my transformation and I couldn't wait.

I'm one of the lucky ones – I didn't need huge amounts of surgery or beauty procedures to feminise myself. I wasn't your typical masculine-looking man with dark hair, chiselled features, big feet or hands. I was slim, hairless, fair, and I've been told that I had angelic facial features. But when I began to present as female, my facial hair did trouble me. By the end of the day traces of soft stubble would appear on my chin, making me paranoid. I tried as hard as I could to hide it with make-up, covering my chin and upper lip area with orange lipstick underneath my foundation. I'd seen on You-Tube that the orange lipstick cancels out the dark colour of the stubble. But I didn't really have dark hair – I just had a shadow of stubble. My make-up was layered on so thick, I looked like I was going on stage, especially when I teamed it with pink lipstick. Once, walking through Hackney, a man shouted, 'Oi CoCo, the circus is that way!' at me. Maybe I had found my inner clown after all.

I returned to the skin clinic desperate to start the process and begin to see the changes. I had the same beautician as before and I lay down, ready for my first full treatment. The beautician said, 'If it gets too painful, let me know and I'll stop.' And so it began. After thirty seconds I needed a break – it felt like the side of my face was on fire. My trans friends had reassured me that laser hair removal wasn't painful. 'It just feels like you're being slapped in the face with a rubber band,' they had said. But this felt like I was being stabbed multiple times, as if a hot pin was being dragged through my delicate, sensitive skin. Every time the beautician fired the laser I jumped. I felt like I was in an episode of *Casualty* and she was trying to restart my heart with a defibrillator.

Once both sides of my face had been tortured, it was time to move on to my chin and upper lip. Nothing I had ever experienced equalled this pain. I could feel the shock and smell the laser burning every individual hair. Once the treatment was over my face was bright red and excruciatingly sore. I was smothered in aloe vera gel and given an ice pack to cool me down. The beautician told me to keep my face clean, stay out of the sun and avoid hot showers or saunas for the next twenty-four hours. I was thankful that I had cycled to the appointment and didn't need to get on public transport home. It literally looked like a child had painted a bright red beard onto my face using a felt tip.

I booked my next appointment for five weeks' time. I didn't want to go through the agony again but I didn't want to keep shaving either. I had no choice – agony it was. It was the first of many sacrifices I have had to make in order to become the woman I want to be. Over the course of three years I had many sessions of laser hair removal. In total I've spent £800 on treatments to keep the hair at bay. Thankfully, over time it felt less painful. I jumped and wriggled less every time the laser was fired. Very gradually the strength of the laser was increased and very slowly my facial hair disappeared. By the end of the sixth session I noticed a big difference, and was happy with the results. I didn't need to shave every day and my face was smoother overall. It had been worth the initial torture. From then on, every four or five weeks it was 'zap-zap' laser time.

As my transformation progressed, I eventually told the clinic about my transition and started arriving for appointments in female clothes. It was daunting at first, but I knew that Amber had been through the same process and that many other trans woman had undoubtedly used their service. When it came down to it I had nothing to worry about.

As time rolled by, I received my deed poll forms on 18

April 2012. I needed to have a witness so I asked I I to sign the forms. It only seemed right, as she was my first friend to learn about my plans. This was a huge step in my transition and something else that cost money – £36 to be exact. As I sat down to sign my name, it occurred to me that I would also need a new signature. I began scribbling 'Rhyannon Wagg' over and over again in various styles at various speeds until I was happy with what had developed. There and then I gave up my old name of Ryan and adopted for all intents and purposes the new, improved name of Rhyannon. The legality of my new name was a pivotal turning point in my transition. It was statement and a beginning. I now regard this date as my second birthday, marking the day I started really living.

Even though this was such an exciting moment, full of the promise of the future, I remember feeling sad. It was hard to say goodbye to Ryan, even though I was so looking forward to living as Rhyannon. But it was onwards and upwards – it was time to announce my new name to everyone and to start living full-time femme. Now that Rhyannon was officially recognised, I could legally change everything else. Until you're in the throes of such a life-changing event you don't realise how much you need to amend. I wrote a list of everything that needed to be updated:

- Passport
- Bank account

- Driving licence
- Phone contract
- NHS (doctor's records)
- Email addresses
- Insurance
- Gym membership
- Gas and electricity accounts
- Internet account
- Website
- Facebook
- Twitter
- eBay
- Spotify
- Amazon
- Asos . . .

. . . and the list went on.

Some of these were easier than others and happened at the click of a button, but for many I had to send copies of the deed poll to prove my new name and identity. It was money well spent but the process took several months to complete. I had to come to terms with the fact that this wouldn't be an overnight transformation.

When I changed my NHS status from male to female, I started receiving monthly letters asking me to go for smear tests – which was funny although totally inappropriate for my situation. With regard to my social media accounts, it proved slightly more difficult. I had been silly on Facebook, often changing my name, making anagrams of words and playing around. I didn't know it at the time but Facebook only lets you change your name up to a maximum of five times. I'd already used up my allocated allowance so I couldn't change my Facebook name to Rhyannon Styles. Instead I had to start all over again and create a completely new profile. In many ways this felt quite apt – it was exactly what I was doing in my life. I was starting from scratch and learning who I was all over again. I was a baby, with the benefit of having thirty years of life experience.

With a new name in tow, I started to present as female whenever and wherever I could.

YouTube became my classroom, where I found crucial insight from other trans girls. I picked up tips on how to feminise your appearance by changing your wardrobe. I didn't have the finances to replace my entire wardrobe in one go, so instead I bought feminine items of clothing and teamed them with what I had. Looking back, it was a frightful combination. I looked like a walking jumble sale, but I did what I could. Local charity shops, vintage stores and cheap high-street shops were the easiest places to navigate. At the time I believed I completely passed as female – most probably because this is how I so desperately wanted to be perceived. Sometimes I was surprised when onlookers called me out. I felt like a girl, I was a girl – so why couldn't others see it?

I was once waiting at a bus stop near my house in Hackney. I was minding my own business and drinking a coffee. Two women caught my eye – I noticed the way they were looking me up and down. After a while of them scrutinising me, one of them asked, 'Are you a boy or a girl?' to which I looked away, shame-faced. She proceeded to repeat herself, saying, 'Tell me, are you a boy or a girl?' At that point the other woman joined in and they started to sing, 'You're a man, it's a man.' Faced with this humiliation I decided to walk away rather than answer their questions. As I was escaping I heard them shout, 'Batty man, batty boy' after me, before bursting into laughter. They caused quite a scene and I was left feeling hurt, embarrassed and afraid.

I'm thankful that this incident is the worst prejudice I've suffered since my transition. Many others are not as lucky as me in this respect. According to a report by James Morton of the Scottish Transgender Alliance in 2008, 62 per cent of trans people have suffered transphobic harassment in public places. I soon became accustomed to people staring at me on public transport, whispering into their friends' ears. The glaring, bright lights of the tube carriage are not the most flattering, making it impossible to hide under them. This heightened my anxiety and caused me to over-plan my journey. Whenever possible, I would cycle.

This felt much safer. To my great disappointment, it was plain to see that I wasn't passing as female – to others I simply looked like a boy wearing girls' clothes. One time a teenage lad followed me around Tesco, informing fellow shoppers, 'That's a man.' I clutched my basket and quickly whizzed around the shop before I lost my temper and threw a can of baked beans in his direction. But at times like this, when I felt like giving up altogether, I would always turn to my Nan Goldin photography book. *The Other Side* was my rock during the trying times. The book depicts various trans women at all stages of transition – it covers the whole spectrum. In dark moments it helped me realise that I had to brush off others' reactions. Happiness would come from confidence, peace and belief in myself.

I have been fortunate to live in Hackney, which is such a diverse borough of London. This diversity has allowed me to blend into the background. The area is full of so many different minorities and ethnicities that in a sense we all help camouflage one another. It's such an eclectic place and it has allowed me to thrive. I saw other trans women in Hackney, at various stages of transition. I witnessed how the public reacted to them too, which helped me prepare for the worst. I was in the supermarket again where I saw a trans woman fixing the self-service checkouts. When she finished she headed off towards the toilets. One of the other employees shuddered as she walked past, shaking her head and screwing up her face. She wore a look of disgust and it distressed me. I wanted to report it to the store's manager – it was blatant transphobia.

In the early days I walked around with a foreboding sense of paranoia and anxiety, always on the lookout for shifty glances or comments from strangers. My head would constantly derail me to a negative place, a default of shame and fear. Perhaps not everyone was judging or saying bad things about me – it would be nice to think that this wasn't the case – but that's how I felt at the time.

Those first few months were challenging. Everything was different. Not only had I changed my name and adopted a new presentation but I was also sober. The amount of energy it required to transition, and the resulting tumultuous emotions, often floored me, but I was determined not to take drugs or drink alcohol to numb the discomfort. It would be too easy to disappear into a bottle or a whirlwind of drugs. I had to face up to the fact that such teething problems were part of the process and the reality of my new life. Looking back, I can now say that I am better for these difficult times, which built my resilience. I'm stronger having survived.

I didn't expect my local shopkeepers to notice a difference but the change was immediate to them. If you've been going into the same shop for over three years to buy your soya milk, people begin to recognise you. This is one of the reasons I loved Hackney; I loved the sense of community, spotting the same faces on the street. It made me feel secure. When I slowly started to introduce Rhyannon, I initially selected which shops I would feel most comfortable approaching. My local greengrocers on Chatsworth Road had a difficult time with me. One day it was 'Hello, mate!', 'Cheers, mate!' and the next day they ignored me. I found that people would avoid making eye contact if they felt awkward. It was clear that my transformation was making certain people uncomfortable, which was hard to come to terms with. I didn't blame them, though – I guess that change creates uncertainty, which in turn makes people uneasy. I would have to get used to it.

The first time I went into my local coffee shop dressed femme, it was awkward to say the least. I felt uncomfortable about them feeling uncomfortable. I'd been going to this coffee shop for years – they knew me and my order off by heart. It took me forever to build up the confidence to go inside, but I couldn't put it off any longer. A girl can't live without coffee. It was early on in my transition so I was still experimenting with my style. I was dressed up to the nines, wearing one of my more eclectic outfits that looked like a Christmas tree. As I entered the café the shock on their faces was plain to see – they didn't know how to react. Gone were the jovial chit-chats and pleasantries. Really, all I needed to do was to breeze in, saying, 'I'm Rhyannon now, can I have a soy flat white?' But at the time I felt that the only way of translating my new identity was by showing up as Rhyannon and acting as if nothing had changed. It took me a while to summon up the courage to go back but I'm pleased to say that I'm one of their regulars again now. Once they got used to Rhyannon they welcomed her with open arms, and they have witnessed my transition over the last four years.

My postman Owen also took the news well. Naturally, a postman knows the names of everyone on the street. For years, Owen knew me as a man called Ryan. But one morning I had to answer the door to collect a parcel addressed to Rhyannon. (I'd received another eBay dress!) At the door Owen asked, 'Who's Rhyannon, has somebody new moved in?' It was 8 a.m. and I was wearing a baggy T-shirt that definitely didn't scream 'girl'. For a second I thought about lying and telling him a new girl had moved in, but I liked Owen. We'd been chatty ever since I'd moved into the area and I wanted to be honest. I admitted to him, in the simplest terms, that I was now Rhyannon. I didn't say any more than that – I didn't need to. To my relief, Owen just replied, 'Good to know, enjoy your day,' and it was never spoken about again. And over the course of the next two years while I remained at that address, whenever I saw Owen it was completely normal. This exchange felt surprisingly easy, especially as it was one of the first times I'd spoken up directly to a stranger. I was definitely growing in confidence.

Over time, Rhyannon became someone who everyone knew and accepted. It has been over four years since I became Rhyannon and sometimes even I forget my past life spent as Ryan. Sometimes it slaps me around the face and I think, 'Oh yeah, you were a boy once.' In these moments I almost can't believe it. Often when I am recalling memories with friends, they will refer to me as Ryan before justifying themselves with 'You were Ryan then.' Although in my own mind I may have completely switched to Rhyannon, I know that I will never erase the memories of Ryan from others. Those memories are theirs, not mine, and I'm OK with this.

As a trans woman you shape your identity in several ways. A lot of it comes down to appearance – how did I want Rhyannon to dress? What style would she have? How would she do her hair? In the early days I went through a real pink period – everything I purchased was pink. Hot pink, baby pink, fuchsia – you name it. To some degree I was trying to use the colour as a statement of femininity. It's crazy to think that I, of all people, fell into this stereotypical trap. At this stage I was trying everything out, and I guess I didn't have the luxury of going mad for pink as a little girl.

Hair plays a big part for trans women. At first, I found it affirming to have long hair, which helped shape a more feminine appearance (from the back anyway!). I didn't have a particularly girly hairstyle – it was more like a messy Eighties rocker. One day I decided I wanted a fringe and headed to my local hairdressers. My face shape didn't suit a fringe, it only accentuated my square jaw, but I liked it, it felt fresh. I looked more androgynous than explicitly female, but many of the girls I knew wore boyish clothes too, so I embraced it. Weeks later when the photographer David Bailey was taking my portrait, he came over to me, lifted up my fringe and slapped me on the forehead while cheekily asking, 'Tell me a successful woman that has a fringe' – I immediately grew it out.

I became attached to black skinny jeans and tight long-sleeved T-shirts teamed with Converse trainers. When it came to shopping I did anything I could to avoid changing rooms. Charity shops are great for this as you can generally duck in and out without being noticed. But high-street stores often have gendered changing rooms, which are breeding grounds for questioning gender identity. Some higher-end shops realise the potential in any customer and I had a great experience at one store in Westfield shopping centre. The shop assistant clearly clocked my situation and referred to me as 'she' and 'Madam' throughout my visit. I had an inkling he might be on the LGBTQ spectrum too – that always helps. Others have turned me away from the female changing rooms, informing me, 'The men's are upstairs.' In these cases I was so mortified I'd walk straight out of the shop. It's humiliating to be misgendered, especially when I was trying so hard. I always felt like I was taking one step forward and several steps back. I've had to learn the hard way that I can't control how people read me, no matter how hard I try, and this was difficult to accept in the beginning.

In the early days my femme look was fashioned by wearing a padded bra underneath my clothes and tucking my penis away to hide any trace of a bulge in my skinny jeans. I wore thick make-up because I wanted to feel feminine in any way I possibly could and I disguised my masculine features with contouring. This was all I could manage at that point. I didn't want (and couldn't afford) to have plastic surgery yet and I wanted to start taking hormones first. Surgery felt like another big step that I wasn't ready for yet.

I knew that due to the timeline of the transitioning process, I wouldn't be able to start taking female hormones any time soon. This meant I wasn't going to have my own boobs for another two years, or possibly even more. This was a depressing thought. Without surgically enhanced breasts I needed a selection of bras – I wanted my underwear to start reflecting how I felt. I wanted to feel like 'me' underneath the clothes. But I didn't know where to start – I didn't have breasts and my chest was as flat as a washboard.

Trying to navigate the lingerie section in Marks & Spencer is like trying to find your way around London without a map – except M&S is full of lace, chiffon and silk. I didn't know about cup sizes or the difference between balcony, plunge and underwired styles. The same went for knickers. I was used to being size M; what did a size 12 mean? What was considered sexy or frumpy in the land of female underwear? Firstly I needed to find out what I would feel comfortable in but even this felt like a huge task. I often went on shopping trips by myself but was too freaked out to buy or try anything on. When I walked around underwear shops I felt stupid. All the advertising plastering the store walls only highlighted what I didn't have, triggering my dysphoria.

I slowly braved buying knickers, although at first they were just multi-packs of badly decorated briefs or big pants in plain black. These undergarments didn't make me feel sexy or look attractive, but even so, they felt like a huge leap. They felt more in keeping with my new identity and at least I'd finally thrown away my boxer shorts. Frustrated and confused, I reached out to a female friend. H kindly offered to take me bra shopping and it was reassuring having her introduce me to this new world. We were looking for a bra that would be easy to pad. At this point I was still using bags of rice for padding, but after some coaxing I bought a pair of clear rubber 'chicken fillets' from Primark. We chose a selection of bras that H thought would fit and headed to the dressing room. But the experience was disheartening. I felt like a man trying bras on, the process really didn't fill me with joy or positivity. Instead of making me feel feminine, it only highlighted what I didn't have.

Eventually, after lots of running back and forth around the shop we found a size that fitted me – 34A. I decided to buy two bras in neutral colours – nothing frilly or fancy or ultra-feminine. It was just for practicality at this point. I used these bras solidly for the next two years, wearing them under everything – they were almost like my armour. I also experimented with the size of padding, to humorous effect. At times I must have looked ridiculous.

Wearing a bra was difficult to get used to. At first I would often forget to put it on under my T-shirt. I would be halfway down the street and then, 'Oh bugger! Where's my bra?' I was so used to not wearing a bra for the first thirty years of my life that I had to reprogramme my mind and my routine and adjust to a new way of dressing. I was so used to feeling fabric brush against my nipples, it was strange for that daily sensation to disappear. When I went out dancing with the girls to let my hair down, I didn't like how hot my chest got. It would become all sweaty from the bags of plastic covered by my top, creating the illusion of breasts. Having breasts was something a thirty-year-old 'male' was going to need time to get used to.

Breast implants is the pathway for many, but it wasn't what I wanted or could afford. I did a quick Google search and found prices starting from £5,000. However grumpy and impatient I felt, I knew I wanted to take hormones to see what happened to my body naturally through this process. This was always my priority over surgery.

It's quite some feat trying to fit female garments on a male body that has gone through puberty. Clothes for women allow for wider hips, smaller waists and bigger bums than my body naturally had. Once bra shopping was conquered, it was difficult to find 'female' clothes that fitted a 'male' body and supported me in all the right places. Through trial and error and a tsunami of tears, I slowly adjusted to a new wardrobe – despite the many challenges my body presented to me.

The first summer of my transition was hard, really hard. I didn't feel at home within my body yet. I still looked different to how I imagined myself – I still looked like Ryan. I wasn't allowed to bask in the summer sunlight because of the laser treatment I was receiving on my face. I felt hot, sticky and uncomfortable – even in the safety of the shade. During the winter months I snuggled myself into a big coat that protected me. But in the summer I had nowhere to hide. I couldn't bear seeing everybody sunbathing in the parks wearing little clothing and enjoying themselves. The fear of my make-up sweating off and running down my face like an ice-cream prevented me from joining in. I wore baggy T-shirts and shorts in an effort to hide my masculine body while simultaneously trying to feel feminine, but it didn't work. I wanted to be free and effortless. I wanted to run around in summer dresses and low-cut tops like all the other girls, but I physically wasn't there yet. It would take four years before I felt comfortable doing this.

It was a difficult period, but I got through it. Thankfully, I was sober and able to talk about my troubling feelings during my twelve-step meetings. But all the while, I felt like I was still waiting for my life to begin.

Chapter 9

TRANSCENDENCE: CHANGES

On 21 June 2012, I received a letter from the Gender Identity Clinic. I was really excited to receive it but it turned out that it didn't contain happy news. It explained that a referral from my GP alone wasn't acceptable due to commissioning arrangements from the clinic. I would need to be assessed by my local secondary care mental health service, and a copy of that assessment should accompany the referral. I was completely gutted and the letter reduced me to tears. I felt like my life was at a standstill and I had yet another hurdle to jump over. I'd already waited three months since my initial appointment – it felt like prolonged agony. I experienced mounting impatience and frustration with the system that was holding me back. I called my transgender friends to vent, but they immediately put me in my place. 'Sister,' they echoed, 'it's gonna take some time.'

At my next appointment with Dr Ashrafi, I was in full

femme mode. I was using the name Rhyannon and I wasn't happy. Dr Ashrafi was kind and sympathetic – he could tell I was fuming. But the next appointment with my local psychiatrist wasn't available until September. I blurted out, 'September! Are you having a laugh? That's three months away!' Dr Ashrafi placated me, reassuring me that I looked great and that everything, over time, would be OK. As frustrating as it was I had no choice but to accept that it wasn't going to be an overnight transformation. I had to summon patience, courage and strength within myself to continue.

I couldn't handle the thought of waiting to start hormone treatment. By this point I was obsessively watching YouTube videos of trans women, soaking up any information I could find. I was desperate to look more feminine and to lose my male body. Unhealthily, I compared myself to trans women who had transitioned years before, who looked beautiful and, most importantly, female. It made me feel uncomfortable and irritable. I knew that when I stripped away the padded bras, removed my make-up and looked in the mirror, I was a man.

I buckled under the strain, deciding to take matters into my own hands – I wanted to play god and speed up the process. I searched online and found a website where I could buy black market hormones. Some of my trans friends advised against it, citing how dangerous it was and that I wouldn't know what dosage to take. Others said,

'Do what you need to do to feel happy.' I thought, 'Fuck it, what's the worst that can happen?'

I nervously ordered a pack of sixty-four 2 mg tablets of oestrogen called Estrofem. As I clicked the 'buy' button online I had that nervous jittery feeling in my stomach that you get when you know you're doing something wrong. But that didn't stop me – it felt exciting. I was desperate to begin the medical side of my transition and nothing was going to get in my way. When the tablets arrived a week or so later, I was thrilled. I immediately showed them to Gus, who questioned my motives. 'Are you sure that's what you want?' It was what I wanted – more than ever – and the pills became my secret.

The little blue pills came in a cute round dispenser with a pill marked for each day. As much as I was looking forward to taking them, I held off doing so right away. There was so much to think about. I wondered how my life was going to change and how I would feel. I thought about the feminisation process. Was I really ready to develop breasts and other coveted female characteristics? For so long I had day-dreamed about turning into the woman I'd always envisaged myself to be, but now something was holding me back.

Gus moved out of our shared house just before the 2012 London Olympics began. Our lives were separate and the relationship was over. In reality it had been over for quite some time, but living together kept us close. I remember walking around the supermarket when our break-up hit me.

I had tears streaming down my face as I was trying to find the quinoa. I suddenly felt very alone. I'd lost my partner and my closest friend. But I reminded myself that it was my decision and I was thankful that Gus had supported me for so long. Many in his situation would have abandoned me. I still loved him, but I had to come to terms with the fact that it wasn't meant to be. We both had to move on with our own lives, no matter how hard it would be. I had so much I needed to work through and I wasn't ready for another relationship any time soon. First, I had to learn to love myself.

I worked through the heartbreak of my break-up with the help of our new housemate, Delly Dot. She lent a sympathetic ear over cups of rooibos tea and chocolate biscuits. All of my female housemates, Del, Molly, Angela and Rebecca, helped me with my transition. It was like a female coven offering much-needed support and acceptance. I was surprised and grateful at how quickly they adapted to my new name and pronouns. They abbreviated my name to 'Rhya' and used 'she' or 'her' as they introduced me to their friends as a woman. It was also great having heterosexual males around who were on hand to give me honest advice about my outfits. I'd ask, 'Does this work?' or 'Do I look hot?' and they'd be like, 'Nah, ditch the fluoro tights!' It was a relief to be supported by such wonderful people.

At one stage a room became available in our house and we had to look for a new flatmate. I was early on in my transition and many aspects of 'Ryan' were still present. We soon found a new housemate but we hadn't discussed my transition when he viewed the room. This was a source of much anxiety for me – what if he wasn't prepared to live with a trans woman? If he invited friends over, how would they react? What if he flat-out rejected me? I texted him and asked him to come over, knowing I would have to be honest with him. It turned out that Alex was completely fine with it. He said, 'As far as I'm concerned, I'm living with three girls.' I can't tell you how brilliant it was to hear him say that.

It was my housemate Molly who had advice for me when it came to body hair. I was shaving my legs daily, hating having hairy legs, especially in the summer. My legs weren't hugely hairy compared to others but it made me feel masculine when I looked at them. I wanted to have smooth, feminine legs. We had a lovely big bath, but it was becoming a chore and very time-consuming shaving every day. Molly suggested using an epilator or hair-removal cream – I opted for the cream as it was cheaper. But the product burned me and I immediately came out in a rash. The fact that I had decided to also treat the pubic area was big mistake! I swore off using the stuff ever again.

Another friend suggested waxing. I wondered if I was brave enough, and whether the beautician would be trans-friendly or ask unwanted questions. But I knew I needed to summon the strength to ditch the Bic razors and go to a beauty salon. A close friend pointed me towards a local salon and told me to wear a loose-fitting garment. I was really paranoid about my genitalia and how I would be able to hide my penis with the waxer being just inches away. I'd never been in such an intimate situation before – except during sex and seeing the doctor. This was going to take courage. I decided to wear two pairs of pants over the top of my dance belt. I tucked my genitalia tightly out of view, giving the appearance of a completely flat genital area. It was very painful but I was so relieved with the illusion that it gave me the strength I needed.

During my first visit I laid down on the beautician's bed and promptly shut up. After all the trouble I'd gone to downstairs, I didn't want my voice to reveal that I was a man. I wasn't trying to trick the waxer into thinking I was a woman, I just wanted the experience to be as comfortable as possible. I didn't want any negativity or hostility because I was trans. In the end the appointment went really smoothly (just like my legs!) and the waxer said very little to me except, 'Is the temperature OK, Madam?' If she did realise that I was trans she didn't make a point out of it and I was relieved. I was also pleased to discover that waxing wasn't that painful – I think multiple tattoos and the torture of laser hair removal have increased my pain threshold.

You always need a first-time experience like this. You need to break through the wall and realise that it's never as bad as you think it's going to be. Particularly in the service and beauty industry – people should just want your custom. Nowadays, because I am more confident in myself, I don't worry like I used to. I often wait for the waxer to do a double-take. When I take off my clothes and lie on the bed, it's obvious what's going on in my underwear. The beautician will look at me and then look again, quite confused. It amuses me – maybe more than her! I love how your legs feel the day after a wax. It only occurred to me recently that I should make more time for myself and indulge in beauty treatments. It really does make me feel more feminine – it's simple yet effective.

In June 2012, it was time to bid farewell to my sister and her girlfriend. They were returning to Australia, having decided to live there permanently. I knew I wouldn't see them again for a long time so it felt important to say goodbye as Rhyannon. I had been dressing as Rhyannon full-time for two months at this point, undergoing monthly laser treatment, but I still wasn't taking the hormones. We arranged to meet at Birmingham New Street station and spend the afternoon shopping before going for dinner. This was the first time anyone in my family would see me dressed as a girl. Because I was comfortable being Rhyannon in Hackney where I often blended in, I didn't think the West Midlands would be too much trouble.

I remember standing in front of Greggs bakery at the train

station, waiting for my sister and her girlfriend to appear at the top of the escalators. I was hiding behind my sunglasses, trying not to stand out among the provincial types. I was wearing very, very tight denim shorts, an orange and brown checked shirt, and an apricot scarf tied into a bow in my hair. I was trying my hardest to blend in, but I didn't look like anyone else. Far from it. A lot of my early outfits were very out there – loud and outlandish, bursting with what I deemed to be feminine features. Wild patterns, crazy colours, sequins and glitter galore. This kaleidoscope of colour and texture made me really happy. I'd be dolled up to the nines but the effect just wasn't right. I didn't look overtly feminine – I looked like a dressing-up box. I'll never forget my sister's face as soon as she saw me. Shock was written all over it – as if to say, 'Oh my God, what is he wearing?' She remembers this moment (and how disastrous I looked) clearly, and we often laugh about it today.

When we were walking around Birmingham people were staring and whispering in my direction. I didn't actually notice it – I'd become so used to people looking at me that I hadn't realised. But my sister saw it all and it upset her. My voice still sounded masculine because I hadn't yet undergone voice therapy, which meant that while I was browsing the shops people only heard 'man' regardless of how much blue eyeshadow I was wearing. It was a difficult experience, but I can now say that without difficulties you don't grow.

I wanted to have my ears pierced as a feminine state-ment. The only body part I'd had pierced in the past was my eyebrow, which didn't last long. The first piercing was rejected by my body and grew out. The second looked ugly after about six months, so I let the hole heal up. I still have the scar today so I'll always remember that painful process. In Birmingham my sister took me to a tattoo and piercing parlour near Chinatown to get my ears done. I don't know if the man holding the piercing gun knew I was transgen-der but he was definitely flirting with me. Maybe he was trying to diffuse the awkwardness – it was a great distrac-tion. With two clicks it was over and for the next six weeks I had to make do with stainless steel studs until I could treat myself to the hooped earrings I truly desired.

On reflection, my sister remembers this day as the moment she realised her brother had gone. I wasn't fully formed as Rhyannon yet, but I'd made enough subtle changes in my dress and attitude to suggest that I was becoming a different person. I was well on the way to transitioning into a new woman. I was glad that my sister witnessed these early moments and supported me through-out her struggle to understand it. I'd survived an afternoon in Birmingham and waved 'hello' and 'goodbye' to my sis-ter but I still had much further to go.

Years later, my sister gave me some much-needed fash-ion advice. I pulled the same denim shorts out of my drawer and slid them on over some black tights. When Danielle walked into the room she looked me up and down, screwing up her face. 'Sister,' she said, 'you're not seventeen any more. You're a lady now.' This was priceless advice and I had to agree with her. I took off the shorts (but I didn't throw them away). I'm incredibly grateful that my sister and I have become close friends as we've aged. It's brilliant to be able to go shopping together, something we couldn't do when we were young. Our queerness has brought us closer together than ever before.

When September rolled around, it was time for my appointment with my local psychiatrist. Once again I prepared myself to regurgitate my life story. I was desperate to get the referral; nothing would hold me back. On the day I wore my usual attire: skinny jeans, a bright pink jumper with sequin detail on the shoulder and white Converse trainers. My hair was tied up and I trowelled myself in make-up. During the forty-minute appointment I sat very still in the chair, telling the doctor the facts. I knew I had to tell the truth and that my story and experience warranted the referral. I was transgender and it needed to happen. As the doctor heard my story, he wanted to know how long I had felt this way. He wanted to hear evidence that proved it. I remember him questioning what clothes I wore at the weekends. 'Do you wear dresses?' he asked. 'Of course,' I confidently answered. 'I wear dresses and high heels.'

Once my time was up, the doctor said he didn't think it would be a problem to refer me to the clinic as I showed classic symptoms of being transgender – like cross-dressing all my life and feeling happier when presenting as a female. It was great to be understood and I felt an overwhelming sense of relief that things were moving forward.

In October, I received the doctor's review of the appointment. It was a two-page detailed description of my life. As I read it I was horrified to discover that he referred to me as a man throughout the report. At the time of our appointment I had already legally changed my name and my NHS gender was registered as female. But his referral only contained the pronouns 'him' and 'his'. This felt like a betrayal from a medical professional who was meant to be on my side. The doctor also addressed my choice of clothes, noting that although I wore make-up and feminine clothes, they were essentially just trousers and a sweater. When I read this I was gobsmacked! I wondered if he had looked around the waiting room that day. Many other women were dressed in trousers and a jumper – after all, it was a chilly September morning. I didn't see a single soul wearing a short sexy dress and high heels. I couldn't help but think the doctor's attitude to female apparel was stuck in the 1940s.

At the end of the letter his conclusion read, 'I would consider Rhyannon as someone who has a typical transsexual disorder (gender identity), and who clearly has thought about this for a considerable period of time.' As I read his words, I stumbled over them. I didn't agree that being trans was a 'disorder' – it felt completely natural to me. But even so, I was thrilled to get the referral. Next I would have to wait for my appointment to come through, so I braced myself for surviving the cold winter months alone as Rhyannon.

With a long stretch ahead of me, I started to think about hormones again. I had become very impatient, desperate to fast-forward the process. One day I threw caution to the wind and thought, 'Let's just see what happens.' So I popped my first blue pill. At first I didn't feel anything unusual but this changed a week into my new regime. I started to feel different as the oestrogen began to release into my bloodstream and pump through my veins. I didn't instantly feel like Wonder Woman, but I wasn't far off. It felt like stepping into a lovely warm bath, having a cuddle with your grandma or curling up with your partner and watching wildlife documentaries. The hormones gently wrapped my body in soft, warm ribbons of love. I finally understood what all the fuss was about – it was like licking a lollipop for the very first time. I floated around on fluffy candy-coloured clouds as my body awakened to new experiences. The sensations were incredible. I couldn't believe I had held off for so long and I had no regrets.

Quickly, my skin started to feel softer and more sensitive. When I touched surfaces or fabric brushed against me, I felt every fibre. Taking the oestrogen pills increased my positivity and enhanced my mood. I felt relaxed, comfortable and downright heavenly. It calmed down my anxiety – the familiar negative voices in my head slowly started to disappear. I looked at my reflection in the mirror, feeling like I was finally moving forward and accepting with relish that I was changing. I eagerly anticipated what would happen to my body.

I started to notice that my nipples were painful to touch, and very erect all of the time. They stuck out from my chest like pink hard-boiled sweets. I would touch them and instantly regret it. I would forget when I took a shower, accidentally knocking them with my arms and shuddering with pain. This was called 'budding' and it was the beginning of breast development. As my nipples became small mounds, I thought about the fact that after a while this development would be irreversible. I was growing breasts at thirty years old and it felt totally natural. My body was catching up with my mind.

One day my friend Caron called to have a chit-chat. I was eager to tell someone about my secret. I excitedly confessed my pill popping to her but she hit the roof, subjecting me to a tirade of reasons why I should stop. I listened to her as she warned me about the dangers of embarking upon such a life-changing transformation without medical guidance. She chastised me, reminding me that the pills could contain a cocktail of lethal ingredients. Waiting for Hormone Replacement Therapy on the NHS would be a far safer solution. She told me to stop – it was loud and clear.

I decided to call a trans woman who I was very close to, Mzz Kimberley, for advice. In her wonderful Detroit rasp, she said, 'Honey child, you're playing with fire! I've known many girls who do it but I wouldn't.' Although I didn't like what I was hearing I was thankful to have women like these around me. I came to the difficult realisation that I was doing something against my better judgement and that although it felt amazing, it was also dishonest.

I stopped taking the hormones after about two months. In my heart of hearts I didn't want to stop but I was afraid of what the clinic might say knowing I'd embarked upon the process myself. I put the little blue pills back into my knicker drawer and tried to forget about them. Slowly my lumpy nipples retracted, my anxiety returned and I felt masculine once again. I was back to square one. Emptiness crept up inside me, flooding me with low self-esteem and the crushing desire to kill myself. It was clear to me that oestrogen was exactly what I needed to stay positive and alive.

It was predicted by Nostradamus that Doomsday would fall on 21 December 2012 and the world would end. I hoped his prophecy wouldn't come true because I felt like I'd only just started living. By Christmas time the planet Earth was still orbiting a giant ball of fire in the Milky

Way and I was still very much alive. I was seven months into my transition and everything had changed. My London bubble had adapted to my life as Rhyannon. Some of my friends occasionally slipped up and called me Ryan and 'him' but it was gradually diminishing. I greatly appreciated how hard they were trying.

As I waited impatiently for my next appointment I had another important dilemma to consider. How was I going to tell the rest of my family? The thought of going home for Christmas was hanging over me. I couldn't imagine turning up as Rhyannon. My thrifty and jazzy attire was far too loud for my sleepy village. At this point only my sister was aware of my transition, so I couldn't just turn up and be like, 'Surprise!' We had so much to discuss, it just didn't feel like the right time. So I made the decision to pack Rhyannon away for one last time as I returned home. That Christmas was the last time my family saw me as Ryan.

On Christmas Eve, I rummaged deep in my wardrobe to find any clothes that looked male. I decided to wear a pair of plain jeans, a grey sweatshirt and trainers. I tied my hair up into a messy top-knot, ditched my padded bra and took off my make-up. It was like stepping into somebody else's life – it didn't feel like me at all. I felt embarrassed, and dreaded running into anyone I knew. I even avoided the local shops so as not to confuse the shopkeepers even more. How would I explain where Rhyannon had gone? It felt like a betrayal. I was desperate to have a drink – it was the one time a double vodka would have been handy.

On the streets of Hackney my status changed immediately. I reverted to being seen as a boy within seconds and it was a scarring experience. A stranger referred to me as 'mate', which I hadn't been called in a long time. I shook it off but was deeply distressed. To make matters worse, the trains heading north were all cancelled. What should have been a simple two-hour journey home took five hours. When I finally reached my station where I was being picked up by my mother, I was in a stinking mood. 'I'm not doing this again' was the first thing I said, greeting my mum. It wasn't a good start to the trip.

My family are settled around three villages in the Midlands, and every time I'm home I have to do the rounds. I reluctantly drove around in my mum's car, counting down the hours till I could leave. I wasn't in a Christmassy mood at all – far from it. I remember visiting my Nanny Marge, who was ill that year, bedridden for over a week. I turned up holding a bouquet of roses, which instantly put a smile on her face, though I remained glum. She kept asking me what was wrong, saying that I didn't sound like my usual self and that my sparkle was gone. I brushed off her questions and tried to deflect the conversation. I wasn't there for very long, but I know that I left a lasting impression that I wasn't well. It was a similar scenario when I visited my father and his family. I turned up sulky and defensive, unwilling to reveal anything. I retreated completely into myself. My sombre mood and lack of life triggered concern from my relatives. They could tell that something was seriously wrong.

The day after Boxing Day I packed up my bag and leapt out of the door. Freedom was only two hours away. As usual my mother and Ian came to the train station with me. It was a tradition that Ian would wave me off with a white handkerchief – it made me chuckle every time. At this particular send-off they wouldn't have comprehended the significance of the goodbye – they were saying good-bye to Ryan. As I journeyed back to London, I knew with total conviction that I had made the right decision to transition. Being regarded as male again had made me desperately uncomfortable and unhappy. I had felt angry and sad and utterly trapped. It didn't feel good lying to my family but I felt like I had no choice – I needed to protect myself.

Once I was back in London I jumped into my wardrobe and hugged my clothes. I was so relieved that I could return to living as Rhyannon. I inhaled deeply as I stepped back into my life. I changed into my favourite winter clothes and trotted out of the house in my red pixie boots to meet some friends. It felt fantastic to be back.

Unbeknown to me, my family were on high alert. As soon as I left they rang my sister to find out why my behaviour at Christmas had been so out of the ordinary. She soon had enough of being in the middle of this furore and insisted that I tell them, suggesting a letter to explain everything. I knew that I couldn't go on without telling my family. I was hiding in London and it was becoming harder and harder. Whenever they phoned, they would call me Ryan – it was like retreating into my old self every time. I felt like I was living a lie. I didn't need to pretend any longer or be ashamed of who I was. I wasn't a child any more.

I had been thinking about writing a letter for some time. I'd started to type little passages on my laptop whenever things popped into my head. It wasn't going to be a quick paragraph in a throwaway email, I owed the conversation much more than that. It wasn't something I wanted to rush and regret further down the line. It was important that I was honest, truthful and fair. I needed to address the facts and be real. But I didn't know where to start. I had so much to cover, I needed to break down the transitioning process for them and reveal many personal things. I prepared myself to be totally honest, because I needed them to understand as best they could.

As I began writing, I kept composing parts of the letter and then hitting delete. I couldn't face it. I wrote many versions until I found the right way to tell my story. It took me weeks to finish. It was incredibly hard laying myself bare like that, and imagining my family's reactions. It's not easy reading your life back to yourself in black and white – you'd think I'd be used to it by now but it's still difficult. I decided to accompany the letter with the psychologist's referral to the GIC. I wanted my family to know it was a medical condition and I was treating it with care. It started off like this:

Ever since I was young, from when I can remember, I have felt a sense of being different and was confused about my identity. What I didn't know then is that I suffer from gender dysphoria.

Gender dysphoria is a condition in which a person feels that there is a mismatch between their biological sex and their gender identity. For example, a person may have the genitalia of a man, but gender identify as a woman. This mismatch can cause feelings of discomfort that are called gender dysphoria. Gender dysphoria is a recognised condition, for which treatment is sometimes appropriate.

The biggest hurdle was admitting this to myself, which has happened and I feel very happy. I always knew the time would come when I would have to tell you, as this affects you as much as it does me.

2012 was a big year of change for me; the decision to become single, sober and healthy is paramount to my decision to start transitioning from (physically) male to female. In April 2012, I changed my name by deed poll from Mr Ryan

Edward Wagg to Miss Rhyannon Wagg. I have changed my bank accounts, passport, driving licence, medical records and all the other records that I can. I can't change my birth certificate yet without seeing a specialist at the clinic.

In London I present as female, I wear women's clothes and wear make-up every day. I use female toilets, people call me 'her' and 'she' and this makes me very happy. It finally feels that I am living as I should.

My plans for the future include starting to take oestrogen, which is a female hormone. This will begin to change my body into looking more female in appearance. I will get an appointment at the Gender Identity Clinic and start talking to specialists about the assistance that is available to me on the NHS.

2013 will see a lot of change for you too; I hope that we can all get through this together. Obviously I know that this news isn't going to be easy for you. I want you to know that this isn't a choice for me; I am not simply identifying as a trans woman because I like women's clothes more than men's. I have no choice; I cannot live my life as a boy. It is just not who I am.

Spending Christmas with you was so painful for me. I have not worn boys' clothes for over six months, I rarely answer to Ryan any more and I flinch every time I get called 'him'. I also felt like I was doing you an injustice; I am lying to you which I don't like doing. I cannot go forward in my life pretending any more.

I want to be happy and I'm sure you would want that too. I can't determine what your reaction to this change is going to be. Deep down I think you will adjust over time and accept me for who I am. It's not going to be easy telling other family members and friends, but this is something that I want to talk to you about. I still hope we can have a relationship in the future. I'm sure you'll need some time to let all this sink in. Call me when you're ready to talk.

I want you to know I am incredibly proud of who I am.

I sent two separate letters, one addressed to my mum, the other to my dad and brothers. It was my immediate family who should know first. Uncles, aunties, cousins and grandparents would follow once I'd spoken to my parents. The letters made quite a package, bursting at the seams with my most intimate life story. I didn't waste any time, heading straight to the post box. With every step I had a sinking feeling in my stomach, I felt sick to my core. With a letter in each hand I quickly slotted them in before I was tempted to throw them away.

Posting the letters felt surreal – it marked the moment that everything was going to change. I prepared myself for the consequences, steeling myself for whatever they might be. There was no going back now. I stared at the post box, feeling like it was a ticking time bomb, waiting to explode. I imagined my mother opening her letter and the look on her face. I didn't want to cause my family any pain, but it was the only way. I thought about how the course of their lives would be changed forever.

The day after, I didn't regret my decision but I was filled with anxiety about the result. Would they reject me? Would they accept me? I wasn't sure if my parents would call me or not and I waited with baited breath. After a few days my heart sank, as I still hadn't heard from them. I turned to friends for solace who all echoed the same sentiments. 'Be patient, this will take some time.' I had done what I needed to do but patience was not my forte – it was going to be a struggle.

At some point in the next week I caught up with my sister. Danielle had been in contact with my parents and she told me they were shocked, confused and upset. These emotions didn't come as a surprise to me but it hurt nonetheless. I wondered if I should call them and talk everything through, as I so desperately wanted to make it right. But my sister advised against it, arguing that they needed time.

Time went on, with January and February passing by, one grey day at a time. I couldn't wait for spring to arrive and for my first appointment at the GIC. It felt like new beginnings were just around the corner. In March it was my thirty-first birthday and I wondered what cards would arrive in the post. On the day of my birthday I sifted through the mail anxiously. All the cards from my family, bar one, were addressed to Ryan. I knew I shouldn't expect anything less, but it didn't evoke the usual birthday cheer.

There wasn't a card from my father but I did receive one from my mother. It wasn't addressed to Ryan or Rhyannon – the envelope just said 'R'. This felt like progress. I was overjoyed that my mum had sent something. It had been nearly two months since I sent my coming-out letters and I still hadn't heard from them. But the card gave me hope that I hadn't been forgotten entirely. It buoyed my spirits.

Soon, spring arrived. Cherry-blossom trees saturated the Hackney pavements in pink confetti, the clocks moved forward and the darkness retracted. In May I received a letter from my mother's partner, Ian. This was totally unexpected and I was in complete shock when I opened it. I was so relieved that he had made the effort to write to me, and I was overwhelmed with emotion. It was the first of three letters from my parents – a method of communication that we clearly felt most comfortable with. Letters were safer, less emotional territory. Ian explained how my mother was feeling and the reasons why she hadn't been in contact.

You are, in your mum's eyes, Ryan.

Ryan, the baby boy she brought into this world and whom she watched grow and develop into a son she felt so proud of. Now, in her mind, that person, that son, no longer exists. In her mind, when the inevitable meeting takes place, she will be meeting someone she has never known before. Your sexual identity has never been a problem for her; however, the gender change you have embarked upon is, to her, something akin to bereavement. This letter is to reassure you that, although you have not heard from, or spoken to your mum for some considerable time, she still loves you as much as she did, and always will do.

It was incredibly difficult reading this letter. Although I appreciated Ian's honesty, it really hurt. It hit me how much my decision had affected their lives and I wondered how long it would take before everything went back to the way it was – or if it was even possible. But I was thankful that the daunting period of zero communication had come to an end. Moving forwards would now be about time and patience. All in all, it would take a year for my mother to be able to talk to me.

It wasn't long before another important letter arrived. In July, the Gender Identity Clinic notified me that they had received my referral. I was totally thrilled and nervous at the same time. They apologised for the delay in processing my referral, which they blamed on high demand for the service – who knew there were so many others out there like me? I filled in the accompanying forms right away and sent them off, praying that it wouldn't be too much longer until my first appointment. In the end I didn't need to wait long at all – the following week I received a telephone call. Dr Ashrafi and my friends were right; time and patience were crucial for this journey.

It had been sixteen months between my initial doctor's appointment and my first appointment at the GIC. Sixteen months is a long time to wait and the suspense was killing me. Such waiting times are a harsh reality for trans people. The 2012 Trans Mental Health Review estimated that 32 per cent attending gender identity clinics face a wait of one to three years for an appointment. But I constantly reminded myself to be thankful for the NHS and the fact that my transition was possible. I needed to be grateful and appreciate what was about to happen.

The day before my appointment I was scared, anxious and excited as I decided what to wear and planned my journey to the clinic. It was a monumental day for me, the beginning of everything I'd been waiting for. I was about to embark upon a path of transformation and self-discovery, and I couldn't bear for anything to go wrong. I hardly slept the night before as the next day's events churned around in my head and I obsessively over-analysed everything I was going to say. I kept waking up, paranoid that I would sleep through my alarm clock.

When the morning arrived, I was a bundle of nerves – I could hardly eat any breakfast as the butterflies in my stomach fluttered around. I downed three cups of coffee, worried that I might fall asleep on the tube. This only made the butterflies metamorphose into heavy bricks that banged around my insides and made me constantly need the toilet. I took deep, restorative breaths as I shakily applied my liquid eyeliner. In my nervousness it smudged all around my eye, making me look like a mime artist. I may have gone out in the past with a face full of black eyeliner but this day was different. I ditched the eyeliner in favour of big red lips and started again, hoping not to turn into Ronald McDonald.

The Gender Identity Clinic is based in the opposite side of London to me, in Hammersmith. The journey would take around an hour and I was completely paranoid about anything that might interfere with my getting there punctually. I was convinced that a civil war would erupt or that London would suffer an imminent alien invasion. At times like this my head will do anything it can to torture me and drag me through the wringer. To be on the safe side I gave myself two hours to travel there. That way I would have enough time to walk part of the journey if anything disastrous were to happen.

I arrived well in time, surprised when I was faced with the clinic. The world-renowned gender specialist clinic was above a branch of Sainsbury's Local. I had built it up so much in my head that I had been expecting some kind of grand Victorian hospital. I sat nervously in the waiting room, filling out the appropriate forms as various people shuffled by, clutching folders. The door continually buzzed as visitors came and went. Sitting on the beige cushioned chairs I was surrounded by the full spectrum of trans people. I saw an older lady wearing a grey wig who reminded me of the comedy agony aunt Mrs Merton. A young androgynous person with long black hair and patent pink Dr Marten boots spoke with a Lancashire accent to their mum. Directly next to me was a FTM (female to male) trans man with a large rucksack who'd come all the way from Wales, staying in London overnight at the local Travelodge hotel. I realised how fortunate I was to be able to simply jump on the tube.

After what felt like forever, a man poked his head out of the nearest door calling 'Rhyannon Wagg'. I sat down in the interview room, buzzing with excitement, high on caffeine and nervous energy. The morning sun beamed through the window, flooding the room with white light and scorching the back of my neck. The seventy-five-minute appointment flew past as I told the doctor everything. I put my life into context and spoke the absolute truth – I didn't conceal a single thing. I stared at the walls during the painful, difficult and embarrassing moments when I had to be really honest about who I was. I looked at the swirls and circle diagrams drawn on the whiteboard. For the first time in my journey so far I felt like I was being listened to rather than quizzed. I knew that I was in the right place and that I would finally be able to find help.

We discussed my family, and I explained that I hadn't physically spoken to them since December. When he asked how I coped at Christmas, I replied honestly, telling him that I had presented as male. He immediately raised an eyebrow. 'Oh really, so you haven't been living in full female role since last April?' he asked. 'Full female role' is otherwise known as 'Real Life Experience' (RLE) – where transgender individuals live in their desired gender role full time. I explained that it was only for three days and it was borne from a place of necessity, not desire. I reiterated how uncomfortable I had been, how it had made my skin crawl. But he replied that you need to be living in full female role for a minimum of a year before you can be prescribed hormones.

When I heard his words I wanted to blow my brains out with a shotgun. Internally, my emotions caved and swallowed me whole, but I tried to hide behind a brave face. I immediately regretted telling the truth. But I was trying to be as honest as I could – I had spent so many years lying to myself and to others that I was sick of it. Desperately holding back tears I asked the doctor what would happen next.

He explained that hormones are only prescribed at your second assessment, which wouldn't be until December at the earliest. He would leave the decision to the next clinician who saw me.

At the end of the session I was given a paper slip so I could have a blood test. An endocrinologist would review my current hormone profile in order for me to move forward with treatment. With my fate in the hands of someone else, I took a deep breath and reminded myself how lucky I was that I'd made it this far. I reassured myself that it was a small hurdle on my journey and that it wouldn't break me.

During 2013, my career took a U-turn. I'd begun to feel uncomfortable on stage – the performances were not matching my new gender identity. As part of The LipSinkers, people still viewed me as Ryan, mistaking me as a drag queen and not a transgender woman. My performance work needed to evolve just as I would, but it wasn't possible overnight. I was still in the process of working out who I was, which I couldn't do while performing on a stage in front of the public. Transitioning required so much energy, time and patience that I needed the space to devote to it. I needed to briefly take myself out of the limelight. I broke the news to The LipSinkers just as we made our Edinburgh Fringe Festival debut. It was a tough decision but the right one. It was unfair to the rest of the gang and our audience if Rhyannon's heart wasn't in it.

In September I pressed the pause button. I craved security while everything else was in a state of flux. I wanted to do something that would guarantee an income and routine while I was trying to negotiate my new place in the world. In true Rhyannon form I did something completely out of the blue – I enrolled on a college course. Based on my joy of styling wigs for my shows, I decided I'd make a great hairdresser. I enjoyed experimenting with my own hair and I wanted to see if I could succeed in making others look beautiful too.

As the new school term began, I found myself in a classroom twice a week with women of all ages and different backgrounds. This experience was absolutely vital for my transition. On the very first day I announced that I was transgender to my classmates. As soon as the news was out it was as if tumbleweed was rolling across the floor – the room went completely quiet. David, our teacher, broke the silence by saying, 'And I'm gay!' The LGBTQ community is very nurturing and I was grateful that he took it upon himself to announce his sexuality like that. Not that it mattered, but it did diffuse the confusion of my classmates.

It was surreal being back at school again. I was surrounded by sixteen-year-old girls who had just finished their GCSE exams. They schooled me on everything they read in *Heat* magazine. They laughed at me when I didn't know that *TOWIE* was the abbreviation of the reality TV programme *The Only Way Is Essex*. But they didn't know who the opera singer Maria Callas was, so we called it a draw. We were worlds apart but we educated each other. I learned a lot from these girls and they were vital in shaping my identity.

I found myself relearning maths and English as part of the qualification. One afternoon the teacher announced, 'Today, girls, we are going to learn how to use a comma.' I couldn't help thinking I'd be better off lip-syncing to Johnny Cash dressed as a volcano in some far-away field, but I persevered. My performance days were on hold for the time being.

My classmates were fascinated by my transition and asked lots of questions. The most obvious was 'Do you have a penis?' or 'Are you going to have boob implants?' They were questions I'd become used to and I easily shook them off. 'Do YOU want implants?' I'd reply. One woman called Mariana had been to South America and had a boob job, an arse lift and a tummy tuck. She wasn't shy about telling people and she kept offering me discounts if I wanted to get anything done with her in South America. I politely declined her offer.

I schooled the class by advising them how to address

trans people and what pronouns to use. I wanted to reinforce the idea that we are cool, normal people. I was pleased to see that they liked my honest stories and the energy that I brought into the classroom. Occasionally the wrong pronouns would be used when addressing me and 'him' would creep into the room when we were doing a blow dry. I'd blame the hairdryer for turning me bright red and hoped my client didn't realise why.

For the first time since I'd been living as Rhyannon I was having direct contact with the public. As part of the course I started to look for a part-time job in a hair salon as a junior assistant. After several interviews, I eventually settled in a salon in Stoke Newington. This period of my life was a transition within a transition. Aside from my gender trans-formation I was also transitioning into a new career. My part-time job was fun to begin with, but it was very differ-ent to anything I had done before. Instead of going to bed at 6 a.m. on a Saturday morning, I was getting up at the crack of dawn to get ready for work. Such time-keeping would never have happened in the past. Although I enjoyed the routine – it was a welcome break from everything else that was rapidly changing – it was a stark contrast to dancing with Arcade Fire in front of 20,000 people. It was a different reality entirely and I had no choice but to embrace it.

This period of my life lasted just under two years. In this time I built up my confidence as Rhyannon and learned a lot about myself through being submerged in a totally new environment. The salon was a humbling experience. As an artist I was one of the best, I'd earned my stripes on the London cabaret scene and everybody knew my name and my work. Now, I was at the bottom of the ladder, earning £6.50 an hour sweeping the floor and cleaning toilets. These daily tasks deflated my ego and taught me about routine, stability and responsibility.

Although I missed being in the spotlight, I enjoyed my time at the salon. I made new friends and it was refreshing that these people had only ever known me as Rhyannon. As you might expect, I went through many phases of hairstyles, completely ruining my hair with a newfound obsession with bleach. Overall, though, this way of life was enriching for me and it marked another important phase of my growth.

Letter to my Future Self:

Dear Rhyannon,

> *For many years I have thought about who you are and how you will appear. I have wondered where you are and how I am going to find you. I have sculpted you in my mind and in my performances, hoping that this momentary realisation would last forever.*

> *I'm sorry that I often dismissed you and tried to escape you in every way possible. I sought shelter,*

safety and salvation in the wrong places. I wanted to deny your existence because I was scared of the truth. I continually pushed you further away and convinced myself you weren't real.

I don't want to live in shame or denial any longer. I've reached the point where living as Ryan makes no sense any more, no matter how hard I try. I can't pretend any more.

It has taken me thirty years to accept this truth, but now I am ready, I am ready to transition.

Rhyannon, my dear companion, now is your time. I hope I have served you well.

Love always,
Ryan

Chapter 10

TRANSCENDENCE: A JOURNEY

In late September 2013, something unexpected happened. My transition had by no means been a smooth ride up to that point. I don't think transitions are supposed to be bump-free because it's not something to undertake on a whim. To transition is to seriously change your life, your body and your environment. It's massive and the consequences can be complicated and messy. I really wanted to breeze through it overnight, but this isn't how it's meant to be. One thing I certainly didn't expect was to question the whole transition altogether, which is what happened at this time.

In my head, I had made a decision which seemed crystal clear. I couldn't imagine what factors would possibly steer me off course. But the ugly feelings of self-doubt, insecurity and fear managed to creep back into my life. As a result came a period of immense confusion, a difficult chapter in my transition in which I needed to interrogate and examine myself even more.

In mid September my father got in touch. He wrote to me, responding to my original letter in January. He outlined how he felt and explained why it had taken him so long to reply. It was incredibly difficult reading, much like Ian's letter some months before. It was frank and honest – and at points hard to stomach.

In his letter he questioned the motives for my transition. He had looked back at photographs and thought about my childhood, but he couldn't see any gender issues emerging. He couldn't grasp the cause of my actions and my transition was hard for him to comprehend. He had lost Ryan and this was difficult for him to accept. He wondered how I could go about my daily life as Rhyannon and was concerned about the problems it could bring. He went on to say that he continued to think about me, and missed the calls we made to each other. He wished that he could turn back the clock and talk to me about my decision, but it was too late.

As I read his words I broke down with emotion. The reality of his feelings was difficult to process. I couldn't bring myself to read the letter again for some time, and I didn't reply. It hurt too much.

I felt like I had lost everything. All my relationships seemed to be falling apart. My family weren't talking to me, I saw no relationship on the horizon and I hadn't heard from the Gender Identity Clinic about initiating hormone treatment. I felt like I was moving further away from my desires rather than towards them. I was devastated.

Thankfully, I didn't turn to alcohol or drugs to comfort me. In many ways my actions were much more damaging. For a period of a month I returned to being Ryan. My logic was this: 'If you go back to being Ryan, you will get everything back – your family, your partner and your security. You will be loved.' It sounds totally crazy now, but things had got so tough that I saw no other option. I lost myself all over again.

I slowly stopped wearing make-up, padded bras and female clothes. I even went to JD Sports and bought some trackie bottoms – I thought embracing a masculine aesthetic would solve all my problems. I couldn't totally assume my old identity; I found it wasn't as easy as simply swapping a wardrobe. Instead, I found myself somewhere between the past and the present, stuck in a nightmarish limbo.

My friends and those closest to me were confused. I'd said one thing and then gone back on it all. They had only just got used to calling me Rhyannon and now I'd thrown another curveball into the mix. They didn't know whether they should refer to me as Rhyannon or Ryan. I didn't know which felt more comfortable either, so I suggested they went with whatever rolled off the tongue.

My head felt screwed up and my emotions were out of control. I was exhausted and I wanted out. I lost the ability to move forward because I was scared. The thought of continuing my transition was frightening. I didn't know if I would ever find peace within myself, the love from a partner and the security I so desperately craved. All the doors felt closed, I felt utterly trapped. I had reached a point where no roads lay ahead of me. I knew that being a man wasn't the solution because it only made me unhappy and suicidal but I was also stuck, believing that transitioning was the wrong path to pursue. I lost hope in either direction. I was back to square one.

At this dark point of my life, I found a solution that saved me: I talked about it. This was revolutionary to me. I had never done this before; I was used to bottling it up and burying it deep. I turned to my many sober friends and spoke freely about how I was feeling. Their advice was priceless. I took it on board and let myself simply 'be'. I sat back and didn't make any more rash decisions. I decided to allow the universe to lead the way. I told myself that whatever funk I was in would pass – eventually. I had to be patient and just observe.

Once I let go, things started to fall into place. The letter I had been waiting for from the Gender Identity Clinic finally arrived. I took this as a sign and it changed everything. The appointment was booked for 16 December. Finally there was something to look forward to. Hopefully things were looking up.

With a clear path ahead of me, I embraced the feminine and Rhyannon rose once again. It felt incredible to be back with renewed determination. This troubling period taught me one thing: being Rhyannon was the only way forward. Finally, I was back on track.

When my appointment came around, I was slightly more relaxed on my visit to the clinic – I didn't feel the need to arrive an hour early in case of alien invasions. I would make the journey several times over the next six months and eventually it became second nature to me. This time I was going to be assessed by a different clinician, who would decide if I could begin hormone treatment. Once again I felt like I had the world resting on my shoulders, so I slapped on my war paint and headed out of the door.

As with my previous appointment, I filled the doctor in on my life. It felt like a script I knew off by heart. This time I was able to add new information: I told the doctor I was having a break from performing and had started training as a hairdresser. The GIC want to see evidence of people living in their desired gender role. My new job was perfect for this as my pay slips were proof that I was working every day as Rhyannon.

It wasn't long before the topic of the previous Christmas was brought up. I had been terrified of this moment, knowing that my future could depend on it. I had meticulously prepared my answer, explaining the reasons behind my presentation that Christmas. I willed the doctor to understand the desperation of the situation, and to my relief, they understood. I also decided to keep quiet and not say a word about my recent fluctuating 'female/male' presentations. I knew it wouldn't help me move forward. It would only hinder the treatment that I had been waiting a lifetime for. In any case, due to my recent experimentation I was 100 per cent certain that being a trans woman was the right path for me. I loved being Rhyannon so I kept schtum!

Next on the agenda was hormone treatment. We discussed why I wanted to start and what I wanted to achieve. I told the doctor that I wanted to feminise my body because I couldn't feel comfortable with a male presentation or masculine features. I confessed that I had taken hormones in the past and that the immediate effects felt good. But I assured the doctor that following advice from friends I had thrown my black market hormones away. Then it was on to my sex life. The doctor wanted to know how I used and felt about my penis. I explained I hadn't been in a serious relationship for over a year and although I'd had several recent sexual encounters, sex no longer felt like a priority in my life.

The doctor clarified that once I began hormone treatment, my body would stop producing sperm. It was reiterated over and over again that I needed to think very carefully about if I wanted children in the future. If so, I should research banking and saving my sperm. Having my own children wasn't something I'd ever really desired. I knew that if I decided to have children in the future then I would look into adoption or alternatives. The doctor re-iterated that I would need to consider this carefully and I promised that I would give it some more thought. In all honesty, I'd only just started to work out who I was; I couldn't consider much else besides that.

The assessment was much more in-depth than my first appointment and this pleased me. It felt like forward action was in motion and plans were being put into place. After months of feeling lost, I felt supported once again. I could see a light at the end of the tunnel and I prayed that I might finally get the prescription that I desperately needed. Naïvely I hoped that I'd be handed a prescription right there and then, and off I would trot to the pharmacist with a big smile across my face like the Cheshire Cat from *Alice in Wonderland*. But of course, it wasn't this simple. I needed to repeat the blood tests I'd had in July because one of the results had returned as abnormal. Happily, the doctor reassured me that they didn't see any reason why I shouldn't start taking hor-mones. I just needed to hold on for slightly longer.

This felt like the story of my life. Frustrated, there was a small part of me that regretted not seeking a private gender specialist. If I had taken this route I would have been com-fortably on hormones and much further along in the process – if considerably out of pocket. But I bolstered myself with the fact that taking my time in transitioning was how it was meant to be for me. Although incredibly exasperating at times, it gave me the time and space to devote to my emotional and mental health, while working out who Rhyannon was. On leaving the appointment, I took comfort in the fact that the worst was over. So far I'd succeeded in negotiating life as Rhyannon, and overcoming the obstacles presented to me. Soon I would begin treatment supported by the NHS and my body would finally change. I had lots to look forward to.

On 21 December 2013 I headed into the unknown (yet again!). After such a tumultuous year with so many ups and downs, I needed a clean break to evaluate everything. I needed to process all the changes and come to a place of mental and emotional acceptance. As I wasn't yet on speaking terms with my family, I decided to spend the festive period at a Buddhist retreat for ten days.

Over the course of the year I'd been healing myself through meditation. Since becoming sober, I'd become a regular at my local Buddhist centre in Bethnal Green. With fellow sober friends we'd drop in at lunchtimes for sessions of meditation and tea. Inspired, I booked a place on a winter retreat, which would take me right the way through until 2 January. It would be the perfect way of spending the Christmas holidays, with no pressure to do anything else except be me.

Life for the next ten days was glorious. I was surrounded by new faces in the Herefordshire countryside and I was eager to get to know them all. We bonded over tea and ate biscuits in the common room, tucked away in an old school. The atmosphere was idyllic but we had lots to do. In the mornings we were woken up by a bell at 6.30 a.m. to begin meditation at 7 a.m. I loved the morning meditation. You would crawl into the shrine room half asleep in the darkness, and when you opened your eyes an hour or so later, the sun would be shining through the windows with that crisp winter light. An hour later it was time for breakfast before jobs that had to be completed in between meditation sessions. The afternoons were spent walking around the hills of the Herefordshire countryside or practising yoga. There was plenty of time to get to know my fellow retreaters, and I discovered that two were also contemplating their gender(s). Robin, Tim and I fast became friends as we discussed everything about transitions: pronouns, surgery, relationships and family. It was wonderful to talk openly and honestly about what we were going through. It felt like there was a higher purpose for me to be on the retreat and to meet people to whom I could relate so deeply at this pivotal point in my life.

On Christmas Eve, I remember looking out of one of the windows at a town in the distance, at the foot of the hill. It was lit up by sparkling, coloured lights and the sound of carol singers travelled through the valley. This was the only point of the retreat when I felt sad – the reality of being so far away from home at Christmas hit me, but it quickly passed and I took solace in going to sleep. Soon it was Christmas Day. It was surreal to be surrounded by virtual strangers on the day so traditionally associated with family. I had decided to leave my phone at home so that I wasn't distracted – this mission was about soul-searching and finding myself. This meant I didn't receive a single Christmas message that year. Most of us at the retreat didn't acknowledge Christmas Day, although some used their phones and wished each other 'Happy Christmas'. To be honest, I didn't miss the festive celebrations – thoughts of the previous Christmas were still reverberating around in my head. It was only when a fellow retreater Jill whipped out a giant Toblerone bar that I was reminded of the excesses I'd left behind.

Over time we built up periods of silence. These would usually begin after the evening meditation – a ceremony called a 'puja' – and last until breakfast the next morning or, as on the last day, until dinner time the next evening. Being surrounded by and confined to silence does amazing things to your other senses. I remember eating a humble oat cake and spreading it with Marmite and tahini. Amid the silence the oatcake transformed into the most delicious thing I had ever eaten. Every bite created spasms of joy on my tongue.

One afternoon a group of us decided to walk around the surrounding area. We were still in silence and didn't intend to break it. When we approached a small hamlet of houses at the top of the hill we could hear music. As we moved closer we discovered a radio lying by the door of a house where building work was being done. We immediately stopped in our tracks, turning our heads slowly towards the sound we were collectively hearing. The effect was like being on drugs – it was otherworldy. I hadn't heard music like this for days and suddenly Neil Young's voice was floating through the air and drifting into my ears. The small radio emitted a sound that was so pleasing, it felt like I was hearing music for the very first time. Every single note, every single strum on the guitar hypnotised me. It was so pleasurable that we all smiled at one another, acknowledging that we'd shared this magical experience.

In films where they depict cults, you often see people walking around farms like zombies, transfixed, with big smiles plastered on their faces. This is what we would have looked like to an onlooker at this moment.

The retreat worked wonders. I felt free, young and tender again. I remember saying to one of the ordained Buddhists that it felt like I'd opened a window and let fresh air into my life. It sounds cheesy but it felt fantastic. As part of our meditation, I'd sat very still for many, many hours with only my own thoughts for company. This space and still-ness gave me the opportunity to invest much-needed time in myself, to come to terms with who I was. I'd reached a new level of love and acceptance for myself. I accepted the journey I had been on so far and what was still to come. I felt so much stronger for it and it was the perfect way to see in the new year. This inner peace would allow me to shine in 2014 and tackle anything thrown in my path.

I returned to London a new trans woman with new beginnings just around the corner. At the end of January I received a letter from the GIC. It clearly stated that I was allowed to begin hormone treatment but that my blood results were yet to come back. I hastily made an appointment with Dr Ashrafi, bouncing into the surgery clutching my letter and asking if I could start immediately. I was gutted to discover that we would need to wait until we received the results from the blood tests. At this disheartening news I didn't know what else to do except go home and meditate. I called upon my newfound inner peace, determined not to be floored by these knockbacks. They were par for the course.

Eventually, on 14 March 2014, the long-awaited letter arrived. As I opened this envelope my hands were shaking – everything rested on its contents. I knew it contained the information I so desperately sought to finally move forward. The letter confirmed that my blood tests had been reviewed and my levels were normal. My current level of oestradiol was 90 and my testosterone was 24.2. Alongside the clinic's psychological approval I was now able to begin treatment. This was such a joy to read. It had been two long years since I initially asked for a referral and finally, three days before my thirty-second birthday, I was given the green light to start treatment. What a gift!

It was wonderful to be in Dr Ashrafi's office again knowing that everything was about to change. As he wrote out the prescription, the skeleton in the corner even seemed to be smiling at me. Knowing I'd made it through the hardest two years of my life gave me hope for continuing on my journey. I had made it this far and I couldn't wait for what was to come.

This was the guidance we received from the clinic:

Please commence Oestradiol Valerate 2 mg. After eight weeks please obtain blood tests for safety monitoring in the form of prolactin, oestradiol, testosterone, LFT and lipids. If these are normal please increase to 4 mg with the above bloods repeated again about one month prior to her attending our clinic for her next appointment on 14 July 2014.

After Dr Ashrafi supplied me with the prescription, I frantically ran around several pharmacists trying to find one with the pills in stock. I couldn't wait a day longer – I wanted those pills so badly. The prescription was burning a hole in the bottom of my bag all morning while I was at college. During my lunchbreak I finally found a chemist which had the treasured pills in stock. I popped my first NHS-supplied

oestrogen tablet on 23 March 2014 while looking into a mirror at beauty school. It felt amazing – I honestly hadn't
thought the day would ever come. I knew the worst was over
and that I was about to embark on a journey that would alter
my emotional, mental and physical self. I was relieved to
have made it – frankly I was overjoyed to be alive.

From the very first day of my hormone regime I took
photos to document my progress. Every Wednesday I
photographed myself using my laptop, gathering evidence
of the changes in my face. I am still doing this today and I
now have over two years' worth of images. This is particularly helpful when I become discontent or disheartened – I
can look back over the years and see how far I have come.

The aim of hormones is to increase the levels of oestrogen in your body to within a normal female range. It's
suggested that trans women reach and stabilise within a
range of 400–600. I was currently on 94 so I had some way
to go. HRT (hormone replacement therapy) is usually prescribed to cisgendered women – that is, women whose
self-identity conforms with the gender that corresponds to
their biological sex – who are going through the menopause
or, as in my case, to transgender MTFs (male to female)
who want to feminise their appearance. The oral form of
oestradiol tops up the existing levels of oestrogen in your
body. The more you take, the more oestrogen is released
into your system. Although hormones can go a long way in

making you appear more feminine, they cannot perform magical transformations and the results do vary.

I began taking a brand of hormones called Elleste. I started on the usual prescribed dose of 2 mg per day, which you then build upon. It's important not to take too much to begin with because the body needs time to adjust to the influx of new chemicals. I discovered that not only did my physical body change, but my mental state too. The familiar feelings of warmth, comfort and happiness came flooding back into my body. I welcomed these sensations and relaxed knowing that the medical side of my transition was underway. I'd done all the prep work and it was time to let the chemicals take over. I patiently waited for my body to catch up with my mind.

One Saturday night I was treating myself to a cosy TV dinner. I was watching the talent show *The Voice* when for no reason at all I started crying. A lady was singing a cover song with Tom Jones and I just burst into tears – I couldn't control myself. I'd never been like this before; it usually took a lot to make me cry and I would never have wasted tears over a reality TV show. Something had changed in the chemical construction of my body and it seemed I was more sensitive than ever. I turned to my trans friends and asked if this was normal behaviour. 'Girl,' they reassured me, 'this is just the beginning; they don't call them "'mones" for nothing.'

According to my expert friends I should prepare for

much more in the way of mood swings and erratic behaviour. I didn't believe them at first, dismissing it as gossip and scaremongering, but over time it all came true. I hate to sound clichéd but I've now spent over two years on HRT and some days all I want to do is eat chocolate and cry. Sometimes I can be on the brink of tears over the slightest thing and then erupt like a volcano that has been dormant for years. (Life does imitate art!)

Taking hormones comes with health risks – which the GIC heavily stressed during my consultations. Oestrogen can increase your chance of cancer and possible side effects include bloating, nausea, leg cramps, headaches, indigestion and breast swelling. One of the side effects I definitely *did* want to experience was breast swelling. I couldn't wait to develop breast tissue.

As a thirty-something trans person I would have to face puberty all over again. When I hit puberty as Ryan at around the age of fourteen, I immediately noticed the changes. Testosterone wrapped its dagger-like claws all around my body and altered it. I grew taller, developing muscles and losing my puppy fat. My voice changed and became deeper, I started to produce semen when I masturbated and my sex drive increased. I grew pubic hair around my penis and testicles, and developed small amounts of fluffy facial hair. To this day I'm very thankful that I never grew a single hair on my stomach, chest or back. Even my arms and legs escaped with just a fine dusting of dark blond hair – I have been one of the lucky ones. I wasn't a stereotypically manly man and that suited me just fine. At the age of fourteen I didn't imagine for a minute I'd have to navigate puberty all over again in my thirties.

When the time came for me to transition, these masculine traits were exactly what I wanted to reverse. Slowly but surely as the oestrogen flooded my system with spasms of warmth my body started to adjust. Once again my nipples became sore and sensitive to the touch. Every time I went to bed and rolled onto my side it hurt. Every morning I would forget about the buds on my chest and knock them while getting on and off my bike, gasping in pain. I'd read that massaging your new knockers stimulates growth. I'd be in bed every night watching some rubbish on the telly while massaging my chest with moisturiser and praying for growth. Of course, you can't hurry this process along. Patience would have to be my best friend again. It takes two or three years on hormones before you attain full growth. Nevertheless, I persevered, looking in the mirror every day and deluding myself that they'd grown overnight. After six weeks, I noticed that the buds on my chest had started to become small mounds. If I squinted and used a lot of imagination I could trick myself into seeing my new breasts growing.

Knowing that I was going to take hormones for the rest

of my life felt great. I was swimming downstream, enjoying being swept along gracefully by the current of oestrogen, whereas in the past I was struggling against the current. This is the only way I can describe the relief I felt.

I couldn't wait for the first eight weeks to be over. The next step would be increasing the dose from 2 mg to 4 mg and this would mean even more changes. It came around quickly and after my appointment with Dr Ashrafi, more blood tests and the usual protocol, my dose was increased to 4 mg per day. I was now able to take two tablets every morning, which I looked forward to religiously.

During my first year of taking hormones I was working in the salon full-time. This meant many of my older friends weren't witnessing how much I was changing physically. I knew that when I eventually saw them my appearance would come as a real shock. One particular event sticks in my mind. My friends Scottee and James had invited me to their wedding – it was going to be quite the star-studded affair. I couldn't wait to show off my new self – I was glowing. I wore a new dress that I had purchased in America some years before and my hair was bleached blonde and cut into a bob. I felt comfortable and stylish, pleased with the effect of the hormones giving me a more feminine appearance. The oestrogen had transformed my face, redirecting the fatty tissue so that I was less angular. My features became less sharp, softened by the new drugs.

The hormones smoothed my skin, and the spots and pimples caused by testosterone vanished. Over time I was even able to wear less make-up with the effect of looking more feminine, which seemed like a huge feat. A simple eyebrow, minimal eye shadow and a slick of mascara and I'm good to go. A fresh lip is also always helpful.

During the wedding reception many praised my appearance. I loved hearing, 'You look great,' and 'Oh my God, your skin looks incredible, babes.' I happily told everyone, 'It's the 'mones!' All this fanfare felt very encouraging, it was a glorious feeling.

Around this time I had another experience that affirmed my new fabulous self. I was walking around Westminster on my way back from coffee with a friend on a rare day off from the salon. When I was crossing Westminster Bridge, a white van stuffed full of men drove past me. From the wound-down window I heard cries of 'Oi oi' and wolf whistles. This wasn't what I was used to. In the past I would have expected to hear cries of 'faggot' or 'queer'. The van, draped in St George's flags, disappeared into the city and I was willing to let the sexism go just this *one* time. I was relieved to be seen by passers-by as the person who I truly was.

On another occasion I was walking down Kingsland Road in Dalston on my way back from the club VFD. It was past 1 a.m. and the streets were full of partygoers. Out of nowhere came a group of about five lads. One of the men put his arms around my waist and said, 'I'd like to talk to you! What's a girl like you doing on her own?' This was a defining moment for me – I realised that things were different now. I was being viewed differently because I was being viewed as a woman – this strange man felt he had the right to accost me as a female. I wasn't as safe as I once was walking home on my own late at night. Another time I stupidly decided to take a shortcut through a park after dark – something I wouldn't have given a second thought to in the past. A man appeared out of nowhere, acting oddly. He stood in front of me and wouldn't let me pass. Every time I tried to sneak around him he blocked me while smiling to himself. It wasn't funny and I began to get scared. I didn't know how this was going to go – what if he planned to mug or rape me? Thankfully, two people came walking along the path, distracting him and allowing me to run off. These two intimidating scenarios acted as a lesson to me. I was being told loud and clear that I needed to change my mindset. I had to think about every action and bear the consequences in mind.

With the hormones transforming me, it was time to embrace the fact that I was now 'passing'. 'Passing' is a term that I am personally not comfortable with, but which nevertheless makes life as a trans person a lot easier. In the transgender community, for some, 'passing' is the only way to survive, and for others it's not that important. 'Passing' is when strangers – anyone who didn't know your prescribed gender identity at birth – can't tell that you are trans. Personally, I don't strive to pass because I believe we should be able to live in a society where anyone of any gender identity can walk down the street and be accepted. We should be allowed to assume whatever appearance we want to – whether or not it conforms to traditional expectations. If someone wants to look like a male in a dress, then they should be left to it. More power to them. Everyone is different and we're not transitioning to reinforce gender binaries.

Sadly, we don't live in such an accepting society and I am fully aware of the privilege of passing. When I speak to trans women who don't pass, I get a sense of how difficult it can be in public and how unsafe it makes them feel. Often their lives feel threatened. When you're walking down the street in full femme mode, it's an incredible feeling. It only takes one person to call you out and shout 'Man!' to undo it all, and this can be crushing.

This recently happened to me and it was a disturbing experience. Last summer I was staying with some friends in Berlin. One afternoon I was walking out of the lake and back to my beach towel when I heard somebody say, 'That's a man!' in my direction. There I was, feeling fabulous wearing a tight black swimming costume beneath the scorching sun when the abrupt comment floored me. My body, wrapped in figure-hugging Lycra, clearly gave away the fact that I wasn't a genetic female and this onlooker decided he had a right to comment on it. His three words stayed with me – I couldn't shake them off. Some days later I had a breakthrough; I wasn't angry with him, I was angry with myself. After four years presenting as Rhyannon I still wasn't comfortable being called out, unless I was doing it myself.

It is all well and good presenting as female but my voice also needed some attention if I was going feel comfortable ordering a late-night bag of chips. My deep voice would often expose me and at my second appointment at the GIC I confided my fears of speaking in public. I told the doctor about the countless times I would order a coffee and witness the change in behaviour by whoever was serving me. It often made me mute, unable to express myself. I felt trapped, incapable of unleashing my humour or point of view for fear of being viewed differently. Through the NHS I was lucky enough to be offered six speech therapy sessions, which put an end to these debilitating fears.

Before speech therapy I had already been making an effort to speak differently as I felt so self-conscious of my natural male voice. Although I hadn't managed to obtain a female range, my voice was definitely higher than it used to be. My experience in stage performing aided tapping into a higher range, as did watching YouTube tutorials by trans women. Working in the salon and answering the phone also helped coach my voice. 'Good afternoon, Rhyannon speaking, how may I help?' was a sentence I repeated time and time again. I would warm up my voice when I was cycling to work by humming. It helped me remember to use a higher pitch when it was time to have conversations with people.

I loved the speech therapy sessions at the GIC. My therapist was called Matthew and I immediately felt comfortable with him. In the first session he wrapped a contraption around my neck. Two gold-coloured discs were snugly fitted to my throat. It looked more like a fashion accessory than a medical device. I was asked to read a brief paragraph of text in a way that felt comfortable, or how I would usually speak. When I read out loud, the gold discs recorded the pitch of my voice and fed this information to a computer programme. I could see the wiggly line moving up and down as I said each word. Once the paragraph was finished and the data was recorded, the programme would show exactly where the pitch of my voice registered. In the beginning it fell mostly within a gender-neutral zone. The work I had done by myself had moved the pitch out of the typically 'masculine' zone, but occasionally I would dip back into it, especially at the ends of words, where my voice would drop. But I didn't mind this too much, and Matthew said it was a great place to start. We wouldn't need to do too much work.

The idea of the sessions was to identify a place where I could comfortably pitch my voice. I didn't want to sound like Miss Piggy or Minnie Mouse – not all women have high voices and I didn't want to sound like I was straining my voice or that it was fake. My goal was to have confidence speaking as Rhyannon.

Matthew gave me vocal exercises to practise in between sessions and I looked forward to developing my voice even more. One of my favourite exercises was role play. Matthew would go upstairs to another office and phone me. We worked through different scenarios – ordering a pizza, enquiring about an advert, or booking an appointment for a haircut. At the end of every call he would give me feedback about how my voice sounded over the phone. It was fun, and with my sense of humour I often went off on tangents, asking about his journey to work or what he had for dinner the night before. Exercises like these certainly made the idea of talking in public more enjoyable.

Over the course of six sessions, with practice, time and patience, I was thrilled to find that my voice changed. Your voice is like an instrument – the more you play it and the more time you dedicate to it, the better the results will be. In the beginning, it often felt embarrassing talking to my friends in a higher-pitched voice but it definitely signalled a development in my transition, which I enjoyed. When I felt shy I told myself that my new voice would carry me through my transition and beyond.

During our last session Matthew played back my first

recording. I was astounded at how different I sounded. I really had achieved a female pitch – I had found my voice. I remember turning to Matthew and saying, 'My name's Rhyannon,' in my newfound voice. With a smile on his face he replied, 'That's it, that's your voice.' I was delighted that everything was finally coming together – it seemed like my first appointment at the GIC was years ago. Time can often be a drag when you're not getting what you want, but now the pieces of the puzzle were fitting together I felt like I was hurtling towards my new identity.

Timed ticked by until my next pilgrimage to the GIC. It was my third appointment, with yet another different clinician. I was so used to making the trip to the GIC that it had become second nature. I looked forward to the long and slow journey along the District line before walking down to the clinic. It gave me some precious time to think about what was to come. I often spotted other trans women and men making the same journey as me and I always felt a kind of kinship with them.

As always, there was a nervous energy in the waiting room. For many it was clearly their first appointment, and I could sense the anticipation as trans women tapped their stiletto heels on the carpet and trans men rubbed their chins. Looking around at the first-timers I marvelled at how far I had come but I was still incredibly nervous. I feared that at any moment I might be told, 'You can't do this.'

Sometimes I felt lonely in the waiting room, especially when I saw others with their mums by their sides. I still wasn't sharing my journey with my family and this hurt when I focused on it. I tried my hardest to push it out of my mind.

As with my other assessments, we ran through the general questions. 'How was I feeling?', 'Had my circumstances changed?' and 'Where did I want to go with my transition?' By this point I was taking 4 mg of oestrogen a day and loving it. Recent blood tests showed that my oestrogen level had reached 257, which was definitely an improvement, but testosterone still ravaged my body at a level of 22.8. I had decided that I wanted gender reassignment surgery, a procedure that would reshape my genitals and create a neo-vagina. I felt that this was the only way forward. It was the full stop I craved.

I explained to the doctor that the hormones had relieved some of my gender dysphoria but that it hadn't completely disappeared. I felt that my male anatomy hindered me – I wasn't free to do the things I wanted to do. I could never walk down the beach in a bikini or be completely naked in a female changing room and feel comfortable. This caused me anxiety and stress. I also worried that I would never meet anyone who would love me as I was, and that I would remain single all my life. I knew from experience that some people were absolutely repelled when they found out I had a penis. I thought having a neo-vagina would solve all of these problems.

It is essential that testosterone levels are repressed before GRS (gender reassignment surgery) is given the green light. The doctor said he would prescribe me an injection that would reduce my testosterone levels to that of a genetic female. I was warned that this course of treatment would drastically alter my libido and possibility of reproduction. My erections would become less frequent, I would likely stop producing sperm and my genitalia would shrink. I confirmed that this was OK – I wasn't using my penis for anything sexual at that point and I definitely didn't want to father my own children. I left the clinic feeling like I was moving forward as Rhyannon and it was a huge relief. I couldn't wait to get an injection in my bottom every three months. In fact, I had been looking forward to it – Mzz Kimberley would continually ask me, 'Gurrrl, are you on the shots yet?' Some weeks later, I flew into Dr Ashrafi's office eager to pick up my new prescription.

Starting Decapeptyl accelerated everything, completely reducing the testosterone levels within my body. In a simpler form, it castrated me. I very quickly noticed a big difference. I only have to look back at my photo log of weekly selfies to see exactly when I began the injections. When I looked in the mirror I began to see a woman staring back at me. My skin, although already smooth and clear from the oestrogen, became even softer and more delicate – I didn't think it was possible. Almost overnight I grew hips and an arse to be proud of, my skinny frame transformed before my eyes into a slightly curvier shape. It was an uplifting experience. At my next blood test some months later, I was amazed. My testosterone level had dropped to 0.4 and I was definitely feeling the benefits. I was starting to feel more like 'me'.

At the beginning of 2014, I slowly began making contact with my family. My mum had read my letter to her parents who had been asking why I hadn't been in contact recently. My grandparents were shocked and saddened to hear about the reality of my life and the fact I'd been hiding from them for so long. On my father's side, everyone found out because my sister told our cousin, which set off a chain reaction. I was glad really; it saved me doing it. They felt upset that I hadn't told them personally and betrayed by the fact that I'd been living as Rhyannon for two years without their knowledge. This was a massive learning curve for me: be honest with your family, no matter how hard it is! I was grateful that my sister had spoken to my family, preparing them for the fact that I would look different. She had been using female pronouns and was referring to me as Rhyannon, even if some of my other family members weren't.

I knew that it would be a long process with my family. My friend Amber had told me how much time it had taken for her family to adjust, so I was prepared to be patient. She humoured me with stories about seeing her family and how awkward it was, and she urged me to visit mine. 'You have to make the effort,' she said. 'You can't expect to stay in London and them to adjust without seeing you.' She was right. It was time to face the music and introduce my family to Rhyannon.

As I sat on the train heading north, I stared out of the window, watching the city slowly disappear as green fields rolled by. As the surrounding countryside enveloped me, I began to feel very nervous. I listened to Antony and the Johnsons on my iPod in the hope it would distract me from my gnawing thoughts. I didn't know what my family's reaction would be or how the other people in the village would behave. I felt petrified.

I'd arranged to stay at my grandparents' house, so my nan and granddad were picking me up. It was awkward for the first ten minutes – but then it always was initially with my family. It takes a while to settle into the roles of grandparent and grandchild again. At this stage – it was just before I started taking the oestrogen tablets – I didn't look all that different but I was definitely more femme. They needed time to adjust and take me in.

I was over the moon when my nan gave me a big hug as soon as we arrived home. It was her way of saying, 'It's OK. I'm glad you're feeling better.' After several cups of tea for Dutch courage, I initiated the conversation about my transition. I wanted to hear about their reaction to the letters. They said they didn't know if they could ever accept it but they were glad I was happy. They weren't sure if they could ever get used to calling me Rhyannon and they were worried about what others would say. Sometimes I felt angry when they called me Ryan – I wanted everything to be perfect straight away and it upset me. I would pretend not to hear them and say, 'Oh, are you talking to me?' and 'That's not my name.' I'd correct them when they used the pronoun 'he'. 'It's SHE, Granddad, SHE!' I'd say. It became very jovial and we managed to laugh about it occasionally. Spending a couple of days with them helped them see me for who I really was and I was happy that the process of acceptance had begun. Throughout the process of transitioning I have learned a lot about acceptance and tolerance. I have learned to be patient and understanding when it comes to my family getting used to Rhyannon – after all, they knew Ryan for thirty years and have only known me as a female for four years.

Nanny Marge, my ninety-year-old grandmother on my father's side, adjusted straight away. She happily referred to me as 'Rhya' and even introduced me to her cleaner as her 'granddaughter'. Occasionally she would slip up with my name but instantly corrected herself. Even though she is so old, she seemed to understand it immediately and she was relieved that I was happy in myself. We talked about my childhood and she revealed that she wasn't surprised at my news. 'You always wanted girly things, and often wished to have long hair,' she said. She told me a story about when I was young. One Sunday I'd asked if I could wear two of her aprons, one at the front and one at the back so it looked like a dress. Then I asked to wear a hair clip in my hair to which I tied a ribbon. Apparently I wanted to go down the road and show my other grandma, but Nanny Marge wouldn't let me leave the house.

I don't remember this particular moment but it totally sounds like me. Nanny Marge told me that she didn't completely accept my new identity, but that it didn't worry her either – and that was more than fine by me. My happiness was the most important thing to her, and I appreciated this. This was a breakthrough for me. Whenever I visited her after this, we enjoyed talking about my latest hairstyle and whether my bum looked bigger in my skirt. 'Oooh, I say,' she would go, 'you look more and more like a woman whenever I see you!'

Sadly, at the time of finishing this book, my Nanny Marge died on 16 December 2016. I'm sad that she will never see the completed version of this book or see me grow older as Rhyannon. Nan supported and cared for me as Ryan and accepted me as Rhyannon – her unconditional love and acknowledgment of my transition will stay with me forever.

*

Not every new family meeting went so smoothly. The first time I saw my mother as Rhyannon it was uncomfortable to say the least. The roles of mother and son had to be reconfigured as mother and daughter. I was eager to be seen by my family as a trans woman but the memory of Ryan was heavily cemented into their lives. Although I hadn't changed enough physically for them to see a huge external difference, they acknowledged the monumental shift within myself. Happily, my mum's partner was very supportive. He welcomed me with a big hug and said, 'It's good to see you back to your usual self.' By this he meant I had found myself again. It was a stark contrast to when I saw him last, when I was utterly lost last Christmas.

The meeting with my father wasn't as positive, but I had prepared myself for this. He was having the hardest time accepting me as Rhyannon and coming to terms with my transition. I arranged to meet him in the beer garden of the local village pub. I had two birds to kill with one stone; I wanted to see him as Rhyannon but I also wanted to say sorry for my past behaviour. During this time I was ploughing ahead through my twelve-step recovery pro-gramme and I was currently on step nine. Step nine is about making amends to people who you hurt in the past. I wanted to apologise to my father for being so dis-tant as a teenager and not making an effort to keep in touch once I moved to London.

Once my amends had been made and he accepted my apology, we turned to my transition. It was difficult for him to sit comfortably with me wearing make-up and female clothes. He was afraid of what other people in the village would say. I knew first-hand how much some of the villagers liked to gossip and manipulate the truth. As a teenager with fluoro green hair I'd always see net curtains twitching when I walked down the road. But this time around I thought, let them talk. Rhyannon was the truth of who I was and I refused to be ashamed. I couldn't let other people's reactions jeopardise my own emotions and my progress. I owed this to myself.

I tried to explain this to my father but his answer was that no matter how hard he tried, he could never be comfortable with me presenting and identifying as a trans female. Saddened by this news, I asked how my brothers felt. He informed me that they were confused and upset to lose their big brother. I couldn't help thinking that my father was rooted in the loss of Ryan. He was ignoring the gain of Rhyannon, unwilling to accept the person sitting before him. As we wrapped up our fraught discussion, it felt really strange walking up the hill towards his village. We talked about my sister and commented on the overgrown church graveyard – anything but my transition. When I reached the turning to my grandma's estate, we shook hands and said goodbye. It was a civilised and formal ending to our meeting and it was the last time I saw my father.

Although it was devastating that my father couldn't accept Rhyannon, I wasn't angry with him – I couldn't find it in my heart to be. I took the philosophy that I didn't agree with his views and he didn't agree with mine – and this is life. The important thing was that we'd said what we needed to say. We'd aired our differences and I hoped that over time he might come to accept me. But I have made my peace with the fact that this time might never come. I can't expect everyone to be happy for me – and I must be grateful for those who are. After everything I have been through, my own happiness is the most important thing and this is what I needed to focus on. With or without his support, I was going to press ahead with the course of my life.

When the time came to return to London, I breathed a sigh of relief. On the way back, I stared out of the train window once again, looking at the power stations flashing past and reflecting on my emotional visit home. The initial – and the hardest – meetings were done. Thankfully, the daunting period of no physical contact with my family had drawn to an end, and it was the beginning of being seen as a transgender woman. I felt that my family had shown great bravery in meeting me and embarking on our new relationship. I was utterly relieved that they hadn't completely shut the door on me, and that they would support me going forwards. I felt incredibly lucky in this respect, as according to All About Trans, 45 per cent of trans people suffer a family breakdown and 37 per cent have family members who are no longer on speaking terms with them. This breakthrough was the start of regular trips home, to allow my family to get to know Rhyannon.

I have no idea if people in my village know about my transition, and neither does it bother me. I don't need to be ashamed or embarrassed any longer about who I've become. The bullies who taunted me when I was young don't exist for me any more and I feel empowered by this. On a recent trip to see my family, before my grandmother died, I was pushing Nan around the village in her wheelchair when we bumped into my uncle Phil. He was working on a house with his builder mates. While we were having a chat, one of his friends came over to say hello. I could tell that my uncle felt awkward and he wrapped up the conversation quickly. When we returned to Nan's bungalow he phoned, apologising for his sharpish behaviour. Apparently his mate had said, 'I hope I get a carer like her when I get old,' referring to me as I pushed my grandma back up the lane. I immediately told my nan and we couldn't stop laughing. I cherish times like these, when the intricacies of life can be laughed at.

Over time, my family witnessed my bodily changes whenever I visited them. Every four or five months I'd take the train, heading towards the Midlands. I didn't always enjoy these trips, sometimes feeling angry and resentful when they still called me Ryan after so long. But I learned that a transition takes time for everyone. I had to give my family time to accept me, just as I did with myself when I took my first steps down this path back in March 2012. It has taken a long time to build bridges with my family – it has taken four years for us to grow comfortable with each other in the same room. But we are so much closer for it – I no longer feel like I'm hiding behind the face of Ryan and it has breathed fresh air into our relationships. There is great power in honesty. I have exposed myself for who I truly am and they have got to know the real me. This is a wonderful feeling.

Chapter 11

ENTER RHYANNON STYLES

Transitioning has transformed my life in more ways than one. As well as quite literally saving my life, it has opened up new, exciting and unexpected opportunies in both my professional and personal life. I never anticipated that I'd become a columnist for a national magazine. If you told me at the beginning of my transition that three years later I would be sharing my journey with the world, I would have freaked out. I wouldn't have been able to handle it. Everything in life felt too new, too raw. In 2012, I'd been reborn and I needed time to discover who I was. But it wasn't just about me. There was a much bigger picture to be considered.

In 2014, trans actress and activist Laverne Cox raised the bar by appearing on the cover of *Time* magazine under the headline 'The Transgender Tipping Point'. This changed the course of history, heralding the transgender revolution that had been building for some time. In the UK, since

Channel Four screened the life-affirming *My Transsexual Summer* documentary series, the public and the media's view of trans people had begun to evolve. Trans journalist Paris Lees gloriously topped the *Independent*'s 'Rainbow List' in 2013, acknowledging her visibility and prowess in the media. Lees became a forerunner and an activist promoting equal rights for trans people through the charity 'Trans Media Watch'. In many ways her groundbreaking work behind the scenes paved the way for my own visibility to flourish. Beyond trans visibility in the media, the year of 'The Transgender Tipping Point' saw many milestones in the political landscape for the trans community. The government's Transgender Equality Inquiry run by the Women and Equalities Select Committee was a breakthrough for trans rights, as was the LGBTQ charity Stonewall becoming trans-inclusive in February 2015.

Social media – Facebook, Instagram, YouTube and Twitter – has also played a huge role in bringing trans people together. Nowadays you're only a click away from accessing a wealth of information about all aspects of living as transgender. This enables individuals all over the globe to connect, creating momentum and visibility as never seen before. It's empowering and enriching.

In June 2015, my good friend Russella – a.k.a. 'The Fabulous Russella' – invited me to the opening of a MAC make-up concession in central London. This was the type of showbiz affair I'd missed so much when I was a hair-dresser. But this time around I was recently self-employed and I couldn't wait to have some fun.

At the party I was reintroduced to PR wiz Mandi Lennard who was responsible for the event programming. I hadn't seen Mandi since my days of performing with Jonny Woo and The LipSinkers at Bistrotheque. 'Do you know Rhyannon Styles?' Russella asked Mandi, introducing me in a fabulous fashion. At this, Mandi looked confused, not recognising me straight away. I reminded

Photograph © Cameron McNee

her that I used to be the performer 'Ryan Styles' and she soon pieced together the puzzle.

Weeks later, I received an email from an editor, Kenya Hunt, at *Elle* magazine. Following Mandi's suggestion, *Elle* wanted to know if I would be interested in sharing my transition story in a regular column for the magazine. Trans issues had blown up in the media, and *Elle* was one step ahead of the game in searching for a transgender columnist. I had to read this email over and over again, and it took several times before I believed it. Once it had settled in, I let out a rather loud 'YES!' and ran off to share the news with my housemates, who jumped for joy with me. This was exactly what I needed at that time. I had just left a career that wasn't satisfying me, and it felt like I was being handed a golden ticket for my re-entry into the world. It was the perfect way of saying, 'I'm back and I'm Rhyannon now.'

In the past I had only ever written scripts for my performance work, small biographies for my website and arts council applications. Never in a million years did I imagine I would be writing think pieces about Germaine Greer or revealing my personal life on a global platform. Little did I know how much I would enjoy it! I replied to Kenya's email saying that I would love to take the job. After several exchanges and meetings, we planned my first column and a video shoot. It was really happening and I felt so happy. I couldn't wait to share my journey – I knew that I had plenty of experience and anecdotes that people would love to hear. I was totally confident that it was the right thing to do.

I am thrilled that mainstream media and pop culture has picked up on trans issues and is catapulting trans individuals to new heights. Trans people are finally receiving the respect, equality and stardom that are so deserved. In 2015, Rebecca Root appeared in *Boy Meets Girl* – a BBC2 drama based on a trans woman navigating life in Newcastle. What was so remarkable about this show was that the lead trans character was played by a trans woman. This was a real victory for trans visibility. *EastEnders* also followed suit, employing a trans man to play a trans character – a milestone for a daily soap opera watched by millions. It was also fantastic to see American transgender model and actress Hari Nef recently appear on the front cover of *Elle* – a first for a UK publication. I'm proud to be affiliated with this groundbreaking magazine.

Back in 1961, the model April Ashley, thought to be one of Britain's first transsexual women, was outed by the *Sunday People* newspaper with the headline ' "Her" Secret is Out'. Ashley, who had been modelling for *Vogue*, was immediately dropped by her agents and never modelled again. Her book *The First Lady* reveals how being 'outed' as a transsexual impacted upon her public persona, leading to unemployment and the disintegration of her personal relationships. Ashley is just one example of the many trans people who have had this happen to them. It's a far cry from Hari Nef's *Elle* debut and Caitlyn Jenner's very public coming out on the front cover of *Vanity Fair* magazine, which literally broke the internet.

'The New Girl' column only exists because I am fulfilled and happy within myself. For years I was hiding who I truly was, unable to accept the truth or tell anyone that I was transgender. I was plagued by insecurity, self doubt and fear. This is such a stark contrast to where I am today. I am finally where I am meant to be and it feels great. This is reflected back to me by many of my column readers, who reach out to me with positive comments on social media sites like Twitter, Facebook and YouTube. I love reading what they have to say and I'm really happy knowing that people are engaging with me positively. It's surreal to know that one of my *Elle* videos 'Sister, You're a Lady Now' has now been viewed over 86,000 times. (That wasn't all me, I promise!)

It was only recently, when a friend said to me, 'You're the face of a movement', that my visibility as a trans woman really clicked. Previously, I regarded my *Elle* column as simply a platform for sharing my journey. Unexpectedly, I became a spokesperson for the transgender community and a figurehead within the media. This is a position that I relish and I'm thrilled that my voice and experience is part of the wider consciousness. I'm proud to be carving the way for trans people and raising all-important awareness.

By default I have also become a role model to those who are considering a transition. Readers reach out to me, saying that my honesty and bravery has helped them immensely in finding the courage within themselves to transition. This pleases me so much. I didn't have a role model when I was at my lowest, so the thought that I might help people find themselves when they are lost is hugely gratifying. I am thankful that I might be of service to a community that has helped and supported me while I was finding my own identity. I am proud to say that my visibility as a trans person enriches me and many others.

I have been lucky that many amazing opportunities have been made available to me because of my *Elle* column. I have been invited to speak and contribute to panels that discuss gender, identity and sexuality. It seems that all those years of hosting a pub quiz week after week prepared me for such public speaking and I love doing these events. Last year I also landed a cameo role in the BBC2 drama *Boy Meets Girl* where I played a trans woman alongside fellow trans journalist Paris Lees. Paris was a great cohort as we waited in the cold, drizzly car park of Granada Studios in Manchester. We sat in our cosy trailers and gossiped about everything from clothes and music to boys. It was surreal to be a stone's throw away from the set of *Coronation Street*, and I marvelled at how far I have come.

To top it all, in 2016 I was shortlisted on the *Independent*'s

'Rainbow List' (a list of the most influential openly LGBTQ individuals in the UK) as 'One to Watch' due to my media visibility. This was an incredible accolade and it certainly made me feel good about the level of honesty I bring to my stories.

In truth, around the same time the *Elle* column first landed in my lap I had already made the decision to turn my back on hairdressing in favour of becoming more visible again. One evening in May 2015 I went to see an exhibition by Mx Justin Vivian Bond called 'My Model/MySelf'. Bond is a New York-based artist who I'd had the pleasure of meeting several times before and I was grateful to call her my friend. Since our first meeting almost ten years ago we were both now describing ourselves as trans – a label that drew us together even more. At the exhibition, Vivian was installed in the window of the gallery, performing in a pink dress, as if posing for photographers on the red carpet. While I watched Vivian shift between poses, I got caught up in the sheer power of performance. I couldn't help thinking about what the Australian performer Dallas Dellaforce had whispered into my ear the previous summer: 'Don't forget, darling, you are a star!'

For some time I had missed performing – my creative muscles weren't being exercised and I had started to feel trapped. For so many years, performance and cabaret had been my outlet. Without it, I no longer felt like me. The harsh reality of hairdressing was also setting in at this time. The hairdressers in my salon thrived on their passion for hair – a passion that I didn't share. When I saw my colleagues exhausted, tired, hungry and thirsty after not stopping for eight hours on a Saturday, I knew it wasn't the life for me. After seeing Vivian at the Vitrine Gallery, a spark was ignited in me and I handed in my notice. I knew I had to go and do what I do best. The salon had served me well and it was exactly what I needed for that period of my life, but it was time to move on. It was time to resurface as Rhyannon Styles, and be bold and proud of who I was.

So here we are today, at the tail end of the 2010s and trans people have come incredibly far. People like me didn't exist in the Eighties, Nineties or Noughties. We are visible in the media, demanding to be seen. We have infiltrated and saturated mainstream TV, music videos, magazines and social media. We are role models to the younger generation. Role models that I didn't have, but so desperately craved. As individuals we shine; as a community we thrive.

We see fewer people use scathing language like 'she-male', 'sex change' and 'chicks with dicks'. Trans people appear less in humiliating news headlines and punchlines to bad jokes. Finally, we are treated with the dignity and respect we deserve.

I sincerely hope that the next generation of trans people

will feel much safer and more supported, able to reveal themselves and embrace who they are. I was depressed and contemplating suicide for most of my twenties because of my gender dysphoria. But I have managed to turn it around in the last four years, and here I am today. I am loving life, taking pleasure in every single moment. Transitioning has saved me.

As well as the many developments in my professional and public career as Rhyannon, my personal life also experienced a period of change. Most notably, my love life. I feel that now is a good time to recap my relationship history for you. I want to briefly talk about the past before I bring you right up to date with my relationship status today. But first, I want to outline that sexual identity and gender identity are two distinctly different things. This is important for me to stress as many labelled me 'gay' because I wore women's clothes. And I, too, fell into this trap as a teenager. But this is wrong, and while I can understand this mentality in the 1980s, there is no place for this kind of thinking today.

Because I was born with a penis I was labelled as 'male' and because I was attracted to other males, this was labelled as 'gay'. It turns out that both of these labels were wrong. Over time I realised that just because I had sex with men that didn't make me gay and just because I was born with a penis that didn't make me male.

My sexual desire has not changed throughout my life – I'm attracted to all genders and I have no primary focus. On the other hand, my gender identity has changed. (You're reading the book all about it!) But my sexual identity is not connected to my gender in any way. I'm a trans woman because this presentation feels comfortable to me, not because I like men. Besides, many trans women's sexual preference is for women, which totally debunks this out-of-date theory.

Growing up, trans role models weren't available to me. But there were gay males who I could relate to – Boy George and Julian Clary all flaunted a femininity I understood and connected with. When I moved to London and lost the shackles of small village life, I finally felt free to explore my desires towards men. It was liberating! My first boyfriend in my early twenties was called Peter. I remember when we went to G-A-Y nightclub for his twenty-first birthday. While we were dancing he decided he'd rather listen to the Smiths on his portable cassette player than whatever music the DJ was playing. He put his oversized 1980s headphones over his ears and spun all over the dancefloor. Boys with generic haircuts drinking fluorescent alcopops looked at him like he was crazy. I loved Peter for that.

On my return from Australia, before my induction at clown school, I crashed in Peter's bed. At the time we were both suffering from high levels of anxiety and uncertainty about our future. We had both finished university and didn't feel financially secure. Our artistic careers, though exciting, felt unstable. I was thankful I was moving to Paris but I knew it was just a short-term fix. It was all too easy for us to fall back into familiar patterns, and I started sleeping with Peter again, craving comfort and stability. We shared a bed and each other's bodies. I was hiding, running away from making a life-changing decision, which in hindsight was part of the process.

At a later date, a mutual friend informed me that Peter had heard about my transition. Apparently, his response was, 'I'm going to have to have a word with him about that!' Sadly, we never did get to have this chat because Peter Alexander tragically died in September 2012. At his funeral I introduced myself to his mother. The first thing she said to me was, 'You look like an interesting woman.' I would have loved to have seen the look on Peter's face at that. Peter was the first person that I loved, and when he died so suddenly I made a promise to myself to never hide who I am from anyone again.

At the beginning of my transition I didn't have the headspace to date. Following my break-up with Gus, I focused all my attention and energy on me, myself and I. In many ways I was discovering the world with fresh eyes and I needed to devote myself completely to this task. On one occasion in a nightclub, a man approached me and asked, 'I need to know if you're a man or a woman.' Immediately I answered him by saying, 'I'm transgender.' His response was 'Oh,' and off he went into the night, never to be seen again. This conversation was typical during the early years of my transition. People were attracted to me but unable to pinpoint my gender or my sex. When they found out that I was transgender they instantly rejected me. It was a cruel twist of fate that when I finally learned to love and accept myself, others rejected me. These experiences really hurt and I often felt that more doors were being closed than were being opened.

Once I felt more secure within myself and comfortable within the presentation and role of Rhyannon, I began to date. It took two years for me to be able to give my attention to someone else. As suggested by the girls in the hair salon, I joined internet dating sites like Tinder, OK Cupid and many others. These dating apps had previously daunted me, but I knew it was the right time to tackle them. I felt much better knowing that I was established on hormones and my confidence had grown. In short, I felt more like me. I created profiles on the various sites and nervously uploaded selfies. I didn't have many photographs of the 'new' me so when the salon was quiet, we undertook a little photoshoot as I posed for the girls.

In my profile blurb I stated the facts: 'I'm a pre-op transgender woman.' After my experience with Peter, I had to honour my promise to myself. I hoped that people understood that 'pre-op' translated as pre-operative, meaning that I still had a penis. When it came down to it, many failed to realise what it meant (I didn't blame them!) and it took some explaining. But I was in for an even bigger shock. To my surprise, many didn't know what 'transgender' meant either. I was asked more than once if I was a woman who was turning into a man. This only served to highlight people's preconceived and outdated images of male-to-female transsexuals.

One of the many challenges I faced was having to explain myself over and over again. Once an initial 'like' or 'match' was in place, so began the conversation about what was in my pants. These endless messages became so dull after a while that I decided to change tack and conduct an experiment. Without intending to meet anyone I changed my profile information so that it didn't reveal that I was transgender. The results were just as I expected, I instantly had more 'matches', 'likes' and invitations to date, and not a single conversation about my genitalia. But I knew that I would never find a suitable partner by hiding who I was. So I went back to being explicit in my description. As a result, a small minority of people reacted badly to this revelation.

Men were cruel, ignorant and rude with their words. Like cowards they insulted me from behind the safety of their phone screens. When I spoke up and called them out on their prejudice I was instantly blocked – it was the end of the conversation. I was appalled by this hypocrisy. It was OK for them to throw negativity my way, but when I challenged them, it was a different story altogether. When I explained that 'pre-op' literally meant I had a penis, I would get responses like, 'Can I cut your dick off?' or 'How big are you?' These messages were hard to stomach and I regretted being visible. In these cases I immediately deleted them, thankful that these men had shown their true colours straight away. It seemed that dating as a trans woman was a minefield. I had never experienced anything like this while I was a man dating males. I had never been shamed because of my body or my gender expression. Quite the contrary, my femininity had always been accepted and embraced.

Luckily, there were exceptions to these trying experiences. A handful of people didn't think it was an issue that I had a penis. Some of them had messaged me on the strength of my pictures alone and didn't even read the blurb. There were a couple of men who came forward, wanting to know more. They had never dated a trans woman before and largely considered themselves heterosexual but they were attracted to me and wanted to go on a date to explore this. I instantly pointed out to them that wanting to date me didn't mean that they were gay. I may have had a penis, but they were attracted to me because of my feminine attributes, not my male ones.

I was eager for new experiences too, particularly in dating and relationships. Without any expectations, I was willing to give it a try. I took the plunge and took them up on their offer of a drink (even if mine was a fizzy water). It would be a learning curve for both of us.

It was very exciting getting ready for my first date as Rhyannon. At the time I was living with my friend H so I had an expert eye on hand and someone who I trusted to help me select the right outfit. Together we chose a simple black dress, brown boots and my camel coat. It didn't feel like a grand outfit, but we were only going for a quick drink on a Sunday afternoon. We hit the nail on the head because I looked and felt fantastic. My confidence shone through and I'm sure that the person I was meeting picked up on this too.

During the date the main focus of conversation was my decision to transition. This didn't feel intrusive – in fact it felt great to talk to someone who wasn't judging me and was simply curious. It was nerve-wracking meeting a stranger, but I reassured myself that they knew I was transgender and were comfortable with it. Because I was already in Rhyannon-mode, I didn't feel the need to adjust my body language or speech. I was the person that I wanted to be and I didn't need to be anyone else. Although my first date didn't lead to anything serious, it was a liberating experience. It gave me the confidence to date as Rhyannon and many more dates proceeded. I had reached a place of acceptance around who I was and in turn this self-assurance was attractive to other people.

Months later, I started to conclude that the dating sites weren't catering to my needs. More often than not, I heard the same thing: 'You're a very pretty woman, but not my cup of tea.' With these constant knockbacks I began to feel deflated and unattractive. By this point I had moved house and was living with two gay males, one of whom kept raving to me about the amount of guys who were using Grindr to look for trans females. Grindr is a dating app for gay males, and for this reason I'd never used it. I assumed it was only for men, so I never regarded it as an option to meet people. It was a revelation to me. Once I'd signed up, my experience of Grindr was far better than Tinder – I found the users more accepting and complimentary regarding variant genders. As I've mentioned before, the gay community is very nurturing and open-minded.

On Grindr I met people who were explicitly attracted to trans women. The trans attraction was present for a lot of men, including many who identified as bisexual, bicurious or whatever. Several men also stated that their own sexuality was fluid and couldn't be defined as straight, gay or bi. Their sexuality was constantly evolving and my femininity was attractive to them. It felt like a win-win situation. This pool of men was the one I needed to focus my attention on and I dived right in! With this revelation I gained more experience dating as Rhyannon and it felt wonderful. Each date felt like a learning curve. The more I spoke about who I was and the journey I had been through, the better and more confident I felt. It was really exciting to express myself with honesty and not be scared of the outcome. There was no rejection, no negativity and no prejudice. For the first time as Rhyannon I was complimented. These men told me my body was beautiful, sexy and hot. I melted every time and these comments awoke me sexually.

Talking about sex is complicated and trying to describe my sexual encounters removes the passion, the infatuation and the pleasure. But I'll try not to let you down. I don't want to say that I never enjoyed sex when I was Ryan because that would be a lie. It would be massively unfair to my previous sexual partners because I clearly did enjoy it – I was always at it! I had a high sex drive and desired the same from my partners. I enjoy sex now just as much as I did back then as Ryan. But having sex while being accepted as a trans female is mindblowing. It is an altogether different experience to having sex as a male. This difference in the sexual experience is not down to me. As someone who has had sexual encounters as both genders, I can safely say that it's down to my choice of partners.

In my experience, men who are attracted to trans women approach the act of sex differently to gay men. Unlike homosexual males, they have sex with cis and trans women. They rarely have sex with men and they don't identify as people who are attracted to masculinity. And as a result, the sexual experience with them is completely different. Where they touch you, where they kiss you and how they have sex with you – everything is approached differently.

When I grew breasts it was a bonus for everyone and it feels amazing when I am touched by my partner in this newly formed area of my body. What was once only slightly sensitive now feels electric to the touch (when done correctly!) by the influx of hormones entering my bloodstream.

There was a period of time when I was incredibly sexually active and I felt alive. But during the course of my transition my libido has fluctuated – sometimes I've really desired sex and other times I've forgotten about it completely. My trans girlfriends warned me about the loss of libido and the inability to produce semen. And after a year of testosterone-reducing injections these characteristics slowly crept up on me.

In the middle of 2015, my libido had completely diminished due to the side-effects of my medication. I rarely thought about sex, and if so it was just a passing thought.

This was a stark contrast to my sexual imagination in the past. But nonetheless, I still found people attractive and I continued having sex, even though I wasn't able to maintain an erection. (I'll leave that to your imagination.)

Due to the changing nature of my sexual desires, I began to crave something more. During my sexcapades I hadn't met anyone who had wanted anything more than casual sex – which was fine to begin with. But over time, my perspective changed. I wanted to develop in other areas. I wanted to know who Rhyannon was in a relationship. I wanted to know if it were even possible. I needed to cut down the noise and focus. I decided to have a break from the dating apps, which were distracting me from my primary purpose of finding love.

Before I threw in the towel I decided to check one last website. It was a specialist site for people who are attracted to trans women and I hadn't looked at it for months. Once I logged in I discovered a message waiting for me, a response from a person I'd messaged nearly a year before. I had forgotten all about him because I didn't get an immediate response at the time, reading the silence as 'I'm not interested'. It turned out that the real reason he hadn't responded was because he was in a relationship.

When I read his message, my heart skipped a beat. I was really attracted to the person in question and extremely excited that he had responded. I nervously picked up the conversation, hoping that I wouldn't have to wait another year for a reply. I was so glad that I had decided to check the website before I gave myself a break from dating. When I think back to this moment today, I consider it to be very timely. I had to let go of all the other distractions in order to find the person who could potentially be a game-changer for me.

Within days we had swapped numbers and as the conversation excitingly moved forward, I was eager to meet him. During our conversations over text he charmed me and some days later we had our first date. I was completely smitten.

For our first meeting we kept it low-key and local, but as soon as he walked into the bar I instantly felt butterflies in my stomach. He looked exactly like his pictures on the website, and I was so happy when he put his arms around me and kissed me on the cheek. He bought me a Club Mate soda and our conversation began. Up until this point, I had no idea what he was called as we hadn't revealed our full names on the website. I had been using the moniker of 'Rebelle' and he had used 'Ry'. He laughed when I told him my name was Rhyannon – which is his sister's name. I couldn't believe it when he said his name was Ryan. When I explained the significance of this, we both laughed about it. In the bar that night Rhyannon met Ryan all over again and there was something beautifully ironic about it.

(I know it's just a name, but it's cute!) We had chemistry, there was no denying it. Our connection was obvious from the very first kiss and many dates proceeded.

Weeks later, while lying in bed together, Ryan turned to me after we had finished kissing and said, 'I really like you.' I'll never forget this special moment – I admired his honesty and confidence. Most importantly, I really liked him too! This was it, I was finally ready for a relationship. I was comfortable enough within myself and blossoming in my new identity. I had learned to love myself and was ready to love someone else.

Ry is the first person I've had a relationship with since I began my transition. We have a compatibility that works on many levels. Ryan identifies sexually as queer and in the past he has had relationships with cis women. But he has admired trans females since he was young and I am happily his first trans girlfriend. Since becoming Rhyannon, Ryan is the first person to show me respect around my identity. He enjoys me for who I truly am and this is a spectacular feeling. Being cherished, loved and admired as Rhyannon is something I always dreamed of. I couldn't have wished for a better lover and in the days when I was scared and lonely I never thought this would happen. I'm so glad that I was wrong! I am so happy that I found Ryan.

Chapter 12

TRANSCENDENCE: IS THIS THE END...?

On 27 April 2015, it was time for my last assessment at the Gender Identity Clinic. This appointment was with yet another clinician – in total I have seen four different members of staff, excluding the speech therapist. The purpose of this assessment was to provide a second opinion for gender reassignment surgery. As part of the NHS criteria you need to be living as a woman full-time for a minimum of two years in order to be eligible for surgery, so I took as much evidence as I could. This even included a photograph of me in the college magazine when I won a hairdressing prize. Everything and anything helped – I didn't want to jeopardise my chances at this point.

I was very nervous at the appointment – I had waited so long to discuss the life-changing option of surgery. Our conversation was frank and to the point, discussing the surgery options in detail. I was asked if I wanted a cosmetic or a functioning vagina. I was certain that I wanted a functioning one, for the purpose of sexual intercourse. In this case, the vaginoplasty operation would invert the penis, creating a vaginal cavity. The scrotum would make the labia, and the tip of the penis is formed into a clitoris, meaning it's possible to get sexually aroused – it sounds incredible and very intricate. The operation takes between four and six hours.

I was warned about the possible complications of surgery. Prolapsing vaginas, loss of sensation, inability to orgasm, loss of vaginal depth and bleeding were all potential outcomes. The psychologist reiterated that instead of thinking 'it won't happen to me', I needed to get into the mentality of 'it could be me'. This made me shudder. I was reminded again and again that it is an irreversible operation.

I was also informed about vaginal dilation, which is essential in order to keep the vagina open. I would need to significantly dilate my neo-vagina and be very regimented for the initial year after the vaginoplasty. The dilation process during the immediate weeks after surgery is very intense. It involves inserting perspex rods, which are shaped liked dildos, into the vagina, and keeping them inside for prolonged periods of time. In the beginning you need to dilate four times a day for thirty minutes. And regular baths are needed to keep the vagina clean. As your vagina heals, you can slowly reduce this regime, but if you're not sexually active dilation is essential to ensure the vagina keeps it shape.

The doctor informed me that having somebody to care for you is crucial following your discharge from hospital. Ideally, you need to have help on hand for two weeks to wash towels, change bedding, cook food and help in any way possible. I was advised to take up to eight weeks off work post-surgery before easing back into the saddle gently. The pain would be significant but directly afterwards, in hospital, I would be on morphine. Once home I could take ibuprofen and paracetamol to ease the discomfort. I would be sore and prone to infection while my neo-vagina was healing.

As the operation is provided on the NHS, I expected another long wait – it could take up to nine months to get a consultation with the surgeon and another six months before surgery. I quickly did the maths and worked out that late 2016 or early 2017 would be my rough surgical date. This was also dependent on whether I had enough penile material to work with. If I had been circumcised, this would hinder the possibility of the operation without enough skin to use in the inversion. But this didn't worry me – I knew what I had would be enough. I was also informed that I might have to undergo laser hair removal around the base of my penis and testicles. This is a safeguard, to prevent hair growing inside the walls of the new vagina.

Results of a recent blood test were also in. My oestrogen levels were still too low and the doctor suggested increasing my dose to 6 mg a day. Happily, the Decapeptyl injections had succeeded in stabilising my testosterone level at 0.4.

As my appointment wrapped up, it was surreal to think that my next meeting at the GIC wouldn't be until after surgery. The influx of information felt very overwhelming – there was so much to take in and consider. I felt a mixture of emotions leaving the centre that day. As I walked down a road I'd grown so familiar with, I thought about how far I had come, and what was going to come next. Once again I would have to wait for the next and final stage of my transition.

I had to think long and hard about the potential surgery looming ahead of me. I knew many trans women who had undertaken GRS or who were, like me, making the steps towards it. I didn't know a single trans woman who had decided to keep their penis. Like developing breast tissue at thirty-two years old, I wondered what it would be like to have a completely new body part aged thirty-five. I've had my penis all my life – and even though I wanted GRS, I couldn't get my head around the idea of my penis being inverted to create an entirely new space on my body. What if I didn't like my new vagina? Would I regret surgery? I thought about the stress and pain I was going to put my body through, weighing up if it would be worth it. Growing up, I never saw a girl's vagina and thought, 'Ooh, I want one of those.' When I had sex with women I didn't think, 'My life will be complete, once I have that.' Even backstage in dressing rooms with burlesque dancers and strippers, 'that's the thing I need' never crossed my mind as I looked at the vajazzled crotches.

I had journeyed through my transition regarding a neo-vagina as the finishing line. I assumed that when I was anatomically correct, life would be a dream. A part of me thought that life would be a fairytale once it was complete. Although I knew this was a fantasy, sometimes it was the only thing that kept me moving forward. Now that the reality of altering my body was just over a year away, I wasn't sure if I was comfortable with it.

While attending my multiple GIC appointments, I didn't think I had a choice. I thought I had to say that I wanted a vaginoplasty in order for my prescriptions to be given to me. I thought I had to want the surgery in order to become a woman. But the person that I was in 2012 and the person I am today, thinks quite differently. If I were to repeat my experience at the GIC today, I would be honest about how I felt and discuss the options of a non-binary existence. I had never thought about an alternative reality. Could I identify as a woman and keep my penis? Could I be accepted in this world? My next question was, 'Whose acceptance was I looking for anyway?'

I have never hated my penis. Many trans women experience feelings of resentment, anger and revulsion connected to their penis, but this never really applied to me. I'd experienced feelings of shame from time to time, but ultimately I thought about it as a piece of flesh that hung between my legs. Put simply, I use it for urination, masturbation and sexual intercourse. The only time my penis really bothered me was when I was trying to hide it – stemming from the fear that others would notice it and say, 'That's a man!' This was connected to other people's perceptions of my gender, rather than my own. For others, this piece of flesh defined me as a male, a label that I didn't feel comfortable with.

I thought about my transition in relation to my sexuality. I'm primarily attracted to masculinity, but masculinity doesn't always have to come with a penis. I would also say that I find something extremely sexy about the kindness and softness of femininity. Once again, such femininity doesn't have to come with a vagina. I don't ever want to rule out the possibility of a relationship based on genitalia. I know from personal experience that people are much more than this. I wondered if my desire for a vagina was reduced to the rigid logic of: 'I'm a woman, so I need a man. A woman has a vagina and a man has a penis.' I knew that this was a prehistoric thought pattern, and I was surprised that I had believed it. I was shocked that I had fallen into its trap, given that my very existence refuted it. There were many reasons behind my surprising acceptance of this out-of-date logic, many of which could be tracked to conditioning when I was growing up. In the 1980s, boys were boys and girls were girls – it was as simple as that. But I knew better now. It was time for me to think more about the space that I could occupy as a *trans* woman.

At the start of my transition I was pushed away by some people I wanted to date and have sex with because of what was between my legs. This hurt. It felt that every possible relationship was being shut down because I was transgender. One of my main reasons for wanting GRS was the hope that I wouldn't suffer rejection any more. I thought carefully about the other reasons for wanting surgery. I wanted to feel comfortable in changing rooms, swimming pools, gyms, saunas and on beaches. Anywhere that involved revealing my body or being naked troubled me and I didn't want to carry this anxiety all my life, I didn't want to be called out when people saw I had a penis. I felt utterly frustrated that everything in life had to be so gendered. These societal labels felt rigid and inescapable.

For many trans people, there is safety to be found identifying and passing as 'male' or 'female'. However, this is not everyone's desire. After the 'Transgender Tipping

Point' came another movement, championed by social media. There has been an increase in people describing themselves as 'non-binary', which means neither male nor female. It translates as not wanting to comply with the out-of-date definitions of 'female' and 'male'; it is a rejection of these restrictive labels. In terms of pronouns, many have decided to adopt 'they', refusing to be categorised as 'she' or 'he'. 'They' means everything and all. This movement has recognised that there is the potential for more to exist. Identifying as 'non-binary' moves beyond the physical and further away from the anatomical. This was something I identified strongly with. I started to think about labels, which are simply words that somebody else decided should fit us. The world might revolve around these anachronistic terms but I didn't need to play along with this game. Surely it was my choice to decide who I was. My gender is mine to choose.

I decided to reach out to trans friends who had undertaken GRS. I grilled them about the nitty-gritty details, my main focus being sex and relationships. I knew that I wouldn't use my vagina for giving birth, so its secondary purpose of sexual intercourse was my priority. Many said they enjoyed having sex using their vagina – that their bodies now matched how they felt about themselves in their minds and as a result the sex was incredible. Some preferred to have anal intercourse with their partners, finding it more sensual. Others revealed that their vaginas couldn't accommodate a larger penis, which could be awkward and painful.

I wanted to find out if anyone had been rejected sexually because they used to have a penis. Lots of my friends revealed they had suffered such rejection. In some cases, men who wanted children in the future were unwilling to start a relationship. Many were frustrated that this fact of their past defined them and ultimately stopped people from experiencing the love they could offer. After such honesty from my friends, I came to the conclusion that I was putting too much emphasis on life being a twenty-four-hour sexathon. Having a vagina was about so much more than sexual intercourse. Instead, my energy should have been focused on self-care, self-love and self-acceptance. With the reality of surgery so far away, I pushed it to the back of my mind for the time being.

On 8 December 2015, the universe slapped me around the face with a curveball. I wouldn't have to wait for GRS after all. Over the years I'd been waiting patiently and all of a sudden it was going to be delivered early, just in time for Christmas. I received a letter from St Mary's Hospital explaining that NHS England had agreed to transfer many patients to a private hospital in order to reduce the waiting times for surgery. This option was made available to me. This meant that after an initial surgical assessment,

I could have surgery as early as two months later. From a surgical perspective, if I didn't need to lose weight or have laser hair removal around my genitalia, I could have a vagina as early as April 2016. This was nine months earlier than originally planned.

This new information completely spun me out. On the one hand I was excited about the finalisation of my transition, but on the other hand I was petrified. It was time to get my thoughts straight – I had to be brutally honest with myself. Did I wholeheartedly believe that surgery was the way forward for me? And if so, was now the right time? After much agonising and soul-searching, I still wasn't 100 per cent certain. Since my initial referral my thoughts had significantly evolved and shifted, and many doubts weighed on my mind. If I was absolutely sure that surgery was the right move, I would have snapped at the chance. But I couldn't be certain, so I couldn't proceed with confidence. This wasn't an operation to have on a whim – it would remould my body and my mind. I sincerely believe that when something is right you feel it within yourself and similarly, when something conflicts you, you know it deep down. You feel both with equal force – you feel it in your gut. I had to follow my instinct.

I discussed the operation with Ryan, as it would affect him too. He offered me some thoughtful words, pointing me in the direction of wabi-sabi, a Japanese philosophy.

Wabi-sabi is a belief in transience and imperfection. Derived from Buddhist teachings, it is a beauty that is imperfect, impermanent, and incomplete. In Ry's words, 'Nothing is finished, nothing is perfect and the only constant in life is change.' This philosophy resonated powerfully with me and related to my transition perfectly.

I loved my last six months with Ryan. I took pleasure in the fact that he enjoyed my body and he made me feel more like me. The relationship taught me to accept who I was, how I looked and what others found attractive about me. It helped me realise that there are people in the world who prefer a trans aesthetic. I didn't need to alter my body to please somebody else. The choice would need to come from within myself. We talked about how our relationship might be affected by surgery. We both agreed that the relationship didn't hinge purely on our bodies, but the operation would change things and we couldn't be sure of the outcome.

The big revelation came one month into my relationship with Ryan. Out of the blue I started to have erections and I was able to orgasm. It was quite a shock the first time – I never thought it would happen again. My immediate reaction was to feel like I was going backwards in my transition rather than forwards. I was confused – what did it mean? I didn't know if I could enjoy the sensation without feeling guilty. I kept asking myself, 'Am I still a woman?', 'Is this

OK?', 'Am I allowed to enjoy this?' It took a while for me to accept it. I needed to reassure myself that the pleasure was mine to own, something to enjoy and feel grateful for. I needed to step outside the binaries that were shackling me. Once I managed to let go, the sensation felt really, really good. Now I can happily dive into an orgasm and I am thankful for every single one.

This milestone changed everything. Could I go through with the surgery knowing I might never orgasm again and could possibly lose feeling altogether? An orgasm is a natural joy and a blessing. Was I willing to risk it for an operation that I was beginning to regard as cosmetic? I also questioned if I would feel trapped once I had a vagina. Once it was done, there was no going back. What if I *still* didn't feel comfortable and complete in my body? I started to wonder if it was more psychological than anatomical. There were times when I wished I could test-drive a vagina. How could I confidently claim the need for a vagina without understanding what it feels like to have one? I knew for certain that I would never go back to living and presenting as a man called Ryan (that's me, not my boyfriend!) – my former identity was definitely in the past. But would a new body part enhance my life as I previously imagined? Would it really solve everything? Such thoughts and questions tormented me, going around and around in my head and keeping me up at night. As exhausting as it was, it was necessary. I needed to have this dialogue with myself. I needed to address these issues.

After much introspection, I came to a decision. The more I thought about it, the more certain I was that it wasn't the right moment to have GRS. As a result, I turned down the opportunity to have surgery in 2016 or 2017. I needed more time. I needed to ask myself more questions, interrogate myself and continue this internal dialogue. I wanted to experience life living, breathing and identifying as transgender. I owed it to myself to be honest about my feelings and authentic to myself. I needed to own what I already had. I wanted to speak up and present another possibility.

I remind myself daily that only living in the present will make me happy – I needn't worry about the past or try and predict the future. Right now, I'm living exactly how I want to live and it feels amazing. For the moment I'm happy and content having the body that I have, and this doesn't make me any less of a transgender woman. What's in between my legs doesn't dictate anything, I have transcended this minor detail of my life.

I don't think of myself as someone who is between two opposites, because I don't regard my male and female 'genders' at opposite ends of a spectrum. It's the end of 2016 as I write this and I'm throwing out the labels, the assumptions and the rulebook. I won't let anyone else reduce my gender to either female or male; my identity is an energy that is unique to me. I feel that as my transition has progressed, my male and female self have actually become one. Ryan and Rhyannon have become one.

However this is labelled, and regardless of how uncomfortable this might be for others, I see it as a spiral of two equal parts circling around a central point of love and acceptance. For now, I want to continue my transitioning journey to the undefined space that exists beyond my vision.

There is *no* end . . .

EPILOGUE: RHYANNON RIGHT NOW

I know I said that there is *no* end . . . With my transition I don't think there ever will be. Nothing has an end, things change and consciousness evolves. But this is the end of my memoir and I wanted to leave you with a current taste of my life to bring you right up to date.

It's all over the internet that I am transgender. In the past this was an identity I ran away from, and now, in contrast, it's an identity that defines me. It's an identity I am proud to inhabit. Since I embraced Rhyannon I've never felt happier. I can't stress enough the fuller sense of self I now have. I can say with conviction that I am true to myself, and this feels phenomenal. The strength I have found from living as my legitimate self has saved me. I'm tempted to say, 'I wish I'd done it sooner,' but such things only happen when the time is right. I'm a big believer in this. And I've got the rest of my life to look forward to.

I don't tell everyone I meet, 'My name is Rhyannon and I'm transgender.' I don't feel the need to make this everyone's business. If people enquire what I do, I say, 'I'm a writer and a performer.' Sometimes I reveal that I'm *Elle* magazine's transgender columnist, but it really depends on my mood. If I'm asked outright, 'Are you transgender?' I happily respond with a proud, 'Yes!'

Transitioning is a really big deal. Society tells you directly how to live your life and when you break these rules, it's really hard. I'm amazed at how far I have come as an individual. But, despite my feminine appearance, many people still read me as being a man. It may be that I'm so relaxed and having a laugh with my boyfriend that my voice drops slightly or that I'm wearing a swimming costume that reveals elements of my body that aren't female.

But ... I'm cool with this. I am so comfortable being trans that these instances no longer worry me. If people understand me, then great! But if people have a problem with my trans identity, it's about them, not me. I'm more than happy to be visible as transgender because it helps to break down the taboos around being trans.

My relationships with my family continue to improve as we come to a place of understanding and acceptance. This process has taken longer than I anticipated. However, time is on my side. It's bound to take time to adjust to something as mammoth as a transition, especially as when I began mine

I had been Ryan – son, brother, grandson and nephew – for thirty years. It's hardly surprising that people still slip up occasionally by using the wrong pronouns and name. I can't hold anyone responsible for this. Together we have come on a huge journey, which has required massive amounts of patience from both sides. And we are closer for it.

My relationship with my partner Ry continues to move forward as we learn, play and grow together. Ryan's love for me has enabled me to establish more respect for myself and feel even better about the person that I've become. I feel very lucky in this respect.

My style continues to evolve as the seasons change and I gain confidence around my new body. I look back on the outfits I used to wear and laugh, especially as these pictures haunt me on Facebook. Pencil skirts are a staple in my wardrobe – the fit of these skirts makes me feel so fabulously feminine that I can't get enough of them. I also like wearing trousers, which actually make me feel feminine and really complement my long legs. For me, my trans identity expands beyond the wardrobe. As I've progressed through this amazing journey I've discovered that I have to feel comfortable within myself before I can even begin to dress my body. It all starts on the inside.

Even today I am still questioning who I am. I think it's important for me to accept that I am constantly changing and shifting form, especially as I take hormones which continue to alter my body. I constantly reconsider what labels and words I use to describe myself. During the first few years of my transition I used the labels 'trans woman', 'trans female', 'pre-op', 'girl' and 'she'. I finally felt at home. I have recently begun to describe myself as 'trans-femme' because this is the closest definition that I feel comfortable with. It announces that I am trans but also fully femme. I don't think this terminology is too descriptive and it doesn't reinforce the dated binary interpretations of gender.

Right now I'm totally happy with the way my body is and I believe that this acceptance around who I am will continue for many more years to come. There is such a preoccupation with trans people's genitalia and surgery. For me, surgery won't make any difference to how I choose to label or not label myself. My trans identity is so much more than physical anatomy.

When I was little, my sister had a pretty jewellery box. Inside was a ballerina that denoted one idea of feminine beauty with her dainty waist, pink tulle skirt and gold hair. This was a representation of femininity that I felt I would never achieve, but one that I sought. Years later I had a ballerina tattooed on my right arm as a symbol of the femininity I now feel. It illustrates the journey I have undertaken and the trans femme/woman I have become.

My experience of transitioning continues to be life-changing but I wouldn't have expected anything less. Nor would I want to change it for the world. For anyone who is considering a transition – prepare yourself, you're in for a bumpy but thoroughly enjoyable ride. Buckle up and make the most of it! Be brave, be proud and be true to you. Set yourself free – I promise it will be worth it. And for anyone out there who knows somebody who is transitioning . . . tell them how wonderful they are for doing it!

ACKNOWLEDGEMENTS

I would like to thank my friends and family for supporting me while I shape-shifted around and within a form. You have been gracious in your actions.

Thank you . . .

Mum and Ian for acknowledging my transition.

My little ginger sister Danielle for all your patience and mediation.

Ry C. Brown for putting your fizzog in front of my fizzog over a Club Mate and continually making me happy. (Luvs ya!)

Sam, Bruno and the catfish of Lake Tegel in the summer of 2016.

Kenya Hunt, Lorraine Candy, Hannah Nathanson and everyone at *Elle* UK magazine for giving me the opportunity to tell my story.

Mandi Lennard for the incredible recommendation.

Christina Demosthenous at Headline Publishing for pushing forward and editing this book.

Dr Ashrafi and NHS England for supporting my transition.

The twelve-step recovery programmes of London and Berlin, one day at a time.

The Fabulous Russella. It's great to see you!

Billy Clibery, Caron Geary, Daniel Schreiber, Eva Prinz, H Plewis, Jade Johnson, Larry Tee, Lyall Hakarria, Marisa Carnesky, Michael Nottingham, Richardette, Sam Ratcliffe, Sitron Panopoulos and Stuart McKenzie – thank you for picking up the call and for keeping me on track.

Sarah Ainslee, Georgina McNamara, Jennifer Higginson, William Baker, Cameron McNee, Nick Knight and David Bailey for documenting my life so beautifully.

I wrote this book while listening to: Planningtorock, Blood Orange, Max Richter, KLF, David Bowie, Nick Cave and the Bad Seeds, BEAK>, PJ Harvey and Dead or Alive.

In memory of Nanny Marge and Peter Alexander.

Rhyannon Styles, 2016